MUSIC
HERE AND NOW

ERNST KŘENEK

MUSIC
HERE AND NOW

Translated by Barthold Fles

NEW YORK / RUSSELL & RUSSELL

CONTENTS

TRANSLATOR'S NOTE

THIS translation was made under the supervision of
the author. The translator wishes to thank Mr. Philip
King, who has read this version and has made many
valuable suggestions.

B. F.

THEME

THIS book will survey the entire field of Western music, not just the music of America or the musical events of today; it will examine its problematical features and endeavor to explain how they developed. "Here and Now" sets the tasks incumbent upon professional and amateur musicians, as well as laymen, at the present turning point in music's history; it implies that these problems can and should be solved at once. In granting that human affairs are products of history, we should never forget that history is produced by the deeds of mankind.

One of the chief purposes of this book will be to show that not all contemporary music is "modern," or, as I would rather say, new.

Throughout history, the only music of lasting importance, contributing tangibly to the evolution of new artistic thoughts, means of expression, and methods of construction, has been progressive. An intention to symbolize a steadily increasing degree of consciousness by musical means, to intensify the emotional expressiveness of music, has always been the common denominator in historical mutations of the art.

In the nineteenth century, however, this view was considerably dimmed by the inertia which increasingly affected the mentality of the middle classes. Owing to the social development of that period, they enlarged the musical public to an extent previously unknown and became the most powerful factor in the distribution of music, without contributing to its spiritual advancement. Their attitude was corroborated by a romantic aestheticism which overworked the emotional immediacy of music as an almost exclusive prerequisite in evaluating it.

Hence the extraordinary difficulties which real new music has to face in our day in emphasizing articulate construction and lucid consciousness.

I reject the idea, advocated by some people, that a thorough change of extramusical conditions, such as social or political conditions, is needed to solve the problem. Evidence that mutations of this kind do not achieve the improvement is too convincing. The moral and intellectual forces embodied in art are above transitory social patterns.

This book is not intended to be simply a treatise in defense of modern music; it will take up the question of what can be done today to establish a higher position for those elements of music, and particularly of new music, which I consider the most valuable. Since my point of view is especially related to the growth of new music, I shall deal principally with this phase of the art and with the problems which new music must attack "here and now."

MUSIC
HERE AND NOW

CHAPTER ONE

WHO IS MUSICAL?

Music, Literature, Plastic Arts

IT IS clear that music does not directly reach as many people as do the other arts. Though it is true that not everyone who sees a play in the theater, who reads a novel, or who looks at a painting achieves the same contact with the real artistic essence of these works, and it is even probable that this essence will remain hidden to the majority of the consumers, yet even those who do not "understand" anything about these arts are in some way affected by works of literature and by the plastic arts, in so far as they have a plainly recognizable physical content. The layman who looks at a painting and recognizes the subject as being a landscape, still life, or human figure will hardly say that he understands nothing of painting. It is sufficient to him that he is able to identify the pictured object; his opinion of the picture will depend, as a rule, on whether he likes or dislikes the subject. It is obvious that his emotional reaction to the subject matter is profoundly influenced by the manner of presentation, therefore by purely artistic values; but in most cases he is far from conscious of that fact. The same is true to a still higher degree in literature. No one who can read at all will refrain from giving an opinion on a book on the ground that he knows nothing about literature. He

13

is convinced that, once he has mastered the physical content, he also has absorbed the artistic value; he probably does not even take into consideration the fact that this artistic value may be something in itself which exists outside or behind the material. And in fact, this question is not so easy to answer as it seems. Evidently one can easily imagine two entirely different novels, both having the Civil War as their subject and yet treating this subject from diametrically opposite points of view with widely divergent results. But in this case they will have the same common subject only in a very superficial way. With one, the real substance may be the progressive attitude fulfilling the dictates of history; with the other, the problem of a tragic conservatism. These are obviously two different subjects, and the artistic form given to them certainly cannot be judged independently from them, as if it were something which exists by itself and which can just as well be taken away from one subject and applied to the other.

However it may be, language does not contain a simple pertinent word for the condition which prevents someone from being directly affected by literature or by the plastic arts; but it does contain the word "unmusical," applied to human beings who are not directly affected by music. The reason for this linguistic distinction is that in music—if we exclude program music and music directly associated with the spoken word, like opera, song, etc.—no concrete objects are visualized. The condition of being affected by music does not materialize by the roundabout way of an extramusical substance. The human being who is affected by art only with the help of the objects portrayed is helpless in the face of music, for it has no such substances or, if we want to express ourselves more carefully, at least

does not give them a name. Such people are probably
no more "inartistic" than many others who think that
they understand painting and literature because they
can grasp the material contents of these arts. But since
to them the road to artistic values is opened over the
bridge of these substances, the road remains closed to
the unmusical, for no concrete substances come to his
aid.

We see therefore that music addresses itself to a
limited circle of people—in fact, to those whom we
designate as "musical." The musical person·is someone
who is directly affected by music, and, according to what
we said before, this evidently means that such a person is qualified to take in the artistic values of a musical composition without the obvious presence of an
extramusical substance. This looks like a very complicated theoretical paraphrase of the generally accepted
idea that the musical person is one who likes to hear
music "because he likes it." Why should we bother our
heads further over an analysis of this quality? Let us
be glad that there are so many people who like music;
and when we are composers, let us write music which
pleases the people. Why then should we continue to
rack our brains over this problem?

And yet I introduced something to speculate about
when I spoke of "artistic values." I mean something
which exists in itself, even without regard to the number of listeners who can grasp it and to whom it is
pleasing.

I shall go further and turn the widespread interpretation of these things upside down. This interpretation,
even if seldom so formulated, says approximately:
"Music is good when it pleases musical people." But
I contend that only those people are musical to whom

good music is pleasing. Thereby the sense "musicality" has been given a relative value, and in order to determine musicality we must ask: "What is good music? And how can we recognize it, if not by its success?"

The quality of each human creation can be judged in the light of its component laws, as well as by their degree of practical value. Exception must be made for philosophical and artistic productions. The mechanical engineer is able to judge if the bridge which he contemplates is good in itself; he knows the rules of bridge building and can determine whether these rules have been properly applied. We laymen do not need the mechanical engineer at all to know whether the bridge is good: if it successfully bears the railway trains which travel over it, it is obviously properly built, and that is all we want to know. But we cannot very well say that a symphony is good because it pleases the two thousand or five thousand or ten thousand persons who hear it. We know quite well that that is not the paramount issue, and that works in which the connoisseur soon discovers outstanding qualities may please far fewer people than other compositions which are unquestionably mediocre. We can designate this fact as the autonomy of music. This means that music develops according to fixed laws which may not run parallel to those under which the spiritual condition of its hearers develops. Of course there is a connection, even a very important and a very interesting one. It is not founded on parallel lines, but rather on a system of dialectics which I shall consider later.

What criteria have we wherewith to judge whether a musical work is good? Obviously these must be found in the sounding substance of the music itself, since we have just determined that concrete substances are not outwardly apparent. Even when these are mentioned, as in program music, the qualities of the work undoubtedly do not depend on them. If a work like "On a Persian Market," which has become a public nuisance, has any qualities at all, they have obviously nothing to do with the title and the ostensible subject, for among the uncounted millions who seem to like the work scarcely anyone can tell whether it is a true portrayal of a Persian market. The value of the piece, if it has any value, must therefore be found in what can actually be heard, in the *music,* and not in the title or the comment which accompanies it. The only thing about this title which actually influences the listener is the fact that he is totally unable to visualize such a subject, for probably he has never been to Persia. Yet, this very vagueness of ideas engenders, in the lazy mind of a person who all his life will run an elevator in Omaha, Nebraska, a pleasant, promising, and alluring vacuum into which he willingly lets the music be poured.

The Material of Music

THE first things to pour into the vacuum are the materials of music. The materials of music are tones, comparable to colors in painting. The number of available tones is infinite. The howl of the siren presents a practical demonstration of the continuity of this limited range, consisting of a limitless number of tones. When music is to be produced, first of all a definite choice must be made from this tone-continuity. It is well known that not all people select the same tones for their musical purposes.

The system which our Western music employs at

present—the octave divided into twelve half-tones at equal distance from each other—is just as little "prescribed by nature" as the old Greek system, which also knew smaller distances, or as that of the Javanese, who divide the octave into seven equal parts. This first formulation of a charter for the sound material takes place really before the actual musical shaping begins. Whenever this goes on, it deals with a material which has already been preformed by history. No composer creates in a vacuum: he is influenced not only by his surroundings but by the fate of music, experienced through the centuries of development. He uses a certain sound language which can be defined by unmistakably recognizable criteria. The listener experiences this sound language in the first place. His experience may be compared to hearing someone talk in a streetcar and suddenly realizing that the language is Italian, even though he is unable to grasp the meaning of the words. It is the material (in this case the Italian speaking sound), the inflexion, the accents which bring about our first reaction.

But it is clear that if we want to know what is being said, we must be able to absorb something more than the mere sound, the audible material of the language. Like language, music evolves in time; by the change of separate language or tone elements, certain time periods are marked or defined. But the composite speaking units—the words—each have a meaning, while these meanings are lacking in a musical picture. Evidently the course of the word picture is regulated by a power which lies outside it. When the connections of the meanings present a general logic which is independent of the language, then the language which expresses these connections is full of sense and its form has been determined by those meanings. Since the units of music do not represent objects from the physical world, we can hardly call this logic to our assistance when we seek to understand, or to demonstrate, the sense of the musical development.

The Musical Thought

AND yet music is in no way a domain of black magic, to which we must despair of bringing a spark of light. In language, it is already improper that the concept and the word exist on two completely separate planes. On the contrary, they form a very close and insoluble compound. It is quite impossible to think of a concept without the word to express it. Words are much more than a means of communicating a concept to other people— words presuppose the fact that an idea can be born into our minds at all; in a certain sense, words are its origin —"In the beginning was the Word."

But as little as a thought can be entertained without the medium of language, just as little can the language exist without the thought. For it is only the thought behind it that gives language its content and meaning; without thoughts, language would be a senseless chatter, an unintelligible succession of sounds, a mere undigested conglomeration of sound material.

Is not the same thing true of music, which, like language, develops its course through time? Is it not here also the thought which gives form, order, and meaning to the sound material in the same measure that it has itself been awakened from its silence by the sound medium and been made to speak through it? In fact, many angles of music which up to now have remained incomprehensible can be explained by this hypothesis, and it is therefore profitable to probe into it further. We must, however, remember that the thought which we are discussing is purely a musical thought, that is, a thought which can be expressed only through the medium of music, never through the medium of words. We must, for instance, strictly avoid the mistake of presuming that the conception of liberty could be designated by the word "liberty" as well as by some clearly defined musical figure. The thoughts of music are not somehow "translated" from the word language into sound language. They are completely original and can only appear in sound. Nevertheless, music has much to do with "liberty," which I shall show again later on; but exactly where the fanfares blare most proudly and where the chorus is most vociferous in its praise of liberty, there we often find the least musical liberty and so the least real liberty.

When this musical thought cannot be expressed by words, how then shall we grasp it and recognize it? Can it be that it is nothing but a ghost evoked by vain speculation? No—one recognizes, differentiates, and values the musical thought according to the extent in which it has ordered, regulated, and molded the material and made it serviceable as a medium of significant expression. Thoughts behind the word language are not recognizable by anything else, either. Nor are the thoughts of the word language expressible in a medium outside of it, for that would require a third medium, an unknown dimension. In so far as the spoken material has sense and meaning, it is indebted to the thought, the existence and power of which, on the other hand, can be discovered only by the stamp which it forced on the material. Likewise music is indebted to the thought for its form and its force of expression. The thought, however, can be recognized only by the fact that it gives this form and force of expression to the material. Just as we measure and recognize the value of a literary work by the richness of its thought and the manner in which this wealth of thought produces a richly articulated original form in the language material, so shall we judge the quality of music according to the richness and versatility of its form, the ingenuity and variety with which individual elements are brought into contact with each other, and how characteristic is the gift of invention reflected in all this. The greater the strength and liveliness with which all this is expressed, the more important is the world of thought which has brought such music to life.

Of course we never can expect—I repeat this once more—to discover the composer's thought in the form of word communication. No matter if we play the "Persian Market" itself another few million times, no musical symbol will ever appear, through any known or unknown magic, which could paint the substance "Persia" more unmistakably than these six letters. But the author only desires us to think, when we hear the rhythmic clanging and stamping, that this work has some resemblance to the actual music customarily heard in Persian markets. This, however, is a purely intellectual detour, which obviously has nothing to do with the question of what kind of thought, if any, is the foundation for that opus. The musical thought can definitely not be extracted from the music by intellectual procedures; it can only be immediately grasped upon hearing, or be made discernible by purely musical analysis, which does not wander around among literary metaphors.

The musical thought is not always identical with the

famous "spark of inspiration"—even though it may be at times. The question "How does one compose?" perpetually occupies journalist and amateur alike. The inhabitant of the modern world of commodities puts the greatest value on picturing the realm of art as a paradise before the sin, as a holy region where one does not "work" but "creates," where one sits in the shady forest, or strolls along the murmuring brook and has "inspirations." In reality, of course, the preparatory labor and the conditions under which a musical work comes to the striped paper are a matter of complete indifference.

Melody and Harmony

THE fate of a musical thought is wrapped up in the musical form which the composer is able to create from the material. That form is the development of music in time. Just as the painter is faced by the problem of how to divide a given surface, guided by the "pictorial thought," so has the musician the problem of how to fill a certain time period with musical occurrences. These occurrences consist of changes of sounds. If one tone or several tones were maintained all the time, obviously nothing would happen and such a manifestation certainly could not be termed music. The processes involving these changes are harmonic and melodic. The fact that we can discern them as such rests upon our faculty of recognizing several tones sounding at the same time, or a sequence of tones which sound one after the other, as units. The rhythm makes its appearance through time periods which are thus marked by the "occurrences," by changing harmonies and the development of the melody. The great battle waged by many music aesthetes as to whether rhythm or melody should be the primary phenomenon seems to me to be possibly interesting, but not of great importance. For even if we could discover unmistakably whether music found its origin in the shouting or in the stamping of primitive man, whether it has been inspired by the song of birds or by human pulsation or the breakers of the ocean, that would not bring us one inch closer to the solution of our present problem. And so my discourse is not genetic, but purely practical. The chronological sequence which I use sometimes has no historical meaning, but serves only to illustrate a difficult point.

Musical thought is first realized along the lines of melody, and that is even in agreement with history, for polyphonic music is a relatively late product in the development of the art; while harmonically organized music, having a compact system of chords, has been known for only four hundred years. Some types of musical thought are marvelously perfect in themselves, such as the Gregorian chant, which does not need any harmonic elements whatever and therefore has not produced any. It was not until polyphony—the simultaneous sounding of several melodic voices—came to be used, that sounds simultaneously produced acquired a distinctive value. From the "horizontal" progress of the single voices—as one calls it according to the graphic appearance of the melodic line on the barred paper—the "vertical" pillars of the chords rise up as static elements and focus attention which formerly was concentrated on the melodic line. Looking back over a period of more than three hundred years in which these harmonic elements have played an increasingly important role, we see that today they largely determine the character of a sound language. These elements are static; that is, in contrast to the melodic element, they do not develop in a time sense; they do not run away from the hearer—and so they are particularly in evidence, suggestive and therefore characteristic of the picture. However tired, for instance, we have become of the diminished seventh chord since Wagner, it is quite typical of a certain sound language (and its usefulness has been worn thin for exactly that reason). But that is no reason why we should forget that these elements are products of a musical thought, primarily conceived along melodic lines.

When the classic composers thought out their melodies in terms of broken triads (as very often they did), it is clear that their harmonies, too, were based on triads. Small wonder that the harmonies of Schoenberg move in a diametrically opposite direction, for in his world of musical thought he prefers quite different intervals: seconds, fourths, and sevenths. In any case, we must remember that the elements of a sound language are not fixed elements in themselves. The triad harmony is as little anchored to some law of nature as any other device. It is, like any other contrivance, a medium in the service of free musical thought. The thought itself has created this medium as an adequate means of expression; changes experienced in historical development have caused it to find new media and to organize the material in a different way. We must strictly adhere to the superiority of thought over means, for only in this way can we succeed in stripping this triad harmony and tonality of the fetishism so often in evidence and so repeatedly marshaled in the fight against modern music. (In Chapter Six, devoted to a full discussion of atonality, we shall have occasion to develop this point at some greater length.)

Articulation and Coherence

WHAT musical thought must first accomplish is *articulation* of material, that is, the clarification of everything which brings order into the change of sounds necessarily required in the course of a composition. The most important elements here are the *accents*. Rhythm, with its multiple succession of accented and unaccented beats, is only the framework of the articulation; it must be filled with musical elements. Here the relation between *consonance* and *dissonance* is of vital importance. Neither of these two concepts is expressed in an absolute sense. The sound material as such contains only the possibility of such a differentiation, as it presents harmonies of various degrees of tensions. By tension degrees I mean the variety of psychological reactions caused by different sound combinations: a perfect fifth, for instance, creates the impression in the listener of a lesser degree of tension than that caused by a major seventh; and so forth. How these differences are applied to articulate the thought depends entirely on the character of the thought governing the material. This is why the effect of dissonance and its treatment are dependent on the historical development of the thought and are not regulated by a definite law of nature.

When all these elements serve the purpose of giving the thought a significant, sharply chiseled, and clear outline, they also make possible the simultaneous connection of several thoughts to the musical form, the higher organism of music. This larger form can be interpreted as something coherent only if a recognizable connection exists between the individual parts. The connection is based on the principle that somewhere a certain element of one part is related to elements of another part. The simplest form of this relationship is exact *repetition;* but the more delicately a composition is organized, the more variable are the forms of the association. Repetition can be extended or modified by processes of lengthening or of shortening, or it may be varied in some other way. From a melodic point of view, an *inversion* may take place, which means that the ascending intervals of the original structure can be changed in equivalent descending steps, and vice versa. Or the development may be retrograde, if we read a melodic figure from the last tone to the first, etc. But very free forms of relationship, in which repetition of the elements has been reduced to a minimum, are feasible, as is often the case in present-day music. All these relationships make use of the elements which the thought has created in its original concept for the purpose of articulation.

Characteristic melodic curves, harmonic features, and rhythmic figures are primarily intended to give maximum significance to the thought, and serve later to create a large entity by their mutual relationship and the many combinations possible between them.

So far I have purposely avoided speaking of definite "musical forms," and have intentionally eschewed the customary term "theme." We shall not confine ourselves to such terms, because we have not yet examined them critically. Generally one is only too ready to adopt the usual terminology, if only for the sake of convenience; and the student often does not realize that he thereby absorbs a whole system of thought, the validity of which is the issue at stake.

Most of the theoretical discourses on music have the character of propaganda or defense. Every new "movement" is violently attacked by representatives of tradition. For this reason, spokesmen for the new movement try to establish it as the only definite solution of all problems, most often because they claim it constitutes a better (or more faithful) reflection of the so-called laws of nature than previous movements. According to this contention, musical progress moves toward a sort of Platonic "Ideal of Music," which is reached whenever a possible accord is obtained between the musical will to create and an unchangeable law of nature. Everything which has so far happened in music must then be considered as a series of preparatory attempts to reach this Ideal Condition; as such these efforts have great merit, or may be in themselves of great value; but they are necessarily deficient, because the eternal law of music has not yet been clearly visioned and time only will perfect our knowledge of that law.

Pessimists are free to assert that this Optimum has already been reached, has even been passed—as in the case of Palestrina, or Beethoven, or Wagner, at your choice—and that whatever has come since is rank deterioration. That contention, though, has nothing to do with analysis but deals only with resentment. But these passionately apologetic assertions prove that music actually does advance in one way or another. Progress has become a little suspect to us who have witnessed greater catastrophes and collapses than have been seen by many generations before us; but if we visualize progress as something bigger than a one-way street which leads straight into paradise, we may as well admit that it exists.

We can discard the ideal picture of music as being merely the projection of the wish-dreams of individual malcontents or reactionaries. But so far as the so-called natural laws of acoustics are concerned, which so far have allegedly been observed with the utmost faithfulness in all new movements, we can state objectively that the development of music has turned more and more away from conditions described by these laws.

The Constructive Moment

ON THE contrary, the advance of music, as with all human progress, consists of an ever greater control over the material of nature. The means employed by thought for its realization in musical material becomes steadily richer and more varied; the form which that thought incorporates in the language is the result of an increasingly careful construction. The composer becomes more and more independent of natural laws. This independence, however, is balanced by a stronger and more vital constructive tendency. In historical chapters, we shall give concrete examples of the composer's increasing emancipation from nature.

After all, it is not surprising that the cry for a natural law is now especially loud, for today humanity has arrived at a point where it does not even know what to do with the results of technical advance. But the claim that everything would become better if we could revert from the airplane to the covered wagon (although several such ideologies are not altogether harmless) would be exactly as childish as the belief that the problems of contemporary music would at once be solved if the musician would only decide to write more triads. (As in the former case, there are, in the latter category, not a few reactionaries who entertain this belief.)

When, therefore, the artistic content, the real essence of music, its advance and its fate are bound up in its

constructive elements, that is, in the entire complex of
the musical figure and in the relationships which
thought succeeds in modeling from the material; and
when, on the other hand, no one can be called musical
who is unqualified to absorb this substance (as we
claimed above as a prerequisite), then we come to the
conclusion that any musical person must perforce be
able to understand musical construction.

General and stormy protest! Should music, then, be
confined to musical scholars? Must all the people who
owe to music many enjoyable hours, in which they give
free reign to their emotions through listening to magic
tones, be insulted by being called "unmusical"? Must
they be excluded from the enjoyment of music? Must
such listeners be deprived of the art and must it be
locked up in the sepulchral silence of libraries in order
that a few long-bearded professors may trace its "construction," which no healthy individual really cares a
straw about? In such involved, scholarly analyses, what
has become of sentiment, that incomparable force which
speaks more directly and more convincingly from music
than from any other form of art? Is it not precisely the
unsurpassed privilege of music to appeal directly to
the feelings of the listeners without any detour of understanding and thought, and thus to open the kingdom
of art to the intellectually unschooled?

It is true that music speaks to the listener without
the medium of abstract concepts—but not without
thought. It is likewise true that music appeals to the
soul—but clearly through thought, which is the language of the emotions. In the language of words, the
emotion is expressed in words which match the concept, to enable the reader (or the listener) to experience this emotion along the line of intellectual compre-

hension. In music, on the other hand, musical thought is itself the bearer of an emotional expression, without any intermediacy of abstract medium. Every melodic or harmonic curve, every increase or decrease in dynamics, every musical gesture is expressive in itself just as every line in the handwriting of an individual is expressive of his mental condition and emotion.

Yet the degree of importance of the expression does not depend on the identity of the subject expressed, as is often supposed, but rather on the psychic fund on which the author draws—in other words, on his talent or genius. Music itself is neutral, like the sun, which shines on the just and unjust alike. Whether the emotional sensation of longing concerns, say, a meal, a faraway sweetheart, or the freedom of one's fatherland cannot be gathered from the music which reflects these emotions. Hanslick, the famous opponent of Richard Wagner, proved that one can, with equal conviction, give to the aria "Ah, I have lost thee," from Gluck's *Orfeo,* the words "Ah, I have found thee," without sacrificing any of the music's power.

Perhaps the elementary strength of emotion in music is overpowering simply because it is completely independent of any physical content, yet that is exactly the reason why music is forced into construction. That does not mean, of course, that according to a puritanical, pedestrian ideology, the unbridled stream of emotion must be placed under control, so that no damage is done and everything flows along nicely and smoothly. Far from it. In reality, the question is one of a dialectical and paradoxical relationship: The more intensive the expression, the bolder and more direct the language of emotion, the more rigid is the construction. Under the influence of a striving for an ever more differentiated, and thereby more intensive expression, the material is changed in a way that enforces an ever more consistent and all-embracing construction. Our historical review will prove this in a concrete manner.

Should Music Be Approached Intellectually?

OUR nice elevator boy in Omaha who enjoys the "Persian Market" experiences but a fraction of the real expressive power of music. He takes part in only a few musical formulae whose expressive significance has been conventionally established by long habit. But must he then first become a music scholar in order to experience the higher emotions when he listens to music? Apparently such a contention is in direct contradiction to the fact that hundreds of thousands of people, upon hearing exacting classical music, experience a satisfying, elevating, and joyful feeling, though they may not understand it. If this were not so, hundreds of thousands would not continue to hurry to such performances. Certainly one need not have mastered the explicit technical issue in order to be immediately responsive to the flow of feeling in nineteenth-century music. But though an individual may never have heard of Beethoven, we must not forget that his reaction is actually based on a human experience of a hundred years, in fact on our entire musical inheritance. The fact that Beethoven has entered into the public consciousness in the last hundred years creates a general mental condition for the acceptance of his music, a condition which we cannot value too highly. But why should the general public of today remain out of contact with contemporary music? Is it because there is enough older music which man, on the strength of his inheritance, is able to enjoy

more easily? For the rest, it is merely prejudice to assume that the spontaneity of the novice's artistic enjoyment is conversely influenced by any technical and
theoretical considerations. This prejudice finds its
origin in the general suspicion of all intellectual efforts,
which in turn finds its cause in the fact that humanity,
seeing itself involved in ever more serious calamities by
its own cultural accomplishments, would rather place
the blame on these accomplishments than try to eliminate the evil by a consistent continuation of spiritual
labor. Nor would it do the enthusiasts and those who
honestly enjoy the old music any harm if they could
be a little informed about its structure and technique.
No football fan has ever found that his enjoyment of
the game is impaired by knowing the rules.

To be sure, the wisdom culled from musical guides
and program notes which the nineteenth century has
brought to the fore and which, for the greater part, has
retained its status up to the present day, is of little
use in tackling the problems of this newfangled music.
The vexation which it has called forth is justified in
every respect—but the opinion that it might, then, be
better to know nothing at all is not justifiable. The
listener who, with the help of a musical timetable
handed to him at the entrance of a concert hall, is able
to identify the "second theme" and the "bridge passage" when they are being played, has no reason as yet
to lord it over his neighbor who simply listens and
enjoys the music. Such stale academic knowledge engenders only a cheap priggishness; the ability of the
willing listener to absorb is strait-jacketed into an
inept system of formulae. And the result will be the
narrow-minded opinion taught by the university extension course, which educates listeners to prejudice. They

soon feel themselves qualified to pronounce anything
which does not conform to rules taught them in "ten
easy lessons" arbitrary, irregular, or intellectual trickery.
For the contention that proper music must be written
according to the approved textbook rules does not prevent the tenderly nurtured wish-dream that this music
was at the same time overheard at nature's breast by the
genius.

A short time ago I heard of a musically uneducated
man in New York who by accident, possibly by mistake,
heard the *Eroica* for the first time when he turned on
his radio. He had a revolutionary experience; never
before had anything like this happened to him; he
had never suspected that something like this existed.
He ran to a friend employed in a music shop and be-
sieged him with requests for further information about
this man Beethoven and his music. He discovered
that somewhere a Beethoven film was being shown and
wished to see it under the guidance of this musical
clerk. He wanted to read books about Beethoven and
to learn everything possible about him. There is no
doubt that this man is on the right road to music. The
overpowering emotion which he experienced was not
enough for him, rather was his emotion so deep that
it did not leave him in peace. It would be of no help
to him if someone were to put a poor outline of the
classical sonata form into his hand and say: "Now you
know how such a symphony is written." Nor would it
do him any good to hear someone explain that Beethoven's music expresses the ideal of freedom because the
master tore the dedication to Napoleon from the *Eroica*
when he found that his hero had degenerated into a
dictator. All that would not mean anything to our enthusiast. What would really interest him and give him

a share in the essence and the fate of music would be to learn to what extent the work which he admired so much reflects in its concrete musical form the ideals which radiate from it; how the ideal of freedom in its most definite historical guise, as realized within the framework of German idealism, determines the form of musical construction to its minutest details; how the transformation of social conditions reacts upon the conception of symphonic form and accompanies its development (always technically traceable in a clear-cut manner, never interpreted from a superimposed literary point of view) to the last Beethoven quartets on the one hand and to Schubert on the other. There is no doubt that our anonymous enthusiast, once caught by his passion for the subject, can be brought to a much deeper understanding of music by such information about the close connection between the inner musical structure and the highly concrete forces of the period —above all, to an understanding of the music of his own time. When he discovers that the latter does not arouse in him the same stormy elemental emotion that is stirred by the symphony of Beethoven, he will, then, perhaps not shrug his shoulder indifferently or superciliously, but he will find this fact (the lack of deep emotional reaction) worth some reflection and will make it a point of departure in his further studies.

How Critics Could Help

WHAT education could and should accomplish in this regard is obvious. I shall have more to say about it at the end of this book. It is a long-range project. But much could easily be done at once to smooth the road of understanding. I shall mention here only the task which is allotted to the music critic. Certainly his influence in general is much overrated—very few newspaper readers read the musical column. It is strange that those in authority in the music field—managers, agents, directors, conductors, etc.—take critics so seriously. The private opinion of a critic, if expressed in a private letter, would never interest them for a second; it acquires practical importance through appearing in a few hundred thousand copies of the paper, even if one knows that only a few hundred of these are being read. Thereby criticism is reduced to the purely commercial valuation to which, indeed, it is necessarily entitled in this commodity world of ours.

The producer of music, as in the case of all commercial products, must keep its ultimate distribution and sales value in mind. Any publicly expressed opinion about this product must perforce act as a deterrent or a spur to the potential customer. Hence criticism itself becomes merchandise, too, for undoubtedly the creators of works of art under review by the critics will strive to influence them so to sway the public, or at least the authoritative personages in the music world, that sales will be increased. To what degree this interdependence may affect certain persons depends on the moral integrity of the individual in question. But the principle of integrity in the field of criticism is just as chimerical as that of incorruptibility in politics. Under certain circumstances even the strictest and most conscientious critic cannot avoid the fact that his opinion is appraised in a purely commercial light.

The critic's important function should be an educational introduction of the work of art and its production to the public, rather than distribution of praise or censure. When two new quartets are played on a

certain evening and the review of the critic reads:
"The second was more pleasant than the first," absolutely nothing useful has been said. The critic should
take the trouble to probe into the artistic intention
of the composers, to examine whether this intention
is realized with adequate means; he must determine the
spiritual quality of the work and fit it correctly into
the larger whole. Only when the public has become
accustomed to consider such a point of view as necessary will it seek in criticism more than the mere information as to whether it is worth while to pay $1.10 for
a seat, because the expert has found the work sufficiently
"pleasant." At present very few critics are willing or
qualified to find out what effect the composer of a new
work intended it to have; this is not always the critic's
fault, for few new works are published today. But even
if the new composition is not available in printed form,
there are ways by which to orientate oneself to it before
the performance. One can, for instance, scan the written score; one can interview the composer, if he is present; one can come to rehearsals, etc. All this does not
always miscarry because of ill will or indolence, but
simply because of lack of time, coupled with the impossibility of finding space for such erudite information
in the newspaper columns. For, since newspapers in the
final analysis are nothing but merchandise, their editors
are first of all interested in the commercial value of the
criticism.

That under these circumstances justice cannot be
done to such a complex phenomenon as modern music
is obvious. Only the most honest critics will wash their
hands of the whole business by frankly admitting that
they do not understand the work. But they do not re-
sign on that account, neither are they discharged by

their employers (as would undoubtedly be the case in the business world). On the contrary, the critics' authority increases, because their admission serves to bolster the self-confidence of those listeners who did not understand the new music either, and so everything remains just as it was before.

No wonder that under these conditions the number of sincerely musical persons is much smaller than it could be; no wonder, above all, that the new music has come to be so dangerously isolated.

CHAPTER

TWO

MODERN MUSIC IS UNPOPULAR

The Plight of Repertory

SEEN from the production angle—in other words, from the composer's point of view—the entire problem of music in our time is one of overproduction and underconsumption, for much more music is written than is played and heard. This condition reminds one of symptoms of the great economic crisis, but the analogy should not be pursued too far. The outstanding success of any industrial product immediately encourages the competitive manufacture of large quantities of identical or similar articles. But in the case of art, the very kind of serious music which is played most often and which is always in demand for repeat performances forms an obstacle in the path of kindred works. The number of sold copies of a successful piece mounts tremendously—printed music is a manufactured product and a commercial article, like any other. But there is no renewed activity in the places of original production, in the composers' studios; the success of one piece easily tends to inhibit the success of another.

By its performance, the musical composition is consumed only in so far as it is absorbed by the listeners for whom it is intended, although it is not actually used up. In another way, development in the last century has shown that the more often a piece of music is repeated the longer its life span will be, for the public desires nothing more ardently than to hear over and over again that with which it is most familiar. The result is that the contemporary composer who likes to have his work performed is threatened by a mountain slide of holy antiquities—and is often buried under it.

Concert and opera have their regular repertory, which cannot be tampered with: their conservation is served by the active work of the most outstanding performing artists. To the new, only as much room is allowed as is left over after the obligations to the usual repertory have been fulfilled. Yet the repertory, in the sense of constituting a supply of works always ready for performance and continuous repetition, is a relatively recent feature in the field of music. Its beginning dates back only about a hundred years. Until that time new works had a considerably higher percentage of performances than the old ones.

When we examine the causes of this phenomenon, a close connection is apparent between the inner quality of art and social conditions. Until far into the time of the classic composers—the late eighteenth century —the core of the musical production process was the *performance,* the real, live tone of music. In comparison, composing seemed relatively a secondary activity, serving more as a technical preparation to the performance than as something which had a spiritual value of its own. If music was to be played and sung, it first had to be written down, but this writing was merely a part of the general preparation, not much more important than securing the proper instrumentalists, rehearsing the singers, etc. To see to the desired performance was the first duty of the musician, who was in the service of the feudal society of those days, or in the service of the church. He had to engage the instrumentalists and the singers, to train them, and to conduct their performances. That notes were needed was self-evident, and that on occasion he wrote those notes himself was nothing which required special mention. It was accepted as natural that the *Kapellmeister,* who was appointed over the other musicians, would use his own compositions for the performance, and new ones whenever possible.

In those days very few composers stood out so clearly as individuals that works by them were acknowledged to have distinctive value and so were performed and repeated in different places. But in such cases the local maestro had no hesitation in making changes according to the needs of the occasion, in replacing parts of the original with inserts by other music masters, and so on. Originality was neither a prerequisite for the composer nor a condition for publication. The ideal was rather an obvious and perfect conformity to the accepted style of the period. Musical themes were not the private property of their inventors, protected against imitation by the equivalent of a patent; the meaning of plagiarism was practically unknown. The composer, as such, did not receive pay for the single performance, not because his invention was original and not liable to repetition, but because at the desired time and in the desired place he, as *maestro di capella,* produced music which brilliantly reflected the generally acknowledged notion of what such music ought to be.

It would, however, be incorrect to report this state of affairs as a golden age. Its stability was only relative; for, exactly as in the history of the greatest masters of the preclassic period, symptoms of individualism became ever more prominent and finally led to the destruction of rigid forms. The progressive element in art, which transforms its essence, its technique, and its material, always questions the integrity of a given style as the ideal of that period. From the biographies of composers like Monteverdi, Bach, and Mozart we know enough about their conflicts with public opinion and the battle they fought with their sponsors to realize how valid this questioning is. But the conflicts between the productive artist and his time were not then so fundamental as in subsequent developments.

The basis of all public musical life was radically changed by the transformation of feudalism into a middle-class society. Theaters and concert halls were thrown open to an enormously increasing number of people, and the operation of music as an institution had thenceforth to depend for its sustenance upon this new audience's desire to buy and its power to buy, a service which formerly was essentially performed by small privileged groups. There is a close relationship between the weakening of the revolutionary ideals of the bourgeois class, which deteriorated and stagnated through compromise, particularly since 1848, and the fact that the artistic advance has found no lively response among the general public.

The concerts which Robert Schumann wrote about in his famous criticism of the eighteen thirties included an astonishing number of novelties. But the policy of the repertory gained the upper hand more and more. This repertory consists mainly of works by the Vienna classics which the bourgeoisie has considered a sort of monument to a concluded heroic period. The exaltation, enthusiasm, élan, and vitality which speak from that music were enjoyed as something separated from

the contemporary scene—as something purely historical. What music expressed in the way of passionate opposition and open protest was completely ignored (most
often in the case of Mozart) or was simply ascribed to
the "titanic" struggle of an isolated genius (as in the
case of Beethoven); and any connection with topical
conditions was carefully shielded from a public trans-
fixed in passive admiration.

The Question of Originality

AGAINST ever growing opposition, the accomplishments
of romanticism and of early impressionism were admitted to the repertory program. We are able to mention only a few composers living today who have successfully invaded the repertory: in the orchestra field,
Richard Strauss, with a few works; Sibelius (limited
more or less to the Anglo-Saxon world); Strawinsky,
with one or two early compositions. Possibly there are
a few more composers in the repertory with limited, or
at most a national, appeal. In opera, Strauss is about the
only composer who has one or two works permanently
included in the repertory programs.

The explanation is found in the rapidly growing contradictions which ruled the musical world of the nineteenth century. The wish-dreams of a definitive, com-
pulsory style still dominate and are further solidified
by the stabilization of bourgeois society. Yet this society, which prides itself on the liberation of the individual from the bonds of feudal and ecclesiastical
guardianship, demands of the artist clear proof of originality. As a result of the inner development of music,
about which more will be said later, composers are increasingly directed to the application of such original-

ity, a feature which becomes, at the same time, an ever growing obstacle to the performance of their works before a public whose ideals of music are becoming more and more petrified. Still, that public is quite willing to allow the rejected artist an aureole in his isolation. He should consider himself well compensated for the suffering which this isolation may bring, because it separates him from the "profane" world of profit, and thus ennobles him. The attic to which he is banned, the better to carry on his titanic struggle and the better to compose, on bread and water, serves as a pleasant annex to the palace in which his master wishes to live, comfortably undisturbed otherwise by the strange sounds emanating from this remote habitation. The thought that posthumous fame is more important than present success allays the guilty conscience of a society which reserves this fate for him.

And yet the dialectic laws which govern these interrelations demand that the trite statement just made, cheap and vulgar though it may be, expresses an unassailable truth. That such a thought can be expressed at all proves the existence of a condition where it is a matter of necessity that a work be made out of material which shall outlast the period during which it is actually being rejected.

In the last hundred years, too, the position of the composer in regard to society has changed radically. No longer has he a personal and individual sponsor, in whose service he is to write and produce music for performance on a certain occasion. Today the composer faces an indeterminable public to whom his opus is brought through an intermediary—a concert or opera manager, or a theatrical producer. Thereby a musical work becomes merchandise, for the producer can conduct his business only in the way prescribed by the economic laws of the capitalistic world. He is not a Maecenas, but merely a merchant who must satisfy the needs of his customers. In the proportion that the character of the merchandise is imprinted upon the musical world, it acquires, rather paradoxically, more and more the consecration of literature. By looking at a graphic picture of the old music we can see how it was written for specified performances, soon to be given. The manuscripts were fragmentary and sketchy. Even in the case of complicated works like operas, little more than the voice and the *basso continuo* were written down; all the rest—even the distribution of the unwritten accompanying parts of the various instruments—were left to a final arrangement at rehearsal, an arrangement which could be based upon the universally known and standardized playing practice. Tempo indications were rare and were limited to a few principal types; instructions as to dynamics were hardly given at all. Music could be written in that way because the works performed generally corresponded to a type which was known everywhere, and little thought was given to its preservation; the written script was merely part of the technical preparation for the solitary performance which was the ultimate purpose of the whole enterprise.

Music Becomes Literature

THE further one advances toward the present in the history of music, the more detailed and carefully executed become the manuscripts. It is evident that not only the entire instrumentation gradually came to be designated specifically, but, in addition, that great care was taken to indicate exactly, to the smallest detail, how the music should be performed. Metronomic indications removed all lack of clarity in tempo indications; directions about dynamics and expressive nuances are today like comments on almost every note—how loudly it should be played, what importance it has in relationship to the other notes, what expressive intent underlies it. The importance is shifted more and more from the solitary performance to the written record, in order that it may result in a similar rendition for the maximum number of performances at any desired place and at any desired time. As the result of the quick change in the general style-picture and its ultimate disintegration, the single work simply does not belong any longer to any given type which could be classified as being universally known. Furthermore, a work is seldom written for a definite, imminent, and scheduled performance: under the force of circumstances the unfortunate composer usually writes at random, and many years may elapse between his composition and the performance. This lapse of time might confuse what today seems self-evident. But above everything the composer who composes "from the fullness of his heart," without the backing of a definite commission, must be able to take for granted, or at least to hope, that his work will be produced often, for only then will it contribute appreciably to his economic existence. In the event that all this does not happen, and to ensure himself at least the consoling chance of a "posthumous fame," he will take great care to prepare such a clear and legible script that after several centuries the score will still convey an unequivocal picture of his intentions.

The more the law of merchandise is imprinted on

musical productions, the more they retire into the written form and approach in character the type of literature which is conserved in the venerable silence of the library. I shall show in the ninth chapter how this development in technique, which has contributed so vitally to the establishment of a dictatorship of the character of merchandise, offers a possibility, unsuspected heretofore, of having music coincide entirely and absolutely with its graphic picture.

Where music has completely surrendered to economic laws, it reminds us most in practice of the old music of the prebourgeois period, which in itself is a strange paradox. I refer to the field of "popular" or entertainment music, where originality is allowed only to the extent that the new work must create the effect of having already been heard a hundred times. Here, too, the ideal is the most brilliant possible presentation of a picture in the general accepted style. The fact that plagiarism is not only tabooed in this sphere but is prosecuted zealously finds its cause less in a concession to the spiritual sense of property in serious music than to a very plausible application of the principle of private property as practiced in the commercial world. Here the product is not intended for a single performance, as with the old music; the real production rests solidly upon the tremendous number of paid performances. The royalty percentage is the basis upon which the creator is compensated for his work. Just as the public pays the cost of building the hall, the lighting, heating, wear and tear, advertising, wages for the musicians, the administration expenses and even the taxes, so does it pay also for the use of the music which is being played—a point of view which can be made clear to the producers only over the latters' vigorous opposition, since they find it more economical to consider a work of art so infinitely ideal that one should never profane it by contact with filthy lucre.

The Royalty System

THE system of royalty is fully justified in the case of popular music, where the public is offered a certain merchandise which it sincerely desires. After all, why should people not pay something for musical details in the entertainment, when they consider it fair and proper to pay a certain amount for all the rest?

In the case of serious music, this system shows the more clearly what contradictions exist in the music world of today. The composer who allows his music to be entered in the regular barter system can soon see from the incoming proceeds what minimum exchange value is inherent in his work. Society, however, is only mildly ashamed of this fact, for it tolerates the condition whereby the best is by no means identical with the most successful. In some European countries, the creators of popular music used to contribute out of their gigantic earnings to subsidies which were used for the support of their less fortunate colleagues in the difficult field. (The latter could divide the contribution among themselves.) Many operetta composers have a secret longing to write a real, decent opera. When Franz Lehár had the good luck to see one of his works performed at the Staatsoper in Vienna, he derived his greatest satisfaction from the fact that at last he had had a chance to write a part for the double bassoon. That had been the dream of his life; but he had never been able to gratify the yearning, because the operetta theaters, for which he had to compose regularly, did not have such an instrument in their orchestras. When those children upon whom fortune has smiled bestow something of their wealth on lonely colleagues, it seems as if they wish to bolster the courage of those bold adventurers who do not hesitate to write for the double bassoon whenever the spirit moves them, even at the risk of thereby making their work less salable.

For the rest, it must be said that of all the people who occupy themselves with music hardly any show a more touching and quite unintelligent respect for the most radically new music than the commercial manufacturers of musical hits. In Vienna I have seen operetta writers, worth millions, who, between excited conferences with singers and producers, would listen in the gallery of the Musikvereinssaal to some modern work which must have sounded like Chinese to them.

The royalty system for serious music has value only if it is expanded to the works of the past, without taking into consideration how many years may have elapsed since the death of the respective composers. The story is told about Richard Strauss that whenever he drew his tremendous honoraria he used to count the bank notes with grim pleasure, saying, "This one is for Mozart, this for Schubert, this for Beethoven." He did this to point out that the large fees which he owed to the establishment of the royalty system had to be considered a sort of punitive tax on a society which permitted those masters to suffer dire want. Even if Strauss's pleasure was greater than his grimness—for he never used to spend any of his money on the graves of the sublime dead, nor did he make donations to any possible heirs—there is something quite pertinent in his train of thought.

The European author's rights are based on the contention that a composer's direct heirs should be satisfied when they have lived for fifty years on the proceeds of his work; after that time the works are in "the public domain," which means that no further royalties are paid on the publication rights nor on the performances. It is alleged that since everyone is allowed to reprint such works, useful competition among the publishers results, so that the works become both cheap and universal property.

A New Suggestion Concerning Royalties

SO FAR, the argument is sound. It does not, indeed, seem necessary that a copyright should remain in the family forever, like so many securities. Hardly any composer, when writing down the first few notes of a composition, thinks primarily of leaving his grandchildren a life insurance in the shape of a successful work. But the composer has other heirs, who more often than not are closer to him in his spiritual experience than many of his blood relatives; they are his colleagues, his spiritual heirs who are born after him, who will continue to develop his artistic thought, to whom his music is an inspiration and an example, and who thereby also may establish that famous "posthumous fame" which results in the tangible success of his works denied to him during his lifetime. Would it not be logical that the spiritual descendants should benefit from proceeds of his work? For if they are working in the same spirit, it is probable that they will enjoy success as little as their predecessors and will be exposed to the same privations.

It is hard to understand why singers, pianists, conductors, concert hall owners, and music dealers should make money today on Beethoven and Mozart, while the spiritual descendants of these masters (no matter how small in stature they may seem in comparison) are forced to suffer the same privations. And if, by some trick of fate, Schoenberg or Bartók should be as popular in a hundred years as Beethoven is today, would it be fair if interpreters and their assistants should again be the only people to profit? No! So long as we are forced to take into account the fact that new art counts for little in its own time, it would certainly be more dignified if serious artists could support themselves out of such a spiritual inheritance, rather than be forced to depend on the gifts of well-meaning colleagues who supply the public with more desirable merchandise.

The greatest objection to this project comes from interpreters. Singers and pianists already consider it a great favor to the composer if they present a new piece, and believe it insolence on his part if he demands payment to boot. It happens often enough that individual performers, and even orchestra associations, refuse to perform new works for the admitted reason that they do not wish to pay royalties. Add to this the facts that the public would rather hear old music anyway, and that old music can be performed with fewer rehearsals and less expense—then why double vexation and lose money besides?

This undignified competition of the innocent dead with the living would stop at once if payments were required to perform any kind of composition. Concert artists assert that such a tax would prove an unbearable burden for their younger colleagues, who often can give their first concerts only by making the greatest sacrifices, and who should not, in addition, be "taxed" for the music which they are performing. I believe this objec-

tion could easily be overcome, if artists already established would contribute a fraction of their huge earnings to the encouragement of their struggling brothers
and sisters through a fund established for that purpose.
Here, too, the question of a sort of spiritual inheritance
might arise. Why, for instance, could not a star conductor or prima donna devote, say, 1 per cent of his or her
income to a fund which would enable young conductors or young singers to give their first concerts? (If
only to enable them to bear the extra expenses caused
by a proviso that the composers—to whom, after all, the
whole industry owes its existence—should not go empty-
handed; or to avoid a fight between composers and performers over the few pennies involved.)

Under the present conditions everything which the
human being produces has a property value. The manufacturer of an object must make sure that he receives
for his labor in manufacturing it an equivalent in the
form of money, which in turn will cover his living expenses. It is not considered dignified to include art in
this point of view; but neither the work of art, nor its
creator, nor the performing artists, can escape the law
of necessity. For the rest, those who are so sensitive as
to reject such a profane viewpoint are usually the very
people who could easily create more dignified conditions for art, even under existing circumstances. Curiously enough, the creators of art seem to be the only
ones to enjoy the questionable benefits of this extreme
sensitivity about financial matters. For when it comes to
the performers, it is considered quite all right to pay
them properly for their work; and there is no doubt
that publishers, concert and opera managers, and agents
can be smart businessmen—they need to be!

84374

Modern Music in the Concert Hall

THE sum total of the musical merchandise on which the above-mentioned business people earn the most constitutes the repertory. The new production does not belong there and cannot get in, because it consists of merchandise which is hard to sell. In Europe after the World War, and in particular in the countries which lost the war, there was a certain flowering of new music, in connection with a general reaction against former conditions and ways of conduct, for which the war and subsequent defeat were blamed. People often went to the other extreme and sought to be introduced to something new at any price, without consideration for quality. Every opera house or concert organization wanted to give premières—and often nothing but premières, at that. For a second performance, the new work in most cases was not new enough any more. In Berlin, which had become the center of the European music industry, a new, epoch-making, and definite style was announced about every season. Musical works were classified very much like wines, according to their vintages, but with this difference, that they did not by any means become more valuable as they grew older. In the year 1929 it was almost a death sentence for a work to be classified as belonging to the style of 1924. At that time Artur Schnabel used to remark with some justice that the first performance of a work comprised both its cradle and its tomb. And yet the situation was ridiculous rather than unbearable, for, in spite of all the drawbacks involved, at least a new composition had a real chance: after all, it was sure of being performed! Had conditions been allowed to readjust themselves, a calmer judgment would surely have prevailed in the course of time; thinkers would soon have admitted that those "epoch-making" accomplishments, one following closely on the heels of another, were really spurious, and perhaps the road had been opened to works of real quality.

The provoking exaggerations of that period have made it easy for the reactionary forces, who recovered rapidly, to denounce even the intelligent encouragement of new music as "revolutionary rubbish" and "cultural Bolshevism." For the rest, it is interesting to note that the catastrophic catch phrase, "cultural Bolshevism," was first used, curiously enough, by liberal journalists anxious to represent the taste of the old-time, steady visitors to sedate, dignified symphony concerts. Consequently it was from those concerts that the new music disappeared most rapidly, if, indeed, the novelties had been able to gain any foothold worth mentioning. Wherever one may play or conduct new music, nowhere is there felt a greater wave of suspicion, ill will, boredom, and impatience coming from the audience and engulfing the platform than in these halls, built sixty years ago and overloaded with gilded ornamentation. Little is now to be found of the spirit which filled them in those days when the vital adventures in music took place within their walls. The reluctance of the public to occupy itself with new musical problems is naturally transferred to the orchestras playing in these halls. For, so far as the orchestras are industrious and ambitious and have a good conductor, they make an effort to find new variations in the old repertory and to present the conventional style with the highest possible degree of perfection. This may be done through breath-taking precision and exactitude (as with the orchestras conducted by Toscanini) or through a fascinating beauty of sound (as developed, for instance, by the Vienna Philharmonic until the *Anschluss*). The latter type of performance, lately become quite popular, shows little appreciation of intensive work done at rehearsals, because beauty of sound depends more on the excellence of individual players than on combined work. Since numerous and intensive rehearsals are a prerequisite for the performance of modern music, these orchestras, if only because of their inner structure, present a perplexed and antagonistic front to new music. Perfect exactitude is just as necessary in the performance of rhythmically complex music (and most modern music is of this type) as with music of a simpler rhythmic pattern, though the average listener may not be aware of it in the case of modern music. Nor does a proverbially discordant type of music give sufficient prominence to a harmonious sound picture. For these reasons, the technical problems brought up by new music generally fail to interest the members of these orchestras. That is why the few performances of new music which still manage to get squeezed in are much less good than might be expected and so carry little conviction. And since the excellence of the orchestra is beyond question, public and critics alike blame the work itself for the imperfect impression created. All this, then, furnishes a convenient excuse to praise the performers for their unselfish attitude, and to remark with a regretful shrug of the shoulders that their valuable services were wasted on an unworthy task. And if, contrary to all expectations, success is forthcoming, the listener can read in more than one critical review that the applause was exclusively for the brilliant performance. The astonishingly discriminating ear of a critic alone can tell the difference between applause for a conductor and applause for a composition.

The Operatic Situation

THE operatic situation is similar. Here, too, the repertory is the only feature on which dependence is placed for the support of the institution. In Germany, where the predominating system is that of a permanent opera house, subsidized by the city or state and open all the year, the business managers of the enterprise are principally concerned with keeping the unavoidable deficit within limits allowed by the public fund which provides the money. Only by giving performances every day will the opera house be able to justify the tremendous expense incurred by a staff of singers, instrumentalists, and technicians hired on a yearly basis. Potential audiences in the medium-sized and smaller towns are very limited in numbers, and consequently only a few works can be repeated often. The result is that operas which can be produced with a minimum of rehearsals must be favored; and those are certainly not new operas. Nevertheless, better and more valuable work has often been done in the smaller houses than in the larger ones. Granting that the resources of the larger opera houses are more considerable, their expenses are higher as well; and their box offices are dependent on famous—and expensive—voices much more than in the case of the smaller institutions. Moreover, the vocal stars are as little suited and responsive to new music as are the Viennese type of orchestras—or even less so. And since little is usually expected of a new opera, it is generally cast with second-rate performers. In this way, the new work starts out under a double handicap, for not only is the public far less interested than it might otherwise be, but one can scarcely expect the audience to receive and register a complete and integrated impression of such a performance. The lack of success, however, causes the management less worry than one might believe, for it encourages the directors to avoid novelties for years to come, alleging that they would be very glad indeed to try them out, but that the last attempt had proved once more that new operas do not seem to be what the public wants, probably because the crop is so inferior. The Vienna Staatsoper has been particularly smart in the use of this pretext during the last few years. . . .

Even where the management has the best intentions, the new opera does not penetrate into the opera house except in extremely rare cases. One waits for special occasions—jubilees, festival weeks, events which draw many strangers to the city—to produce a new work with particularly exhausting efforts and for a rigidly limited number of performances, set in advance. This practice in no way conflicts with a certain type of opera which has developed strongly during the last few years. Works like *Christopher Columbus* by Darius Milhaud, like my *Charles V*, perhaps like *Mathis the Painter* by Paul Hindemith as well, require not alone in the artistic and quantitive sense an apparatus and a preparation far beyond the scope of a repertory organization, but show a spiritual attitude which benefits greatly by being sepa-rated from the usual night-after-night routine. When we award such an opera the honor of festival perform-ance, we must not have in mind the ceremonial atmos-phere surrounding the Bayreuth *Buehnenweihfestspiele*. In the latter, we find a prevalent intention to transfigure monumentally an existing spiritual attitude in an at-mosphere pervaded by rising incense in the apotheosis.

But in the new operas, or at least in some of them, both libretto and music tend to dispel illusions, to question existing conditions, and to bring problems under discussion. For that reason it is right to separate them from the regular theater and opera industry, which tries to adhere stubbornly, if with diminishing force, to the illusionary dreams of the nineteenth century. Prophecy is always a thankless task; but one cannot offer a very favorable prognosis regarding an organism which, according to its very nature, is neither fit nor inclined to absorb new forces to any considerable degree.

Radio

ABOUT fifteen years ago a new vehicle, the radio, came into use and today brings large quantities of music to the people. From the commercial point of view, which I now wish to place in the foreground, the radio can show very favorable conditions for the distribution of new music. It handles such a huge amount of material, which is eagerly bought, that a small part of its time can easily be devoted to a merchandise which appeals to not more than a few of its customers. Unfortunately this is true only of the European radio, which exists on taxes on receiving sets paid by the listeners. When, in the course of long periods of time, small amounts of new music are being used, the administration need not fear that audiences will drop off appreciably on that account. For material which the audiences need and like to hear is likewise offered. This includes news of all sorts, stock exchange ticker reports, religious services, interesting radio plays, language courses, and, above all, unlimited quantities of entertainment music. In spite of this preponderance of popular material, radio stations

which send out modern music are constantly exposed to
excited protests; consequently in Europe little enough
new music is broadcast. When this does happen it is
nearly always owing to one or more individuals connected with a radio station who have a personal interest
in modern music and who, with much cunning and
patience, succeed from time to time in broadcasting
novelties. Yet, much can be accomplished if there is a
strong enough will behind the effort; this is proved by
the broadcasting station in Brussels, Belgium. When the
authorities received more and more protests against
broadcasts of modern music, they published an appeal
wherein it was explained that every station had to send
out certain programs which were of interest to a minor-
ity part of the public.

No one believes (they said) that all those who tune in
on a discourse on a technical or economic subject understand all they hear, but everybody is willing to admit
that such broadcasts should take place. There exists a
group of listeners who like to hear modern music and
they should have the same right as the others. Those
who do not understand modern music simply should
not listen in when it is on the air.

Protests ceased and more people began to listen to
modern music, for no one was willing to admit that he ·
did not understand it.

Although conditions in the American concert field
do not differ greatly from those in Europe, and although
opera does not yet play a decisive role in the United
States, radio in America has quite a different orientation toward new music. Since listeners in this country
do not pay taxes on their sets, the radio must exist on
proceeds from the sale of its time for advertising purposes. But whoever broadcasts music for advertising

purposes will surely select only such music as he thinks will please the largest possible potential audience; consequently America hears a great deal of entertainment music and a few broadcasts of classical music in very good and expensive performances. The greater the cost of advertising, the more profitable, and therefore the better, will also be the merchandise which is boosted. Obviously new music cannot be considered in this connection. Nor is it likely to find a place in broadcasts which the radio company sends out at its own expense— the "sustaining" programs. For the chief purpose of these broadcasts must always be to reach as many listeners as possible, in order that the station or network may prove to the advertising agents that its apparatus is a successful advertising medium. Because of these commercial or practical considerations, the American companies' own broadcasts are not much different in content from the paid broadcasts. Granted that there are a few exceptions, we regret to say that, in general, radio does not bring American music listeners any closer to living developments in music than they were before.

The Case of Richard Wagner

THE last example within living memory of fanatical resistance to what was then modern music is furnished by the case of Wagner. In his case, opposition was changed in a relatively short time to admiration reaching an equal degree of fanaticism. Yet it would be wrong to assume that the same thing will happen to our new music in time, and that the complaints of living composers about a lack of recognition in their day should be attributed to their impatience. When a few decades have elapsed, it is contended, what happened to

Wagner will happen again (providing the new music of today is as good as his) and no one will be able to account for the present commotion.

In reality, the situation is quite different. This will be shown not only by technical analysis, which I shall take up later, but also by the fact that, owing to its nature, new music contains elements which are radically opposed to its classification in the commercial world. The opposition against Wagner was directed against his means of expression. As soon as people got used to these means they acknowledged, with so much the greater enthusiasm, that in spite of Wagner's pessimistic and negative mood, existing conditions were confirmed and established by the spirit of his works. That is why the special institutions founded at that time to encourage the new German music, such as the many Richard Wagner organizations and the Allgemeine Deutsche Tonkuenstlerverein, cannot in any way be compared to organizations which have been called into existence recently, when the present isolation of new music began to be recognized.

After the war, many local societies were organized for the cultivation of new music, and many of these were later combined in the International Society of Contemporary Music, about which I shall have a little to say later on. The reproach has been brought against these organizations that they have locked modern music in a sort of self-imposed ghetto, because in their programs they present it as something fundamentally different from "old" music. Mixed programs which show the similarities between old and new music would be more useful from the pedagogic point of view, it is said.

However much truth there may be in such a reproach, it has no practical application, for managers of great concert institutions fail to give the slightest thought to a systematic compilation of mixed programs with a view to encouraging modern music. If they work out such programs at all, these are pernicious rather than useful. For one can hardly assert that it benefits modern music if the average audience, after having been forced to listen with polite indifference to a modern work, is induced to a deafening and demonstrative applause through a dashingly sentimental Tschaikowsky or an elegant piano concerto. On the other hand, an exclusive schedule of modern works, such as arranged, for instance, at a music festival, creates in the subconscious mind of willing listeners a certain common interest, from which the really good work stands out in sharper relief than if it appears in an accidental setting of old works, where at best it may be accorded the charm of novelty—a purely extraneous quality. At the same time, the new composition is usually under the disadvantage of being submerged by the evident artistic perfection and historical prestige of the old masters. It might be something different again if we could educate a certain group of listeners to a serious and matter-of-fact attitude toward music in general by a systematic demonstration of classical compositions. If these listeners could be brought later to the best of the new music literature, together with the old works, then they might be able to recognize the inner spiritual bonds which unite all good music of all times, all places, and all tendencies.

I can well imagine that the reader may feel I have painted everything in far too somber colors. Isn't contemporary music played everywhere? Isn't a novelty included in almost every symphony concert? Chamber music groups play new quartets, singers sing new songs, opera houses, regardless of material difficulties, make exhaustive efforts to obtain new scores, great ballet companies continuously commission music from living composers, many broadcasting companies do the same— is there really any ground for complaint? Are not complaints caused by the ambitious impatience of a few artists who are not satisfied with all this and want still more?

Certainly it might appear so. But I have spoken of the fate and of the conditions of *new* music. Is all contemporary music new?

CHAPTER   THREE

NOT ALL CONTEMPORARY
MUSIC IS NEW MUSIC

Contemporary, Modern, New Music

THREE concepts are repeatedly employed, indiscriminately and with varying significance, in musical discussions today. They are: Contemporary Music, Modern Music, and New Music. Their promiscuity, which might easily be considered comparatively unimportant and negligible, is only apparently accidental. As a matter of fact, very important circumstances and more or less conscious intentions lie at the root of this carefully preserved confusion.

The concept of *contemporary music* seems clearest, since it is purely statistical. Contemporary music consists of whatever is written by contemporaries of the person using the term. But even here a suggestion of uncertainty insinuates itself, for how broadly or narrowly one should set the limits of what is contemporary remains a matter of judgment. On a merely statistical basis, Richard Strauss and Sibelius must doubtless be considered as belonging to this category, because they are alive. On the other hand, should Alban Berg be excluded for the reason that he is, unfortunately, dead? But if Berg is to be included (which seems self-evident), how far back can, or should, one go? Whatever the decision, it is obvious that other criteria besides the statistical have their effect, although, by and large, there will be agreement as to what constitutes contemporary music. No distinctions of matter and style have as yet been made under this heading. Irving Berlin belongs among contemporary composers quite as positively as does Arnold Schoenberg.

Obviously this concept does not cover the type of contemporary music with which we are most concerned here. It is pertinent to note that the differentiation was clearly marked when the International Society for Contemporary Music was founded sixteen years ago. The English, in whose hands the central direction of the Society was placed, chose the word "contemporary" on the ground that it seemed neutral enough to suit their aversion to a definite formulation of content. For that very reason, the label was rejected by the German-speaking sections, which used the name "International Society for New Music" (*Internationale Gesellschaft fuer Neue Musik*). In effect, the difference was lightly passed over and explained away as a mere formality dealing only with terminology, though in point of fact the distinction was thoroughly fundamental and indicative of definite and separate viewpoints.

Perhaps the two factions might have been able to agree on the term *modern music,* but everyone rejected this. In Europe, and likewise in America, general usage of the word "modern" has a narrower significance than it received at the hands of those experts who sought to introduce it into technical language. The "man in the street" applies the description exclusively to popular music; and in doing so he is quite in order, for this music is as subject to fashion as are hats, modes of "hair-do," shades of stockings, etc. The average person believes modern music to be the opposite of "classical";

his interpretation of the latter designation takes no account of the period in which the work was composed. To such a person, a string quartet by Schoenberg is as classical as one by Beethoven. He thinks of all string quartets as classical *per se,* as similar to symphonies, fugues, suites, and sonatas. (Exceptions may be made for those pieces, perhaps sonatas by Haydn or Mozart, which children practice on their pianos. For many persons, these belong in the category of études.) Your connoisseur is shocked by the misuse of the word, since "classical" represents to him an historically determined style. (Here, again, he differs from the businessman in the musical world who labels as classical whatever in the sphere of serious music has become a world success and thereby a public fetish and a best seller—Tschaikowsky's *Pathétique* and Rachmaninoff's Prelude in C Sharp Minor, as well as Beethoven's Fifth Symphony, though hardly one of Beethoven's last quartets.)

When the specialist speaks of modern music, he means something distinguished by characteristics other than the merely statistical date of composition. He will call "modern" only that part of our contemporary music which emerges from the whole by a visible deviation from tradition in its material, its style, or in some other essential feature.

If, particularly in German-speaking countries, progressive musicians used the term "modern" hesitantly, they did so not merely to guard their work from the suspicion of any association with "fashion." That attitude in itself would be rather ridiculous, for it would indicate an arrogant separation of the high and mighty arts from the profanity of everyday life. Such a protest against subordinating art to the law of supply and demand would have the effect of a meaningless gesture if expressed from the viewpoint of the pseudoromantic artist wearing a velvet jacket and long hair. For the law of fashion is an inevitable result of conditions governing production and consumption, dictated in turn by the law of supply and demand. A composer who voices this protest because he hopes for a world in which exigencies of production and consumption will yield to human dignity more readily than heretofore, will surely be a representative of the really *new music*.

From the outside—and we should not yet go into the inner musical problems—one can define as "new music" the type which, because of its essential qualities, experiences the greatest opposition to its conversion into merchandise.

Deterioration of Music into a Handicraft

FROM the sociological standpoint, this type certainly bears the stamp of newness. For until now, music which was odd primarily because of its newness could after some time be transformed into merchandise. This transformation occurs in the conventionalizing process, which runs its course in approximately two phases: In the first, the public is gradually familiarized with the odd and discordant elements, which then take on the character of a formula, thereby losing their primary, unique meaning. In the second phase the elements become commercialized and are exploited from then on either by lazy eclectics who consciously or unconsciously want to follow in the footsteps of established success, or by the purely commercial purveyors of entertainment music.

The bold harmonic accomplishments of Richard Wagner have long since been incorporated into the normal stock-in-trade of all kinds of *Gebrauchsmusik;* and the clever and exquisite tone marvels of Debussy, which engendered bewilderment and uneasiness at the time of their origin, have become primitive tools in the hands of all the swing music arrangers of Tin Pan Alley. Naturally the element thus made banal remains relatively untouched in the place where it first appeared. At every performance the Prelude to *Tristan* is as daring and original as it was at its première; but in so far as purely material elements (particularly harmonic elements, as I have explained in the first chapter) participate in this impression, no composer can create this same mood any more by identical or similar means.

By the process of banalization, harmonies and orchestral effects, once fresh and daring and full of expression, have deteriorated and paled to the point where they have become part of the conventional, ready-made musical outfit.

The artist cannot prevent this dire fate of his musical inventions at will. At most he can endeavor to hide his opus from the eyes and ears of his fellow men, although he would thereby at the same time remove the ultimate reason for his activity. Once his work is published in any form, he can no longer hinder its transmission into the world of commerce, if it has proved acceptable for business purposes. The greater the public success of his work, the more thoroughly will it be absorbed as a commercial product and the more rapidly will his material be emasculated.

Since music written in the last two hundred years has been subjected to this process almost without exception, any music which deviates from the rule can certainly be called "new" on the strength of that deviation alone. But a glance will show that this term is in no way synonymous with "modern," and most certainly not with "contemporary" music. Large amounts of contemporary music either thrive on material found within the framework of former styles which have long since deteriorated into purely commercialized formulae, or—in so far as contemporary composers nourish any ambition to have their music appear new in some way—produce phenomena which soon take on the commercial slant, and show the usage and qualities of handicraft rather than the creation of art.

Reaction Pure and Simple

IT SEEMS hardly necessary to discuss the first group, that of the epigoni, or camp followers. There have been such persons throughout the ages, men and women whose modest talents can be made articulate only by a passionate fixation on a gigantic figure of the past. They are reactionaries by necessity, as by conviction; they have no desire at all to express something new, for they do not recognize the vulgarity which is their life element as something to overcome. Normally not even a large-minded concept of contemporary music could be attributed to this group, did not their activities in totalitarian states frequently coincide with the ideal of new music propagated by the authorities.

The reaching into the past, to the stylistic elements of the Renaissance, demanded by Italian fascism, is a little less primitive than the immortalization of romantic material ordained in the sphere of German culture. This forced trend is, of course, consistent with the tendency of such movements to revive the real or ostensible splendor and glory of past periods in the nation's history on which to draw for a substantial part of their propaganda. Yet, at least in the beginning, the Italian fascist attitude was not altogether reactionary, as proved by its connection with futurism. Of course it would be naïve indeed to confuse the futuristic brew with something really progressive. A provocative gesture, intended to dazzle the bourgeois, is completely offset by a moderate eclecticism in the pictorial arts, and in music by a thoroughly insignificant and amateurish practice. Nonetheless, this revival of musical features of the Renaissance cannot be called definitely reactionary as a matter of course. In the hands of such eminently talented and cultured musicians as G. F. Malipiero and Luigi Dallapiccola, the inclination is rather toward another species of contemporary music as it is practiced today, namely, neoclassicism.

Neoclassicism

So FAR as I know, the concept of "neoclassicism" originated with Ferrucio Busoni, a fascinating person and an extraordinary thinker, but a man who did much harm without intention. Busoni was not unresponsive to fundamental changes in musical style and in composition methods inaugurated particularly by Schoenberg at the beginning of our century; but he did not like these innovations. Yet the neoclassical theory, which he built up on this antipathy, soon turned out to be a convenience for all those who shared his aversion for one reason or another, or who simply could not keep step with these changes. Busoni's great anathema was directed against late-nineteenth-century romanticism. To him, the movement seemed foggy, distorted, pretentious, bombastic, and formless. Against these characteristics he marshaled the crystal clearness, the cool fire, the lucidity, and the wise economy of the classical composers, especially of Mozart. We may assume that it was by no means Busoni's intention to introduce in this way a convenient and cheap vehicle for mass transportation along the lines of least resistance; but in practice he contributed to the unfortunate situation. Economy and simplicity—these catchwords appealed to anyone who was poor and naïve. And the slogan of aggressive anti-romanticism gave a veneer of graceful progressiveness to his primitive efforts. No doubt clarity of structure is an extremely important element in music. By the same token it is pernicious to acknowledge the existence of clearness only in certain, strictly limited arrangements of musical material. At first sight, the construction of a bicycle seems surely much simpler and clearer than that of an astronomical clock, but one cannot seriously assert that the astronomical clock is "unclear." At least, I can say that it is not clear to me, so long as I am not acquainted with it. But getting acquainted is merely a matter of talent and training. Because one cannot immediately grasp the complex structure of a modern orchestral work, it is not necessarily "unclear" in comparison with a Mozart sonata. It is always advisable to remember that the same arguments were raised against Mozart's works in his time: they were criticized as being ornate, confusing, overloaded, etc. Naturally, Busoni's own considerations were far removed from such primitive trivialities, but many who parade today in the toga of the new classicism are dangerously close to them.

The extent of this new classicism is considerable. The movement has brought to a head many a variation of species, and has joined hands with similar movements and attitudes. They can all be ranged under the same heading: they bend their efforts to avoid, ignore, and supplant all that transformation of material which is covered by the term "atonality." All these many "conquerors" of atonality have this in common with neo-classicism, that they are united in a vigorous and proud rejection of romanticism.

In France the essential nature of the new classicism found ready support under the slogan *clarté latine*. As a result, the earlier works of that really exceptional genius, Darius Milhaud, and some scores by the very lively Arthur Honegger make an effect that is incomparably more progressive than is achieved today by many of their younger colleagues. For a time Milhaud was much taken with this great musical revolution; but the more convenient manner of the antiromantic *clarté* vogue prevailed and, isolated, he remained behind—though in reality ahead, for the others did not follow him. The younger Frenchmen were fortunate in one way: they did not have to overcome the influence of Schoenberg, who was too far removed from them; but since they had to "conquer" something, even though they had decided to follow the line of least resistance, they concentrated on Strawinsky, of whom, indeed, little is now left to conquer.

Strawinsky and Surrealism

STRAWINSKY's influence on contemporary music, which once was so striking, cannot be evaluated correctly if it is viewed as a spiritual influence, for it depends more on a spectacular and turbulent introduction of elemental rhythmic qualities into a condition of musical language softened by Wagner's "infinite melody" and Debussy's harmonic vagueness. Strawinsky appeared, with dramatic suddenness, a crudely prominent personality, sharply and vigorously outlined and vibrant with barbaric force.

Two qualities gave this newcomer a revolutionary and progressive aspect. When Strawinsky used the musical language of atonality in his middle period, particularly in his *Sacre du printemps,* he seemed to take his place alongside Schoenberg as a pioneer of a new type of music. On the other hand, his relation to the sophisticated Jean Cocteau helped to give his utterances an exciting spiritual background. Probably Cocteau knows more about the real situation in music than many of the French musicians, who mostly are content to play around outside the walls of his thought structure, which frequently look mysterious and hard to penetrate.

From this new point of departure sprang many efforts having as their purpose the transmission of surrealism to the field of music. Strawinsky's *Histoire du soldat* may be the first and most important of these, apart from the curiosity cabinet of Eric Satie, that extravagant but limited musician. Here the clinging to traditional means is just as systematic as in the case of neoclassicism, although the share of progressiveness is larger here than in the latter, since destruction, not restoration, is the object. The old material is not treated as if it were still intact and as useful as before, but is regarded as a conglomeration of wreckage, to be built up into a system contradicting the original arrangement. Surrealism causes a shock very similar to that produced by the introduction of really new features. But while the latter is legitimated by the direct impact of something truly novel, the shock felt in surrealism is obtained indirectly by the distortion of old material into a newfangled structure.

Musical surrealism has not found many adherents. Except for what has been produced by a few young French composers, such as Henri Sauguet, by far the most original work of this kind is *Mahagonny*, by Kurt Weill. Generally speaking, it is the text accompanying the music which plays an important and even decisive part in giving surrealism its peculiar stamp. The musical substance, viewed as such, only too soon turns out to be simply reactionary; of attack and shock, nothing much remains. Having seen surrealism splashed all over the show windows of Bergdorf-Goodman's and Bonwit Teller's, and at the World's Fair in New York, I am inclined to be a trifle suspicious about its artistic values. The movement has deteriorated until it has become a craft, and by this deterioration has surrendered the essential individuality required for a really new style in art.

Strawinsky shakes hands with neoclassicism by way of Jean Cocteau and surrealism. And here is the start of that comedy masquerade in which he hides behind Pergolese, Bach, Weber, and Tschaikowsky for so long that when he finally emerges again as Strawinsky, one does not recognize him for himself. His individuality can always be identified in the unmistakable gestures with which his genius animates his figures, but no one knows what has become of his real personality—perhaps he does not know himself, possibly he does not want to know. In his autobiography, written so coolly and with such conscious detachment, Strawinsky speaks of many people and things but is silent about the only cardinal fact of his mysterious career: namely, how he journeyed from the *Sacre du printemps* to the *Jeu de cartes*.

In France, as in all the countries which lived under the illusion of having won the World War, the rediscovery of the *clarté latine* was coincident with a planned return to normality and stabilization. "Enough of adventure and of disorder!" Such was the first cry against continuing expeditions into the unknown territory of atonality. "Enough of German romanticism!" was the second, sounded in the name of national interest. I had a minor argument with an influential personality in the French music world a few years ago, when I defended an interesting work by a young compatriot of his—interesting on account of its original material and compact construction. The authority in question decried as "un-French" those qualities which I admired. When with innocent, modest pride Debussy used to describe himself as *musicien français* on the title page of his scores, he surely never dreamed of the narrow-mindedness of the bigoted superpatriots who will not grant citizenship rights to music unless it shows certain exterior qualities, arbitrarily established by the reigning clique.

Hindemith and the "Musikant"

THE elements in neoclassicism which are really progressive—namely, the accentuation of a new rationality and the increasing preponderance of spirit over the material of nature—have persisted in Germany as little as in France. Fast as the latter country decided to get along with a *clarté* which threatened to turn to simplicity and which completely ignored all those constructive components which lead from Pascal and Descartes to the Encyclopedists, so in Germany did craftsmanship, which emanates from the idea expressed in the words

musicien français, gain the upper hand. Neoclassicism
was taken literally and put in operation by an extensive
revival of the preclassical concert style. The antiroman-
ticist disposition was made manifest by a still more pronounced romantic-retrospective attitude which was not
recognized as such because it was combined with every
species of technical advance.

An unbroken line leads from the activist *Wander-
vogel* (Boy Scout), by way of Hindemith's concerto
grosso style, to the Hitler Youth, of whom it is told that
they give vent to their indomitable spirit of independence by secretly performing Hindemith's *Spielmusik.*
In spite of their seemingly irreconcilable divergencies,
it is not too hard to determine what these phenomena
have in common: an activistic trait, a tendency to
whittle down, a reduction of music from a spiritual art
to a professional craft. And so it is not accidental, either,
that these movements look to the precapitalistic period,
when the guild system prevailed, for their historical
ideal of music. Certain German musicologists even
issued orders to keep all the music composed in the
period from Bach to Brahms far away from the young
(this was, of course, before the advent of the Third
Reich), and in doing so rather fancied themselves as
extreme revolutionists. This attitude is materialized in
the *Musikant* (musical craftsman), an honorary title con-
ferred chiefly on such contemporary composers as went
about their business, hell-bent for heaven, in shirt
sleeves and with daredevilish rhythm. Music of this sort
gave an impression of spontaneity, which is exactly what
one expects of musical craftsmen. The composer is in
order whenever he creates the impression of being a
self-satisfied and contented soul, perpetually occupied
with the musical craft, perhaps more or less obsessed by

it, sufficient unto himself. The result of his exertions is a "kinetic" type of music, that is, music without much variety of rhythm, the kind of music that hurries along a straight line, music that is poor in expression and emotion. In the last few years, the antiromantic parole has obviously been canceled and, by the same token, emotion restored to a place of honor. What sort of practical result has been obtained in Nazi Germany is still a secret. The important thing is that compositions like these cannot come under the heading of "new music," according to the definition given in the beginning of this chapter. The really revolutionary expressionism of Schoenberg had long since been driven out of Germany even before Hitler came to power; and it is unfair to hold the National-Socialists solely responsible for the present reactionary attitude in Germany toward the arts. For this attitude was current there long before and, indeed, prepared the way for that political movement. Be that as it may, this brand of musical kinetics, having the peculiar flexibility which permits a writer to suggest the lofty beauty of Gothic cathedrals or the triumph of the *Volksauto,* the popular motorcar, with equal fervor, employs musical material that becomes more and more conventional.

Folklore, Russia, Bartók

IN THE eastern part of Europe, folkloristic tendencies predominate. Significantly enough, not even the communist revolution could swerve Russian music from a path which it probably would have taken even without that upheaval. In fact, results were the reverse: political conditions in the U.S.S.R. sharpened the reactionary features of artistic development, because, by an increasing separation from western Europe, Russian composers were gradually forced into a primitivism to which they would not have fallen victim in more normal circumstances. At the present time we have come to a point where the Soviet composer is under as much pressure from the nationalistic tendency as are his colleagues in other totalitarian states. Perhaps in his case, the pressure is even greater. Anyhow, social consciousness that is cast in this mold—reduced to an insistence on flat party slogans—calls for explanatory texts to accompany the music. And so it is hard to see how Communism can lure the progressive musician at all. Granted that his development in the capitalistic world is obstructed by economic laws of supply and demand, I fail to understand why he should long for conditions under which he would not only be prevented just as surely from doing what he really wants to do (and prevented, moreover, by order of the government), but in addition would be forced by the authorities to do something which he would not want to do—namely, to set tedious propaganda lyrics to music and to fashion national raw material for the modest requirements of backward masses.

It must be acknowledged that Russia's contribution to new music has been nil for years. It was never very important; but now even the fascinating and successful facility, the smoothness and elegance which characterized Russian music around the turn of the century, have disappeared, not to mention the somnambulistic genius of a Moussorgsky or the gloomy individualism of a Scriabin, men who are completely left without followers.

While most of the composers of the eastern countries move along similar lines, an exception must be made for

Bela Bartók in Hungary and Alois Hába in Prague, together with a group of other Czech and Slavic students. Bartók is almost the only one who succeeds in bringing his penchant for folklore into fruitful relationship with the vivifying powers of the new music. With great ingenuity he avoids abusing the so-called "soil" elements of folk music as an excuse for side-stepping the new problems. On the contrary, he is successful in throwing into relief those very elements of folklore which contradict the hitherto reigning laws of tonality. He is not satisfied, either, merely to serve up the exotic ingredients in a pleasing form, but rather makes it a point to deal with the real problems of new music against the background of material derived from folklore.

We shall speak later of Alois Hába's achievements. They reach their high point not so much in the use of the quarter- and sixth-tones, by which he became known, as in the invention of the so-called "athematic" style. As he studied in Vienna and Berlin in circles surrounding Franz Schreker and Arnold Schoenberg, Hába shows a less pronounced infiltration of nationalistic ideas than most Slavs. His endeavors are guided by a wholly universalistic impulse and deserve serious attention, even if the ideas are not always satisfactorily expressed.

America Has the Floor

ENGLAND and America show the influence of European developments. This undeniable fact is a source of great concern to many Americans, especially at a time when any dark corner in Europe has a tribe (if but a small one) glorifying in a racial music of its own. We hope Americans will realize as quickly as possible that they

have an unsurpassed advantage in *not* being able to
claim such basic qualifications for creating a national
music of America. The claim would be in vain, and
a false effort into the bargain. What Europe was once,
in better days—a spiritual and cultural unit (although
unfortunately it never achieved political unity)—America has actually become in quite a different way. To
wish for an expression of this unity in the form of a
chauvinistic ideal according to the European sample
would mean voluntarily to descend from a high level
to a deep and unattractive one. The genuine American
national ideal, unequivocally imprinted by history, is
the one of humanity; and therefore the road for American music is clearly indicated in the direction of human
universalism. Although the possibilities have so far been
visioned rather than realized, that fact in itself gives
rise to the greatest hopes. Hopes like these are badly
needed, as Europe—in part loudly and in obedience to
the fixed regulations forced upon composers, in part
apathetically and in a tired voice—has spoken against
bothering any further with a musical development
which is progressive in itself and aims at the high ideal
of unlimited human significance.

The American composer who is willing to proceed
along these lines need not avoid folklore elements if he
sincerely feels an innate desire to use them. As an example of how this can be done without sacrificing originality and the progressive spirit, I shall mention the
unique Charles Ives, of whom far too little is known.
Certainly Ives's imaginary world is replete with purely
native rudiments (which faintly remind one of Walt
Whitman); but his musical vision is far from being
provincial or primitive. The boldness to compose in
so "impractical" a manner that his gigantic scores seem

to shun the exigencies of performance is in itself stimulating in a period when conformity is rampant. Assuredly there must be in this country many other persons who are out of the ordinary and who might achieve great significance if they were properly encouraged and their essays recognized as promising.

It is a legitimate desire on the part of Americans to see a period dawning which will be known in musical history as the "era of American music," as the fifteenth century, for instance, was the era of Dutch music. Yet this Dutch music did not acquire its imperishable significance because of its special faithfulness to folklore —of which actually nothing can be found in the venerable scores of the Dutch masters. It was simply the best music available at that time, and that is why it became imperishable. It was the best music of its time because it was the most progressive in its technique and the most universal in its meaning. I am glad to mention that in America I have met an unexpectedly large number of talented, serious, and enthusiastic musicians who are well aware of these circumstances and are willing to tackle the task assigned to them at this most extraordinary turning point of musical history.

Atonality, Schoenberg, Austria

RESERVATIONS must be made in awarding the title "new" to contemporary composers mentioned thus far. The one quality common to them all is their more or less strict adherence to the traditional material of tonality—in other words, to the sound language based on the system of major and minor keys and formulated by the device of the tonal cadence which has had an undisputed reign since 1600. It follows that the outstanding characteristic of the type of music we shall designate as "new" will probably be its failure to adhere to this principle of tonality.

Such music does exist, being, in fact, none other than the so-called atonal music. To its share also fall all the other characteristics mentioned as requirement for a "new" music. Although atonal music has been in existence for about thirty years and has caused a great deal of commotion for at least a considerable part of this period, it has not deteriorated into a craft. It does not fit in with the character of merchandise demanded by our present economic conditions, because it is not popular and therefore is difficult to sell.

As we know, this type of music was originated by Arnold Schoenberg in a city which was, until recently, considered the capital of the musical world and which at that time (thirty years ago) certainly had the right to that proud title. We refer to Vienna. Neither the accident that one of the most radical revolutions in many centuries took place in that city, nor the concrete changes carried on by that revolution mitigate the fact that Vienna was the focal point of the holiest musical traditions and for a long time had been averse to any innovation in the field. The Austrian character is not accurately pictured along the lines so incessantly followed in the Viennese operetta "zoo"—from *The Bat* to *The White Horse Inn*. Involved for decades in a discouraging struggle for life, the average Austrian was imbued with a deep skepticism, an epicurean pessimism, a complete lack of nationalistic feeling, and a rather primitive sense of reality, balanced by a licentious propensity for unrestrained speculation. This unique combination of conservative and radical constituents, whose origin can be explained in detail by the peculiar history of the country, can naturally be preserved only in certain individuals under the present circumstances, for in reality it represents an extremely humane pattern of life; as a type, it has been long since condemned to an accepted oblivion. The "new" music is practically the last thing which Austria contributed to the world's cultural development before her destruction; and the impending catastrophe was clearly presaged in this music. If the prophecy is correctly interpreted, then the destruction may have at least some justification. If thinkers can learn from this phenomenon the direction of the road leading to a world music, then the world will perhaps have derived from its catastrophe the only tangible advantage accessible to it today.

The step from the later tonality to atonality proper was at once recognized as an undefinable radical measure. That was seen in the turbulent reactions which followed the initial performance of atonal music. Even today—and in spite of all the other and (from a material standpoint) incomparably greater distress they have known—witnesses speak with shudders of that formidable concert in Vienna in 1911, when atonal orchestral works were heard for the first time, causing such a riot that the police were called in to separate the fighting factions and ambulances summoned that victims with bloody heads could be cared for. Certainly people were justified in their horror as well as in their fury. The handwriting on the wall may be more horrible in its appearance than what it forebodes; and the prophet announcing the disaster is invariably stoned. Small wonder that this radical step was taken in the very place where the pressure of tradition was the strongest; small wonder also that the reaction here should be most violent. In fact, the appearance of

Schoenberg had a decisive influence on the musical fate of Vienna, even though the ubiquitous "conquerors" there refused to recognize it. Those who did not want to take part in Schoenberg's innovations—and they, under the pressure of public condemnation, were just about everybody—experienced something like a pathological repression which permanently inhibited the normal use of their musical powers. There is no doubt that the ornate, fat, jellyfishlike, bloated character of the newer Viennese style is a kind of sickly degeneration resulting from repressed atonality.

Conservative Trends in Atonality

AND yet, atonality—the purely musical significance of which I shall discuss elsewhere in these pages—is not unallied to conservatism. It has one point of contact with neoclassicism in that both look for a connection with classical music. But while neoclassicism aims at a revival of that external appearance of classical music which shows (though only to the subjective eye) the insidious picture of pure lucidity, *clarté* and *serenità*, atonality tries to maintain the essence of classicism, the compactness and balance of its construction. Schoenberg logically follows the last quartets of Beethoven and ties up to them, with Brahms serving as the connecting link. Here, too, Schoenberg remains inside the purely Austrian sphere; Austrian literature was the only literature in the German language which consciously continued along the line leading from Goethe's humane and universal classicism. The most important witnesses for this assertion are the Austrian writers Adalbert Stifter, in the middle of the nineteenth century, and Karl Kraus in ours.

As a matter of fact, atonality has, in a sense, saved the compactness of classical construction from inroads by romanticism and impressionism. On the other hand, elements of emotional expression have likewise been preserved by atonality for romanticism against a modern trend which adopted from impressionism an uncritical playfulness and which, through its misinterpretation of neoclassicism, fell in with a streamlined kineticism. For the rest, it is interesting to note that the atonal composers, though attacked as rabid disturbers of everything proper and dignified, have never voiced any manifestoes against earlier styles and movements. Such declarations always were of great concern to those whose musical contributions were in inverse ratio to real progress.

Atonality is also conservative in that it has remained true to itself. And so it could not be long before it was found that atonality could not be called ultramodern any more, but was really terribly old-fashioned! Above all, the movement owes this classification to its adherence to emotional expression. At first this expression shocked one by its unusual intensity. The public had always expected music to express something; that was even a desirable trait. But not so directly and not so loudly—incidentally, an objection raised against all "new" music of all times.

But in the years after the World War, music was robbed to a large extent of its function of emotional expression and was brought down to a more carnal level. If it succeeds on this lower plane, it is sometimes entertaining—and that is often the best that can be said of it. The sociological cause of such disintegration is undoubtedly to be found in an increasing number of taboos, indicating the general confusion mounting to such a height that, for the sake of its own conservation, a growing number of things must be kept secret. Superficially this continued and increasing suppression of inner personal liberty is overcompensated by force, "streamlined efficiency," and the like. The ideal of the time is the standardized, devil-may-care "tough guy." Emotional expression is hardly shocking any more, but seems only ridiculous, in any case old-fashioned—an even worse curse. Here is the reason why, whenever an atonal piece is heard in a single performance—a rare enough occurrence!—at least one voice is always raised to say: "Why all this fuss, when after all this is only nineteenth-century German romanticism?"

However that may be, soon it will perhaps not be the worst that can be said about atonal music. . . .

A Personal Remark

NEVERTHELESS, the evasive, reactionary attitude toward atonality on the part of most present-day musicians is understandable. Of course they will never admit that their self-assurance and superiority, their smart and racy progressiveness, are merely the typical overcompensation of a sly escapism. But still, this is the case, as I know from my own experience.

In the beginning of my career, in the early nineteen twenties, I simply used atonal material because it seemed to be the most radical I could find, and because, as a young man of the postwar period, I obviously wanted to be as radical as possible. But I suddenly discovered myself to be in full retreat. I know now that the need for an "affirmation of life" was the innermost force that drove me to this movement. I soon came to feel that atonal music did not contain enough rich possibilities to be just to the positive side of life. From a purely technical viewpoint I was dissatisfied with the disorder and lack of organization which seemed to reign there; but that was a subjective cause, for I never had occupied myself thoroughly enough with the problem of atonality—I had simply employed it as a device which seemed to be as convenient as tonality. In the end, the above-mentioned psychological change was the decisive cause of my change of style. I came in closer contact with French music and with Strawinsky; and I had the feeling, typical for the stabilization period of 1925-1929, that here a way out had been found from the field of wreckage and that now better and gayer times would come. (*Jonny spielt auf* is the best-known evidence of this period in my development.) I tried to find theoretical reasons for this attitude of mine, and conducted polemics against Schoenberg and the twelve-tone technique. I pinned my hopes to the notion that it should be possible, by means of intensive new experience, to make the inherited material seem so fresh and powerful that a primeval sense would emerge from it, that is, that sense which was inherent in it at the time of its first appearance and which speaks so clearly to us from the works of the great masters. I was particularly attracted to Franz Schubert, by a certain affinity of mood and for other reasons; and I wrote in a style which, with respect to my real personality, performed more or less the same function as Strawinsky's masquerades. But my contact with atonality must have been too strong, and my conscience was not at rest. It became more and more evident to me that I had simply avoided a decision—that I had run away from a given problem. I had not realized what a decisive turning point music had reached with the advent of atonality (with all its implications of widening the scope of the art) nor that the continued existence of music would seem impossible and senseless if one did not struggle to the very end with the problem thus raised. For me, there is no doubt that every musician of today must make up his mind objectively about the question. It is not left to his discretion to avoid the issue. Even if he has not yet come in contact with the problem, either because no one has pointed it out to him or because he has intentionally kept away from it, he will unquestionably encounter it in some way.

My previous complaints about the unpopularity of new music will perhaps strike many musicians as being exaggerated. They may say: "Yes, if by 'new' music he meant 'atonal' music, the author is right, for that is indeed unpopular. But thank God! There is a great deal of grand new music which is not atonal. Naturally it is still played far too seldom, but it is not unpopular. It is healthy, affirmative, positive, and unsentimental, and will undoubtedly persist."

I do not know whether people who say such things are as confident as they would like us to believe. Do they fail to see that the "healthy" and "positive" music of which they speak, music which is written wholesale in these days, has in reality no more "success" than the atonal compositions? Do they not notice that it bores the public just as much as the allegedly old-fashioned romantic atonal music is supposed to do? In fact, the boredom engendered by the former is greater, since there is no chance of at least a little oddity.

All this musical positiveness, with its kinetics, folklore, rhythm of modern life, tempo—everything, goes out of one ear as quickly as it came in at the other. Nobody really believes in it. The era of deceptive stabilization has long since passed; humanity has become much more serious than its clowns are willing to admit; and people know very well that life is not so unproblematical as is claimed by those who take it as it comes.

In view of my former confession, my argument in defense of atonality may be taken as an outgrowth of excessive zeal, akin to the fervent protestations of a monk who, after quitting a monastery, tries to prove his repentance on his return, or similar to the enthusiasm of a new convert to his faith. So far as enthusiasm is concerned, I do not claim that atonality, or even the twelve-tone technique, offers the only permissible method of making music today. What I wish to point out is that atonality has introduced so many important and far-reaching problems into music that it simply cannot be avoided, or dismissed as old-fashioned, romantic, Jewish, Bolshevist, German, reactionary, bourgeois, European, hysterical, or anything else; and that we must concern ourselves seriously with these problems before we can expect to achieve further progress.

CHAPTER   FOUR

THE CONCEPT OF MUSIC IN
THE WESTERN WORLD

Western Music Integrated with History

THE newer European music is undoubtedly one of
the most original and characteristic accomplishments of
the Western World. Whereas most of the scientific and
technical feats of our time can be imagined as previously existing in different cultures, and, in fact, have
certain parallels there, the development of European
music since approximately the central period of the
Middle Ages is a unique fact, unequaled by anything in
past or present civilizations.

A paramount criterion in the astonishing growth of
European music is the fact that it has won and maintained a place of equality with literature and the pictorial arts in the world of ideas after lacking such
equality since the beginning of recorded history. Perhaps one does not realize that the standing of music
has not always been so prominent, and that outside the
European world of culture musical art does not yet
have such a position. This condition is recognizable in
the conviction that we know nothing of any important
composer of the remote past nor of the ancient foreign
centers of musical culture. We have no knowledge of
an Aeschylus or a Euripides in Greek music, nor of a
Chinese Beethoven. If this contention is disputed on

the ground that too little remains of Greek music for us to judge and that the meager remnants that have come down to us have been insufficiently deciphered, the contradiction may be taken as an explanation which, to my mind, also excludes the probability that something of outstanding importance has been lost. There seems to be a mysterious law according to which the purely material durability of records of any spiritual accomplishment, and the clearness of the signs used, stand in direct proportion to the significance of the attainment for the mental history of mankind. Despite forces of annihilation, and regardless of the widespread destruction of many documents, Greek literature and philosophy, for example, have survived to give us a clear and comprehensive picture of that spiritual world.

In spite of the ruthless fury of successive generations of barbarians, we have a revealing picture of the ancient plastic arts and of architecture. We cannot avoid believing that the ancient art of painting was not on the same level of perfection, for the very reason that we know so much less about it. And unquestionably the same holds true of music. If Grecian composers had produced anything one-half as significant as the Attic tragedies, then we would most certainly not only have found some reference to it, but would have some more or less decipherable records thereof.

To me it seems quite obvious that we can assume a relative insignificance of ancient music from the mere fact that it did not develop a lasting system of graphic signs or symbols. The clarity of graphic systems no doubt matches the spiritual importance of the contents pictured. While the Greek script is as lucid and unequivocal as the thoughts which it preserves, Greek music did not foster any such perfected system of signs, since music itself was but little developed and therefore perishable.

Our music differs essentially from the music of other centers of culture because it has a history. It owes its present high spiritual rank to the fact that it has become a part of Western history, and could become a mirror of Western man's historical consciousness. The music of other cultural centers has no history, for the reason that it is bound in principle to an unalterable magic ritual. Primitive tribes have no autonomous music; they do not express themselves through a musical medium, since their music is only incidental in a group of similar elements, like dancing and sacrifices, etc., within the framework of their cult and its functions. Whether the number of primitive sacred musical compositions is being increased by new creations or remains unchanged (as seems to be the case in the ancient Chinese music employed in Japanese ceremonies) is a question that may not be uniformly answered for all primitive countries; but in no instance will the new works be so far removed from the previously existing ones as to justify our speaking of an historical development. For the rest, the musical accomplishments of primitive peoples are for the most part recorded in a form which cannot be compared to our system of notation.

Symbol, Thought, Idea in Western Music

THE more permanently and clearly a spiritual work is recorded, the greater will be its place in literature. Literature is the treasure room of thought; and European music is distinguished by the evidence that it could become literature, which means that it could give physical and permanent shape to thought. In other cultural centers music is almost exclusively applied music. Its forms are magic emblems, comparable to ornaments on cultural tools, architectural details on temples, etc. Certainly the totality of these musical elements expresses the philosophy of life accepted by the races and tribes who adopt them. But the ability to give utterance to personal thoughts, to allow each man a representative expression of his individual philosophy of life through the medium of tone—this was reserved for the later European music. Admittedly the process involved in the musical stimulation of consciousness is largely an unconscious process in itself. Although European music has displayed a spiritual significance from the very beginning (a significance constituting the basis of its development), the process *per se* remained unconscious for a long time. An example may serve to clarify this statement.

The cantatas of Johann Sebastian Bach are full of poetic symbols. Actions of the body and of the soul, the beat of eagles' wings, the coiling of a snake, a hundred varieties of movement performed by water, are reflected accurately in an inexhaustible range of musical elements, and particularly by the elements of rhythm and color. The fact that man is actually able to say all this through the medium of music is a tremendous accomplishment of the European imagination.

In the final analysis, all these images, such as going, walking, running, jumping, floating, streaming, flowing, crawling, and coiling, have nothing to do with music. It is only by a very complicated process that they can be transmitted from one's abstract imagination into the acoustic impressions emanating from a musical performance. Yet the level on which this kind of musical fiction is conceived is merely an intermediate station on the road which Western music must follow to penetrate the world of thought. The marvel is that musical images which can be co-ordinated into a richly graduated scale of extramusical concepts can tell us something without the help of explanatory associations. And yet the concept of the "musical theme"—meaning the subject matter of a musical presentation—has no sense at all unless this final concession to abstract thinking is made. Musical images which show a variety of significant symbols are, at the same time, musical themes—forms which have meaning in themselves but are susceptible of developing this meaning fully and exclusively only by entering into certain relationships with other forms: relationships which, in turn, can be completely described in terms referring solely to the constellation of their musical elements.

We cannot understand the language of music without seeing its forms as thoughts; in other words, if we are not under the necessity of entertaining any extramusical concepts in order to recognize the language as an illuminating and comprehensive medium of expression, in keeping with the dignity of the human spirit. That music has come so far is primarily an accomplishment of the productive forces within the art, rather than merely the increasing force and refinement of Western man's receptive faculties. Thus the distinguishing concept of Western music simply is that it *has* a concept, an idea, and becomes itself an idea. How this idea was born is told in history.

Concerned with demonstrating the mutation of the sound language witnessed in our days, as necessitated by history, we shall now try to trace its origin back to the beginning of European music.

Oriental Influence. The Principle of Iteration

THE influence of the Near East has, it seems, been greater than the immediately available traditions of antique Greco-Roman music in creating the basic stratum of European music that is responsible for its historical evolution. The basic stratum is early Christian music, epitomized in the Gregorian chant. In the light of my previous exposition, this first step in giving European music a literary tinge becomes especially important, even if it was then merely a matter of codifying the applied music used in the ritual of the Roman Church. It was natural that early Christian music should be a continuation of Oriental tendencies, since the principal heritage from the Greco-Roman musical tradition was mostly material used for worldly theatrical purposes. Moreover, the type of music adopted was too intimately associated with pagan expression to be serviceable to the new religion. However that may be, the proof that Oriental musical elements exercised a dominant influence on the musical evolution of Europe for a long time cannot be sufficiently stressed. Recent research, notably in the domain of Byzantine religious music, has shown with increasing clarity the connection between the Gregorian chant and the Syrian melodies of the primitive church.

The principle on which the structure of Oriental music is built is that of *iteration*, that is, the continued sequence of the same or similar elements. There is a fundamental difference between iteration and the principles of form active in the Western mind. This difference is so vital that an orthodox Westerner might not even concede the use of the expression "form" in connection with Oriental artistic patterns. We like to associate the concept of form with the image of a structure occupying a certain finite space and following an inherent, central principle of order, or, in other words, a structure adjusted in practice on a three-dimensional axis system easy to survey.

This definition of form is surely too narrow; it does not cover everything the Western mind thinks of as capable of producing form. It is, however, true that we naturally incline to axial concepts, and so look upon symmetry as the paramount criterion of artistic molding.

The contrast to the Oriental method is immediately apparent when we compare western European architecture with Arabic buildings. The proportions and shape of a Gothic cathedral obviously correspond to a clearly conceived three-dimensional plan based on a system of axes. When, on the other hand, we look at an Arabic mosque, we receive the compelling impression that here is a design which makes only accidental use of the third dimension and in reality extends flatly.

The Arabic design has apparently been worked out according to a plan which it is difficult for Westerners to grasp. There are no naves to suggest organization of the space, nor is the space so indicated that, from a given point, one can visualize the entire structure. In a manner of speaking, the building has no height, presenting instead an unexpected and confusing horizontal expansion. Interminable rows of pillars seem to sprout rampantly in all directions, like so many strawberry plants.

Looking at the building from above, we see a conglomeration of cupolas of various sizes rising to the sky in haphazard rows, without any discernible plan.

No orderly symmetrical axes are visible. The principle by which the mass was created, and which somehow holds it together, is iteration; the tireless repetition of single elements, that is, literal repetitions, or with imperceptibly increasing minute variations. On a reduced scale, the single element is an ornament revealing craftmanship; and the results of the exuberant growth of these ornaments, covering the walls and ceilings of Arabic halls of state with disquieting fertility, are what we call "arabesques."

The Gregorian Chant. Free Articulation

THE physiognomy of the Gregorian chant shows many essential traits which point to this iteration principle. Its long melodic chains can be reduced to small individual links incessantly repeated, varied often only by the repetition of a single tone or by other minute changes. We shall need to remember this when, at the end of our historical survey, we reach the extremely modern theory of "composition with basic patterns." Byzantine music, much closer to its Syrian original, demonstrates the principle of iteration still more clearly than does the Gregorian chant, since it lacks those small traces of tonality which might be evidenced in the latter.

At this early stage of discussion, I should not like to touch upon the critical and controversial problem of tonality. For the moment, we should be satisfied with the exceedingly important knowledge, as reported by historians, that Byzantine sacred music is "organized by patterns rather than by tonality"—a statement which also applies to the ancient Russian church music, which was strongly influenced by the Byzantine model.

Another essential trait of this old, exclusively vocal music is its rhythmic structure, primarily determined by the accent of speech. The texts, though plainly written in elevated language and, by that token, different from everyday speech, yet present the rhythmical structure of prose and determine the rhythm of the musical line by their meters. Wherever the melodic line of the Gregorian chant goes beyond the rhythm indicated by its text, often indulging in fantastically elongated and widely curved lineaments, such components are nothing more than variations and extensions of the shorter melodic features, directly created by the verbal accent. Their rhythmic outline is not decided by any force having its origin apart from free articulation of the word.

The Western Principle of Symmetrical Scanning

MANY arguments support the hypothesis that such a rhythmic force has emerged from the other source of European music, from the tradition of western and northern European races, a force expressed in a striving for the symmetry which I have previously indicated as the characteristic mark of Occidental form. Strictly speaking, one can use the term "symmetry" in music in none other than a figurative sense. If we take symmetry in its literal connotation, it must mean that the ingredients in question are arranged at equal distances on either side of a fixed axis. This, of course, would be absurd. One cannot establish axes in a musical composition progressing through time. Therefore, when transferring the concept of symmetry to musical conditions, one usually admits that two separate, but not too extensive, sections are alike in regard to the number of metrical units each contains, and show integral similarities, particularly in their inner rhythmic formations. In reality, a musical structure of this kind corresponds less to the symmetrical structures of the pictorial arts, from which the parallel has been drawn, than to the poetic figure of rhyme which stresses metric parallel lines.

But rhyme is an invention of western Europe. It is not found, as we know it, in either the Oriental or the Greco-Roman languages; and the absence reminds us that the music of the Orient lacks the "symmetrical" period formation. I do not know whether the ethnic origin of this periodicity in language and music has been discovered. Tentatively, one is inclined to ascribe it to the Celtic tribes. In any case, periodic formation (in which rhythmic and metric units predominate in balanced numbers corresponding to the early association of this music to the march and dance) is doubtless a principle which appears in sharp contrast to the free rambling manner of the Oriental melodic structure. This periodicity, implying the use of regular meters, reminds one of the principle of scanning as found in poetry. Therefore we shall call this element of Western music the *"symmetrical-scanning"* component. If the spiritual source of energy in European music is attributable to man's ambition to express himself, then we must acknowledge his good fortune as much as his genius, since the former enabled him to utilize the combination of musical currents pouring over European soil, and to subject them to his need to an extent never before attained nor suspected in the history of mankind. Seen from this point of view, the history of Western music presents a constant and eventful intermingling and interpenetration of the following two basic principles: free articulation, of Oriental origin, and symmetrical scanning, born and bred in the Occident.

Polyphony and the Idea of Balance

THE symmetrical constituent governed secular music, which made use of folklore even in its artistically more conscious forms. Sacred music, on the contrary, seems to have been preponderantly influenced by the Oriental component. The worldly melodies of the troubadours showed clear rhythmic and structural symmetries of homogeneous sections, while sacred music exhibited the irregularly linked linear traits of the Gregorian chant. The penetration of these two principles was concurrent with the birth of polyphony. This, too, was a purely Western product. Whenever the music of the Far East seems to be polyphonic it is solely a matter of *heterophony,* in which the different voices simultaneously execute the same melodic material, diverging only by improvisatory figuration and rhythmic vacillations—a method reminding one of modern "swing" improvisations. In that arrangement, the question of harmony arising from simultaneous sounds—the cardinal problem of European polyphony—plays no part. We may say that the European spirit summoned polyphony to life especially in order to bring those two principles, foreign to each other, together. For necessary as this contact was in inaugurating the glorious history of Western music, the principle of polyphony was equally fruitful for the same purpose.

Both these principles, that of symmetrical scanning and of free articulation, were used in the technique of polyphony, but each in a totally different way. It is interesting to note that European art music first set out to solve the harder problem of organizing the freely articulated sacred music polyphonically. What I have said about the notation and preservation of ancient music applies here as well. Because we have intelligible and partially complete notation of sacred music alone, we may conclude that only sacred music had real spiritual significance during that epoch. There can be no doubt that "profane" music also existed; but it was far less developed and had no appreciable influence on the historical evolution of the art.

With the introduction of polyphony, the concept of *harmony* was injected into the body of music. No matter how artistic, according to the iteration principle, the organization of the single vocal melody of the Gregorian chant may have been, it lacked the extramelodic dimension, that second co-ordinate by which we, who have been used to polyphony for many centuries, are in the habit of checking whether the music is in proper "balance."

The extramelodic dimension is none other than the vertical dimension. To illustrate: We can apply the metaphor taken from the graphic picture of music, according to which passages written underneath each other (harmony) are called vertical, while notes set down one after another (melody) are horizontal. Both dimensions check each other continuously. Whether the music is in "balance" depends on their mutual relationship; and the newer history of music started when this question of "balance" was introduced.

In so far as the symmetrical-scanning principle made use of polyphony, it strove to form the device which today we call "harmony," endeavoring to build characteristic simultaneous tonal structures to emphasize the metrical organization of the various periods. This seems such a clear application of the potentiality of sounding several tones at once that it is difficult to realize how the principle of free articulation could make use of the device. For the freely articulating single voice hardly needed such emphasis of the rhythmic periods. The first higher development of polyphony did not lead in that direction, but rather toward a simultaneous presentation of several voices moving independently (which we call polyphony in the real sense of the term). One can readily imagine that if the polyphonic seed had not been sown in a soil capable of producing the symmetrical-scanning idea, it would have led to nothing more than a heterophony of the type prevailing in the Far East, in which not overmuch attention would have been paid to the identities latent in the harmonies. And still, characteristically enough, the polyphonic principle was discovered nowhere else than in Europe, where the symmetrical-scanning theorem was omnipotent, and made the entire complex of polyphony—the combination of freely articulated voices progressing together—an extremely problematical one. For when, under the influence of this principle, harmonies have a tendency to contrast with each other and to emphasize the symmetry of periods, the situation must considerably counteract the doctrine of free articulation.

Counterpoint. The Role of Aesthetic Opinions

THE method employed by polyphony to fit this new complex of harmony into its scheme is called *counterpoint*. In considering the polyphony of the Middle Ages, we are liable to make the mistake of viewing the complex "harmony" employed as something then available in its entirety, and to judge it from the view-

point of our present-day harmonic theories. But if we
want to examine the problem from an historical angle,
we must remember that the concept of the *triad*—which
to us is the alpha and omega of the fundamental facts
of music—did not exist before the introduction of
polyphony, not even as a possibility and much less as
an experience. We must visualize the world of harmony
at that time as an unexplored, lawless territory. When
several separate voices flowed side by side, but independently, thus continuously producing harmonies, the
whole arrangement obviously made artistic sense to the
medieval musician only if the harmonies were also subject to aesthetic judgment; else polyphony would be
nothing but a quantitative increase in the fabric of
tone without any intrinsic importance.

An aesthetic critical scrutiny of harmonic material
first had effect on the choice of the harmonies to be
admitted. At root, this question of admitting certain
harmonies has been the focal point of all controversies
throughout the history of music; and all the progress
made in the development of the art can be reduced to
a progressive expansion of the number and limitations
of harmonies allowed. The point is controversial by
the very fact that it is subject to aesthetic judgment
and taste. Or, to put it more bluntly, in the final analysis the question of what is allowable permits of but an
arbitrary answer. There is no law outside our own free
opinion by which any interval at all should be excluded as unsuitable for musical purposes. Arguments
based on the science of acoustics, or any other science,
are nothing but supplementary buttresses of whatever
aesthetic opinion they are employed to defend, and have
no objective justification.

It may sound preposterous to call an aesthetic opinion

arbitrary. Is not aesthetics the science of the beautiful in art? And is not the quality of beauty something absolute and independent of our opinions? If there are differences of opinion in regard to beauty, are they not caused by the fact that nature did not bestow upon everyone the same faculty of identifying what is beautiful? Should we not therefore presume that the old masters considered certain intervals permissible because, in their profound wisdom, they recognized them as beautiful? The opposite is true. The old masters selected intervals that best served their artistic intentions, the human spirit being absolutely free and sovereign to choose what it likes. Not until afterwards does the material chosen for the realization of intentions appear as beautiful, in so far as the works thus created are an intelligible expression of spiritual power, the utterances of a genius. But this quality by no means depends on the allegedly absolute beauty of the selected material. Owing to deeply rooted inertia, the human receptive faculty always tries to perpetuate a choice once made under unique circumstances and for specific purposes, and opposes every experiment along the lines of a fresh selection, endeavoring to justify its stubbornness by reference to the "eternal" laws of aesthetics. All problems subject to aesthetic opinions are necessarily controversial, owing to the relativity of such opinions and not to their erroneously accepted invariability.

From this standpoint, the problem of "which of the various harmonies were permissible" depended entirely on the function they were supposed to fulfill. To be permissible, a harmony first had to show that it was necessary in the composition for positive reasons. In viewing the technique of the so-called "strict" counterpoint (corresponding approximately to the musical style of the period from Orlando di Lasso to Palestrina) as it is used today for instruction in composition, one generally supposes that first a codex of admissible harmonies was compiled; that secondary rules were laid down for the simultaneous movement of freely articulated single voices; and that when those rules were followed, the identical harmonies would result. But if we take the historical point of view, we must imagine this process to have been reversed.

In the beginning, practically no harmonies whatever were authorized as self-evident. Each one had to be mastered before it was accepted as legal. Legality was obtained through contrapuntal technique, which proved the harmony under consideration to be necessary if the simultaneously heard voices were to show a constructive coherence in order to give their blending any meaning at all. We are in the habit of formulating the rules of strict counterpoint almost exclusively in negative sentences: "No unprepared dissonances on strong beats; no sixths jumping downwards; no tritone progression," etc. We adopt the negative attitude because we have for long been accustomed to thousands of "prohibited" occurrences in our music, and because our exercises in strict counterpoint are nothing but an artificial and forced return to an historical stage which lies behind us. The medieval rules of composition would look quite different if we were to formulate them, as seen from the horizon of those times, somewhat as follows: "To obtain a constructive relationship between the single voices (a relationship which gives purpose to simultaneous progress), the strong beats should exclusively contain consonances or prepared dissonances; the melody should progress thus and so," etc. The basic thought is that through these rules the series of all possible harmonies, to be considered as unlimited in number, should not be arbitrarily limited; but rather that the few harmonies one would begin to create would be legalized by the contrapuntal arrangement and regulated according to the rules established. Just which few harmonies shall be created first, however, is purely an aesthetic decision.

In basing their decisions on the artistic conscience of the age, our forefathers aimed at polyphony, which had to be justified by "constructive coherence," as previously mentioned. The main device for establishing coherence was simply to apply to the more involved texture of several voices the same relations which formerly ruled over what was set forth by one voice on the foundation of iteration.

Establishment of these relations between the voices does not, *a priori,* determine the ultimate harmonies; but as the harmonies thus created are required to correspond to their own system of rules, that especial kind of "balance" comes into being which is essential in the aesthetic evaluation of Western music. The musical body should do more than obey the law calling for merely one co-ordinate axis; it should, that it may be perfect, fulfill the requirements of the second co-ordinate by the very fact that it submits to the rule governing the first.

Contrapuntal Devices

OF COURSE these two axes—the horizontal (melodic) and the vertical (harmonic)—are not completely distinct from each other. Intervals shown by the melodic line of the single voice are also decisive factors in the choice of admissible or preferred harmonies. Musical thought which is primarily expressed in melodic invention furnishes the harmonic material, creating groups of preferred harmonies which constitute the root words of a sound language, as explained in the first chapter. Here we have an explanation of why harmonies chosen by application of the contrapuntal technique—developed after primitive experiments with the *parallel organum* —corresponded more or less to the intervals characterizing the melodic progressions of the Gregorian chant.

Constructive combination of several voices consists in transmitting the values of the single voices to the total complex. Literal repetition is the most primitive form of unified relationships. (See the first chapter.) This form of repetition is the basis of the iteration principle. For it is by means of continued repetition that the single element takes on the nature of a "pattern" which determines the larger design. Primitive repetitions have their origin in magic, discernible in the hypnotic monotony produced by the cult music of aboriginal tribes, to which supernatural powers were ascribed. A stupefying effect came from incessant melodic or rhythmic repetitions. In its immeasurable advance from the low level of magic, the Gregorian chant had already shown other and varied repetitive forms.

Devices belonging in this category are *inversion* (whereby the direction of the intervals is inverted, so that the ascending formula A-B-D, for instance, would read A-G-E in descent) and *retrogression* (reshaping the figure in reverse direction, from the last tone to the first, changing the order to D-B-A). When several single voices are combined, the rhythmic relations within them gain added importance by being associated with those of the other voices; this in turn allows further modifications of repetition, which in the end results in what we call *variation*. Variation is nothing but repetition having but few recurring elements of the original design.

We know that the art of establishing contrapuntal relationships between the various single voices reached an extraordinary and almost unholy perfection in the later part of the Middle Ages. Romantic aesthetics of the nineteenth century mistaught us to see in the old golden age of polyphony a capricious outgrowth of an eccentric intellectual zeal rather than a remarkable epoch of musical art, and to look on the period as one connected with "scholasticism" and other ridiculous products of the "unenlightened" Middle Ages. Fortunately we are now beginning to entertain different ideas about the alleged darkness of that era, after seeing that we have little cause to be particularly proud of the spiritual enlightenment of our own time; and soon we shall probably have a considerably higher opinion of the Low Countries' polyphony. We shall learn that the tremendous display of elaborate construction indulged in by composers living then was not attributable to a distortion of spiritual power or to any lack of inspiration, but rather that this display was necessary in organizing excursions into the unexplored and lawless jungle of newly discovered harmonies. This hypothesis is supported by study of the development of our latest music, and it contributes in turn to an interpretation of this growth.

The Problem of Tonality

IN THE course of the sublime unfolding of European music to the artistic polyphony of the later Middle

Ages, an element which was not primarily an ingredient of the polyphonic theorem *per se* advanced into the foreground. That element was *tonality,* a concept which gave rise to one of the most insoluble controversies in musical history, especially since tonality, held up as the antithesis of its ideological counterpart, *atonality,* was surrounded by pitfalls of the most dangerous sort. Proceeding with care, we shall attempt to outline what one might imagine tonality to be if we take as a point of departure the historical horizon seen in our short survey. We do not need the concept of tonality unless it expresses something alien to the facts derived from the principles of iteration and of pattern. The idea of tonality can be of use only if it illustrates a set of circumstances outside the constructive relationships observed so far in polyphonic music: that is, if it characterizes an arrangement of material peculiar to most, if not all, of the works of that epoch.

The best-known arrangements common to the pattern—the basic form of medieval polyphony—are the so-called *church modes* (or *ecclesiastical modes*), in which the tones constituting these forms can be presented in six different scales. The scales are schematic arrangements of tones within the range of an octave, according to their pitch.

It is a serious mistake to confuse the fact that the general arrangement in question goes beyond the constructive regulations of the single opus, with the assumption that, historically, it must have originated before this type of music came into being.

For practical reasons, musical instruction usually starts with an explanation of the different scales on which the music to be studied is based (which, incidentally, is perhaps not at all essential). But it does not prove, by any means, that, antedating the music under consideration, these scales (like so many laws of the Medes and Persians) were proclaimed, in some mysterious manner, by nature or by some other exalted legislator, as containing binding rules from which there was no appeal. The fact that the church modes received Greek names (Ionian, Dorian, Phrygian, Lydian, Mixolydian, Aeolian), because they were supposedly derived from ancient Greek tetrachords, should not lead us astray; the former had as little to do with the latter as the eight-voice masses of the Netherlands school with the flute players of Sparta.

Yet today we interpret tonality as meaning more than the possibility of tracing back the tones used in various melodies in agreement with a scheme adjusted progressively to the pitch of those tones. To us, tonality undoubtedly means that it is possible to establish a system of relationships and interdependences between the harmonies that inhabit the area of a sound language. Tonality in this sense is a harmonic principle and therefore has no legitimate place in the development of music as we have considered it so far. It was introduced into music through the influence of the other European autochthon, namely, the symmetrical-scanning component. Within the sphere of this component, where the question is not one of constructive relations between freely articulated single voices, harmonies rapidly had to acquire a very important but quite different value. What could more effectively underline this inherent demand for symmetry (the metrical similarity of sections built along analogous lines) than accentuation of sections by colorful harmonies cleverly distributed according to their respective characteristic effects?

It is not until such constituents recur in the metrically accented parts of a composition that we are again conscious of the fundamental chords to which other chords are subordinated, and of the fundamental tones, later called "tonics," used as the foundations of these chords. To examine the tonalities of the Gregorian chant in this sense seems a vain enterprise. Doubtless repetition of the pattern, involved in the iteration principle, would show the preponderance of certain tones in the melodic line over others; but this would not necessarily give them the character of fundamental tones carrying certain chords, for the reason that no chords were as yet involved. To my mind, it is not the fact that a particular tone happens to be the first in a scale which makes it the basic tone of that scale; for that matter, it might as well have been the fifth or the last tone. A tone becomes a tonic only when the central triad is built over it.

The First Inroad of Chromaticism

IT WAS this second and higher meaning of tonality which started the slow penetrations of symmetrical-scanning music into the sphere of polyphony, because musicians of the Renaissance were beginning to hear the harmonies established between freely articulated voices, with the ears of those who used the harmonies to emphasize the meter. The process accelerated in tempo, and took on striking proportions in the second half of the sixteenth century. It was connected with a tremendous shifting of sociological relations and of the centers of gravity. As divine service was the priest's concern, so did medieval sacred music become more and more the business of the trained and scholarly musician. But now Protestantism introduced congregational singing in church, demanding the use of a novel, or at least of a much simplified, type of sacred music, accessible to laymen. Contrariwise, man's impulse to express himself, responsible for the origin of European music as such, now stirred anew and imperiously commanded that the art take a long step forward. For the first time, the symbolic substance of music received conscious recognition and was made the vehicle of progress.

The new movement was inaugurated under the slogans of *musica ficta* (music as the expression of extramusical emotional qualities) and *stilo rappresentativo* (a style representing such emotions through striking musical symbols). Music was meant to express something outside itself; one should visualize something while listening to it. Technically speaking, the new movement called primarily for a strong accentuation of the chromatic elements, and, after that, for the victory of the major and minor tonality.

Chromatics, the preponderance of half-tone intervals as we find them in Gesualdo and Cyprien de Rore, indicated first and foremost an enrichment of melodic possibilities; but, at the same time, they included the danger of leveling the differences between the diatonic substances by means of an overextended distinction. Both these aspects of chromaticism lie on the road marked out for European music.

In the light of present-day developments, it can almost be said that the major-minor tonality became an intermezzo, bridging the near-victory of chromatics three centuries ago and its present secure triumph. Probably the principle of chromatics could never have prevailed entirely, because the consciousness of tonality (using the word in its higher, harmonic sense) had already penetrated too deeply from the direction of the symmetrical-scanning component.

The system of chromatics, brought into existence by man's increasing need to express his personality and by his effort to make music more eloquent for this purpose, was coincidentally a further development of the freely articulated melodic element, in that it enlarged the possibilities of the melodic line to an extraordinary extent. But this move from the freely articulated quality of the church-mode language to one entirely based on the chromatic system was caught and interrupted by the principle of major-minor tonality which appeared at the same time. So far as the victory of tonality could be partly traced back to the influence of the new chromatics, the latter in turn was thereby thoroughly cut off from its own road to conquest. Within the realm of the established major-minor system, the world of half-tones at first acted merely as coloring (as expressed by the word "chromatics," derived from *chroma,* the Greek word for color), in other words, as an accidental factor interpolated between the legitimate intervals of the diatonic scale.

The step from church modes to the major-minor diatonics represented a unification of the sound structure. The six church modes were differentiated from each other by having two half-tone intervals included in each scale, occurring in each case in a different place (Ionian: C-D-*E-F*-G-A-*B-C;* Dorian: D-*E-F*-G-A-*B-C*-D; Aeolian: A-*B-C*-D-*E-F*-G, etc.); while the major-minor system was an achievement, since it provided an opportunity to modulate between the twelve major and minor keys. These keys, however, were uniform in structure. The concept of modulation was senseless in the realm of the church modes, as the absolute pitch of the fundamental tone of the scale was totally unimportant. People had no ear for it, but were guided by the relative position of the half-tone in the scale to the fundamental tone arbitrarily adopted. In the new tonality, too, it was not until much later that the idea of modulation grew to its full significance. This did not happen until after the tempered pitch allowed harmonic modulations to run through all keys and return to the original point. At the start, the major-minor tonality was both a unification and a limitation of resources. Man's sense of color had to become refined to a degree where he could recognize the twelve shiftings of the same tonality as so many shades endowed with clearly differentiated powers of expression before the new tonality was accepted as richer in resources than the older one.

The Dominant Principle Meets the Emergency

THE focal point of the new musical structure, and certainly the real cause of its victory, was the *dominant*. The chromatic element had gradually eliminated the differences between the old scales. For it is evident that, if one occasionally interpolated a half-tone in the church modes, their chief idiosyncrasy (the position of the original half-tone interval) would become less and less pronounced.

It was the function of the dominant to dispel the chaos which threatened to engulf music through the introduction of chromatics. We shall see what attempts toward order sprang from the second and more successful great invasion of chromatics three hundred years later. The remedy employed to bolster the shaken structure was furnished by the harmonic feeling developed in symmetric-scanning music. Evaluation of harmonies according to their importance in the metric progress and establishment of a hierarchy of chords based on their relationship to the fundamental chord were then originated.

The connection of the triads on the fifth and the first steps of the major or minor scale—the function of the dominant—was considered the strongest and therefore the central harmonic relationship. Whatever may have been the cause of selection, it is undeniable that this harmonic combination came steadily to the fore in the late stages of the church modes. During the threatening chromatic invasion, the dominant effects engulfed music to an extent which actually prevented the growth of a clear key-consciousness in the new tonality. Utilization of this powerful, novel effect was carried too far.

But soon it became evident that a key could have only one tonic-dominant relation, and that the modern key was stamped by the fact that all other harmonic relationships were subordinated to it.

When that was accomplished, the old order was definitely overthrown, the first onslaught of the "anarchistic" chromatic hordes was beaten off, and the reign of tonality in the stricter sense positively established.

The basic clause of its constitution read: "Consolidated harmonic structure." Two tremendous accomplishments characterized its glorious reign: opera and the sonata.

CHAPTER   FIVE

RISE AND DECLINE OF TONALITY

Why Is Medieval Music Unpopular?

A VITAL change in the musical cosmos, a more momentous change than we generally realize, was caused by the fact that from the period of the late Renaissance on, people began to hear music essentially, indeed almost exclusively, through an *harmonic* consciousness. In other words, they began to adapt themselves to harmonies heard simultaneously. To this change we can attribute the strangeness and unfamiliarity of medieval music today. Basically, everything composed before Bach is now outmoded and unpopular. The public knows little about the first hundred or hundred and fifty years of instrumental music. Among the composers, however, who antedated this epoch, a few names only, such as Palestrina, Orlando di Lasso, Dufay, and Josquin de Prés, spring to mind when we think of that period; but what they wrote is almost completely forgotten. On occasion when we hear a little ancient church music, such as is available through the medium of several series of excellent gramophone records, even men of good will find most of it foreign to their taste. To them, the different works all sound alike—an endless, very pure and dignified but lifeless succession of triads. Obviously the ear absorbs less readily than the eye; imagination is more directly stimulated by visual than by acoustical impressions. For we can enjoy one of the Italian "primitives" (Giotto, for instance) without hesitancy or intellectual effort; and if we have any feeling at all for art, the impressions we receive from them are as distinct as those we get from some more modern painters. For example: The absence of perspective in so-called "primitive" painting does not bother us at all nor does it interfere in any way with our pleasure when we look at such works. Yet, in principle, modern pictures are as distinct from "primitive" art as is modern tonality from the old church modes. What is the cause of this deplorable lack of adjustment, this seeming inferiority of our auditory sense as compared to our visual sense?

The answer is that the ear does not easily learn or absorb anything new. Once absorbed, however, the new element not only clings obstinately to the ear, but supplants what has been previously taken in. The ear may be likened to a conservative, somewhat stodgy old gentleman who isn't interested in novel ideas but who is stubbornly faithful to whatever he has once accepted, while the eye has the character of a flighty, fashionable woman, always eager to adopt new fancies and equally ready to drop them at an instant's notice.

To hear medieval music correctly, that is, polyphonically and contrapuntally, requires a psychological transformation which not even your much-vaunted professional musician finds it easy to achieve. This is because the harmonies produced by the simultaneously progressing voices repeatedly push themselves into the foreground; and the more polyphonic the composition, the more compact the mass of chords which we hear. Then, as a purely practical cause, add to this fact our familiarity with the colorful and clearly graduated tonal palette used in our instrumental music, and we see at once why we are liable to hear the old choral music as a single cord of sound, whereas our ancestors were better able to distinguish and separate the individual voices.

We can measure the extent of the change due to the rise of the harmonic style and tonality by the depth of neglect in which the treasures of medieval music lie buried. The newer style was thoroughly harmonic, notwithstanding that a novel and resounding catch phrase, "melody," was soon to become an all-powerful slogan. Until then, musicians in the Middle Ages, although thinking in melodic terms, had not talked overmuch about melody. Of course the fanatics who terrorize public opinion now, as formerly, with their constant and insistent demand for "melody" have something else in mind. They would be exceedingly amazed if one tried to convince them that a mass by Binchois or Willaert is really a melodic work *par excellence*.

In our harmonic period, the public has come to interpret "melody" as whatever stands out in bold relief as a coherent melodic line over an indifferent accompaniment of chords. (The requirement that the "tune" be susceptible of being whistled by the audience on leaving opera house or concert hall was added to previous conditions in the nineteenth century. This condition was imposed by the *petite bourgeoisie*, who felt that they had not received their money's worth unless, after eating their fill, they could, into the bargain, take home a few tidbits for delectation on going to bed.)

Discrimination between melody as the positively valuable and spiritual element in music, and a more or less irrelevant accompaniment, is an achievement of the harmonic period, an achievement which doubtless considerably lowered the spiritual level of music, also impairing to an immeasurably greater extent the audiences' level.

First Crop of Tonality—Opera

IT IS indisputable that the basic features of music were enormously simplified by the reign of tonality and of harmonic structure. We owe these phenomena primarily to opera—that exceptionally pretentious, attractive, and self-contradictory product of the new regency.

The origin of opera is peculiar enough. This musical form, in which expressive qualities manifest themselves in the most striking manner, and in which soul, fire, passion, rage, and all other emotionally accentuated impulses are boldly limned in tone, was invented in cold blood by littérateurs and scholarly amateurs. A group of such persons, assembled in the so-called *camerata* in Florence at the end of the sixteenth century, held philological sessions with a view to reviving the ancient Greek tragedies as faithfully as possible. The result, scarcely foreseen by the learned originators of this scientific research, was *monody* supported by "modern" harmonies—a solo melody accompanied by chords, signifying an amazing innovation as compared to medieval polyphony. Nevertheless, a long time must have elapsed before opera as we know it could have emerged from the pedantic and academic experiments of the *camerata* if the grandiose Claudio Monteverdi had not seized upon this new art form a few years after its invention. It is owing to his efforts that the connection of theater and music acquired in a short time a decisive influence on the character of musical life as a whole.

Monteverdi

IN HIS historical importance, relevant to medieval polyphony and modern tonality, Monteverdi occupies a
position analogous to the place held today by Arnold
Schoenberg with respect to tonality in decay and the
new language of atonality. Monteverdi's early choral
works, composed approximately in the last quarter of
the sixteenth century, were thoroughly in the Palestrina
spirit of late polyphony. Monteverdi was not even particularly "revolutionary" in that sphere, for he avoided
joining the chromatic revolution of a Gesualdo or a
Cyprien de Rore. The stand he took on behalf of the
new "legality," the major-minor tonality, was reached
gradually. One can follow this gradual ascendancy of a
single dominant-tonic function in his successively appearing collections of madrigals.

In *Orfeo*, the first opera by Monteverdi still extant
(1609), the more advanced concept of tonality was not
yet systematically carried through. The large choral
portions of the work were stylistically still bound to the
submerging world of polyphonic development. Where
Monteverdi was vigorously radical was in his subordina-
tion of technical means to the expressive possibilities
of the single-voiced melody, the monody. It was there
that the *musica ficta* celebrated its entire success, and
there that the revolution in music for the sake of expression was at last fully legitimized. Music then began
to articulate emotions that it had never before expressed
and which, with the lesser means previously at the disposal of composers, it had never been able to suggest.
These strong and eminently expressive effects have ever
since caused people to marvel at Monteverdi's operas,

and have been largely responsible for keeping some of them alive. Yet it is remarkable that Monteverdi's success in achieving powerful expression was in proportion to the degree in which he passed the boundary lines of the new tonality already visible at that time, rather than when he realized tonality within its own bounds. Thus the first composer to bring the new theory to its climax injected into it the poison that was to cause its death almost before he had attained his purpose.

The "strong effect" striven for by all composers from then on had its origin in the audacity which exploded the rules—and would one day cause their total destruction. Unexpected harmonic shifts, sudden modulations in utter contradiction to the underlying scheme of the cadence, or at least strikingly modifying it, served to represent violent emotions.

Monteverdi was equally progressive and provocative in regard to the form of his monodies, though here, too, he fulfilled a law in operation throughout the history of music: that progress is always dialectically connected with elements which appear to have been eliminated by its very arrival on the scene.

One might imagine that monody, the newer factor in opera, should have consisted of emphasis on the symmetrical-scanning concept leading to the birth of the new harmonic-tonal style. But the strongest effects in Monteverdi's monodies were made when the form appeared to be freely rambling and articulated according to the exigencies of the libretto. In this he progressed beyond the customary periodical structure of the conventional operatic aria, since his method gave fuller scope and more freedom to expression; and, as we have seen, expression has been the real driving force in the advancement of Western music. Conversely, the freely articulated structure of the solo melody within the limits of the historical framework was technically less "modern," being directly related to the conquered principles of freely articulated medieval polyphony.

For the rest, this latter feature has never quite disappeared from opera. It survived in the recitative, and was even present when simple periodic diction celebrated its most palpable triumphs, namely, in the later Italian *bel canto* operas. The way in which this element again gained the upper hand through Richard Wagner in the nineteenth century is so well known that it need merely be mentioned in passing.

In Monteverdi's early operas the line distinguishing the aria from the recitative was almost invisible. A later distinct separation marked the beginning of the constant struggle between dramatic expression and absolute musical form which has persisted throughout the history of opera.

Within the art form of opera itself, the element of symmetrical periodicity had at first a deterrent influence, as gestures necessary to emphasize the clear delineation of emotion inevitably called for a freer articulation. Nevertheless, the "modern" thought supplied by tonality reposes in the formation of regular periods, explaining why such formation gained the upper hand to a degree in which tonality consolidated its position. To the same extent, opera withdrew for the time being from the scene of expressive development in favor of independently performed instrumental music, a novel feature which proceeded to expand along a line that none had anticipated. (Eventually, of course, opera was to return to expressive development, and we shall refer later to the potentialities inherent in that development.)

Second Vintage—Suite

FOR the first time, the old European-autochthonic component of symmetrically scanning music, originating in the march and dance, conquered the field; and Western man, determined on self-expression in music, discovered a new and surprisingly fruitful region of activity soon after he had brought the drama into a tremendously important relationship to music.

Summarily speaking, the essential acquisition in this new field was the suite—a loose chain of dancelike, symmetrically linked pieces all tirelessly demonstrating the freshly discovered interplay of tonic and dominant; in other words, the basic facts of tonality.

It is interesting to note that, even in the sphere of instrumental music, the roving, freely articulated component did not entirely disappear. As it survived in the operatic recitative, so did it remain, in instrumental music, in the toccata and its related free and fanciful shapes, in which the imitation technique inherited from medieval polyphony also found a place. But the form of the suite remained the backbone of the current development.

The Tonal Cadence

IN THE realm of the suite, the tonal cadence developed its formative power to an ever higher degree. The term "cadence" has a general as well as a specific meaning, similar to the dual meaning of the word "tonality," as explained in the previous chapter.

In general, cadence means a closing formula which can be demonstrated in every kind of highly articu-

lated music. The Gregorian chant already knew endings
of this sort; but it was not until tonality arrived on the
scene that the cadence acquired added importance, containing in a nutshell the essential constructive possibilities of tonal music.

Under the influence of symmetrical-scanning music,
cadence effects, stemming from the function of the
dominant—that prominent association of two triads
whose fundamental tones are connected by a descending
fifth—had already penetrated the later polyphonic music; and it was characteristic of the new major-minor
system that one relation of this kind was necessary to
determine what is called a key. Next, an analogous and
symmetrical connection, that of triads on the first and
fourth steps of the scale in which the two fundamental
tones were equally in the relation of a fifth to each
other, was added to the dominant tie-up. The combination of these two triad groups formed the cadence in
its specific sense, namely, the tonal cadence. The harmonic zones of the tonic (the fundamental triad) and
of the dominant (the triad of the fifth step) were regarded as opposite polar regions. What really happened
in tonal compositions was an unfolding of tension between the two, followed by the establishment of a balance between them. The typical tonal composition
moves from tonic to dominant along a short road whose
course is prescribed, up to a certain point, by the nature
of this particular harmonic relationship, and so back to
the tonic on a more involved path. We see the line of
least resistance leading to a complicated trail and notice
a stronger emphasis on this latter ingeniously organized
and systematically elaborated element, and the re-entry
of the tonic in a preparation through contact with the
fourth step, the subdominant.

In this process, we can readily see how the pattern of the tonal cadence was accepted and retained as the frame for a more or less extensive series of harmonic occurrences.

Harmonic Modulation and Tempered Pitch

THE more substantial the harmonic processes in the section of a score devoted to the return of the tonic, the more clearly the concept of modulation stands out. Modulation is the art of proceeding from one key to another, not merely through a juxtaposition, but rather through an orderly exposition of elements that can be related both to the key about to be abandoned and to the one which is to be established.

At this stage of tonality, music had not reached a point where new keys unrelated to the fundamental tone would be established in a composition for a long or permanent stay. Nor was there any real need for enharmony. In this respect, the invention of tempered pitch in the beginning of the eighteenth century anticipated to a considerable degree a later development of technique in composition.

Circumstances led to the following adjustment. The twelve major and minor keys may be likened to an assemblage of equidistant parallel lines. But the seven fixed points on these parallels, the seven tones of the diatonic scale, are not thereby interrelated, because not all of them are common to the twelve keys. For example: C Sharp in the scale of A Major is not identical with C Sharp in the F-Sharp Major scale and, above all, is not to be confused with D Flat in the key of A-Flat Major. Before tempered pitch developed, division of the octave into intervals, necessary for the production of major and minor scales, was based on ratios of vibration which only permitted the relationship of tones within the scale of which they were a part, and of the "alterations" derived from them by the use of sharps and flats, to that scale.

Tempered pitch brought about a standardization of the tonal material which at last completed the process introduced by the victorious invasion of tonality. Only since that time has it been correct to speak of a fully expanded tonality whose material consists of the "half-tone system," or, if you prefer, of the "twelve-tone system," in which all the twelve tones of the octave are interchangeable links in a homogeneous network. For the term "system" applies exclusively to a primitive and fundamental division of material; and in so far as tonal music was never limited to the seven tones of the diatonic scale, tonality always used the "twelve-tone system." The technique which some modern composers use within the enclosure of the "twelve-tone system" has nothing to do with a "system" in the sense of an original premusical organization of material; and, for that reason, it should not be called the "twelve-tone *system*," but rather the "twelve-tone *technique*," as I will show in Chapter Seven.

The Reappearance of Chromatics Through Harmony

DIFFERENCES between individual scales are adjusted by tempered pitch. Lines connecting the twelve parallels have now become parallel to each other. To phrase it in another way: All C Sharps and D Flats, like all groups of sharps and flats, are identical, no matter in what key they appear. The vitality of our keyed instruments is mainly due to this identification, the piano's ascendancy dating from the invention of tempered pitch. On stringed instruments, however, various tones are not produced by a fixed apparatus, but by arbitrary stops made by the player's fingers. Thus it is possible for a violinist or cellist to differentiate between, say, F Sharp and G Flat. An obvious outgrowth of tempered pitch, although not one readily exploited to its fullest possibilities, is *enharmony*, that is, the right to consider any given tone either as an ascending alteration of the half-tone underneath or as a descending alteration of the one above. As an illustration: The note between G and A could be either G Sharp or A Flat. But the statement implies that, if I modulate from G-Flat Major to C-Flat Major, I can call the latter "B Major" and can easily continue my modulations to E Major and A Major, regions I could never have reached by way of the flats. I can modulate in a circle from C Major through all twelve keys, and arrive again at my starting point, a trick impossible without tempered pitch.

Meanwhile it is noticeable that the resplendent tempered portal through which freedom was found in the structure of tonality provided at the same time a comfortable entrance for the guest who was to be kept away by the erection of the building. Completion of the edifice was intrinsically connected with reappearance of this dangerous and unwelcome visitor, who, in the course of a hundred and fifty years of active burrowing, has succeeded in demolishing the organism. I refer to chromatics.

Johann Sebastian Bach

THE fact that tempered pitch had considerably facilitated communications between all parts of the harmonic territory constituted an obvious invitation to an even more "interesting" arrangement of that "harmonically interesting" section of the tonal composition—the return from the dominant to the tonic. That was exactly what happened when the suite developed into the sonata. As a transition from the former to the latter, the work built up by Johann Sebastian Bach stands historically at the center of the tonal period. Bach was the first to erect a monument to tempered pitch, creating coincidentally the first standard opus for the modern piano, *The Well-tempered Clavichord.* He did not make full use of the resources of tempered pitch, as we understand it in the light of the enharmonic circular modulation just referred to; but he was the first composer to treat the twelve keys as independent units possessing individual timbres.

From the viewpoint of our historical survey, which is intended to be a history of musical structures rather than a history of music, Bach put an end to the rapidly increasing disintegration of tonality through chromatics, by giving a new impetus to the contrapuntal element and making it, for a time, the pivot of musical progress.

Since the beginning of more modern times, counterpoint had led a subterranean existence; Bach was the first composer to bring it out again into the open. His contrapuntal works, above all, his *Art of the Fugue,* leave an indescribable impression of perfection by reason of the imcomparable fashion in which the principle of "balance" is realized and demonstrated. Scarcely any other music so clearly justifies the exigencies of the various co-ordinating systems. Through the use of contrapuntal devices, music in the hands of Bach again approached the character of the freely articulating component. Yet these devices followed the directions of medieval counterpoint both more and less: less, because strict contrapuntal regulations and prohibitions regarding intervals did not apply here and so gave place to greater liberty; and more, because, despite the fact that the entire composition was based on the concept of free articulation, the requirements of tonality had to be fulfilled. These requirements represented a harmonic system perfected in the course of a long process of development, a system inestimably harder to realize than the few basic factors of the medieval church modes. When, in the *Art of the Fugue*, one can turn whole fugues and canons upside down and play them in reverse order, we are not dumbfounded by finding that the stream of the freely articulating voices still makes sense; for one can easily imagine so treating an independently invented voice part. What really amazes us is that, as a result of all these processes, a pure D Minor emerges again, a harmonic picture that conforms as spontaneously to the requirements of tonality as does the original form of the piece. Such phenomena reveal the concept of "balance" with the clarity of sunlight.

Bach demanded more of tonality than that it conform to its own harmonic rules: he taught it to obey the laws of counterpoint as well. In doing so, he checked the precipitate and primitive trend from diatonic tonality into chromatics; and it was owing to his claims on tonality that when the chromatic principle finally came to flower, it was adapted to a standard it might not have attained without his intervention. Even if Bach's writing of harmony and counterpoint had been an isolated phenomenon, his almost supernatural realization of "balance" would have remained a stimulant for all the composers who came after him. Whatever Western music has been produced since Bach, or may yet be forthcoming, must be measured against his standard of perfection.

Examination of Bach's coupling of harmony and counterpoint, the two original components of Western music, discloses that he not only brought a stylistic development to its logical conclusion (as the customary historian is wont to point out) but also initiated a new view of the concepts of repetition and variation. Henceforth, these concepts, having taken on a certain characteristic quality in tonality, were seen in an important new light. It was not until this was realized that the budding form, the sonata, became the standard form of tonality. To that extent, Bach was one of the co-originators of the sonata.

The Meaning of Repetition in the Sonata Form

AFTER the advent of Bach, music seemed to submit to a spell of simplification almost as widespread in scope as the one it experienced during the period of transition from medieval polyphony to the harmonic-tonal style. Initial experiments in the sonata form, made by Stamitz and similar half-forgotten composers in the mid-eighteenth century, were like childish prattlings compared to Bach's sagacious thought structures. But with Haydn and Mozart, European music soon rose again to its full spiritual height.

As previously intimated, the motive of repetition played a special part in tonal music. The repetitive device has a magic origin, preserved in early forms built on the principle of iteration: a constant repetition of the same elements, with the idea of exorcism through ceaseless reiteration. In the development of medieval music this principle had grown to a spiritualization which showed no sign of its magic origin. In tonality, however, repetition has an entirely different meaning; it means the re-establishment of a situation which had prevailed before the introduction of divergent features, such as the establishment of a tonic after a digression into the dominant. Although this occurrence seemed to be on a considerably higher level than the ritualistic exorcisms associated with the iteration concept, in reality the whole thing rested on an equally close, perhaps a still closer, connection with the world of magic ideas. What is mirrored in cases like this is nothing but a naïve belief in the immutability of nature engendered by modern physical science. The belief insinuates that whatever may happen in the meantime, the way of the world remains constant, nothing ever decays, everything remains forever as it was in the beginning; a recognizable objective logic and causality rules all that takes place in the universe. This great myth, served up as rational science, was placed atop its last gigantic monument in Wagner's *Ring*, as demonstrated to us *ad oculos*. There at the end, while gods and heroes perish, the Rhine, a symbol of imperishable and immutable nature, flows along as majestically and serenely as in the opening of the cycle when the river gave birth to the gloomy tragedy. The reinstatement of tonality as the essence of tonal music spells restoration and resignation. Following an epoch of interesting but ineffective commotion, the old order, supposedly ordained by nature, was once more firmly settled; the moral is that it cannot be changed. Reduction of the old order *ad absurdum* was objectively contained in its essence, but subjectively unintended by musicians who constantly found new and more ingenious ways of re-establishing the order which they themselves had first shaken.

The Apex of Tonality. Beethoven

THE sonata derived its significance and its differentiation from the suite from the part dedicated to the return to the tonic, called "development." In development, the themes of the "exposition"—the first part,
leading from the tonic to the dominant—were "worked
up." Now, what does "working up" a theme mean? It
means varying it. We have already seen how freely
articulating music varied its elements through melodic
alterations, such as inversions, and rhythmic changes
like augmentation. Many elements were also varied in
the early tonal music, but mostly by adorning a simple
harmonic framework with varying figurations, as in the
passacaglia. Bach was the first to show how the subtle
methods of polyphony could be used within the region
of tonality, how individually outlined themes could be
diluted into a more or less indifferent motif pattern,
and how one could work contrapuntally with that without losing sight of a previously prepared harmonic plan,
even to the extent of bringing that plan into more plastic relief.

Of such a character was the variation of themes called
into play in that section of the sonata whose function
was to lead back to the tonic. It was not only that this
part was dramatized by a lively and consanguineous
variation which followed the line of increased expression; the type of "working up" led as well to an enrichment of the harmonic detours, legitimizing them in a
destruction of the original metrical symmetry of the
themes which were contrapuntally split and coupled.
Once destroyed, the metrical symmetry stood in need of
repair. As an example: When a first phrase of four

measures is followed by a six-measured after-sentence, the elongation, contrary to the symmetrical-scanning theorem, can best be legitimized by an unsuspected modulation in the interpolated measures.

The penetration of the dramatic spirit into the sonata form doubtless caused the development of sharply contrasting themes. In the sonata's initial phase, this principle was unknown; with Haydn, the "second subject" was often similar to the first. Contrast between the tonic and the dominant regions, rather than between the subjects themselves, was the essential feature of early sonatas. Emphasis on thematic contrast, similar to the harmonic contrast developed in the exposition, did not come until later. Even Beethoven did not follow the new principle strictly, nor without ingeniously glossing over the split in the exposition. This explains why, in studying the expositions in Beethoven's sonatas, one so often has to ask oneself whether they do not contain more than two themes, perhaps four or five, or whether they have been fashioned from a single complex theme.

Beethoven seldom allowed the second theme to acquire the calm and the stability expected of it; he spent much effort in preserving the steady flow of the exposition once the first and parent theme had been displayed; so that here, too, the progression from tonic to dominant remained the main objective of presentation. Nonetheless, the bithematic principle, gaining increased prominence in the romantic period, can be traced back to Beethoven.

Compared to the vivid richness of Mozart's contrapuntal development sections, Beethoven makes relatively a less progressive impression, for he frequently seems a little stiff and limits himself to what is absolutely indispensable; but, for all that, his music strikes one as being more monumental than Mozart's, and even more rigorous. On the other hand, Beethoven was extraordinarily progressive in the thorough economy with which he built up his extensive forms from scanty material. Though creating in the golden age of tonality, when no signs of the imminent decay were visible, Beethoven was the first to anticipate the new era. His last quartets presaged the discovery of a coast where the vessel of European music would seek a haven a century later. The chromatic four-tone motif which had a focal place in these last quartets can be traced through all of Beethoven's compositions back to the works written in his early youth, sometimes assuming the character of what we called a "basic pattern" in ancient music and what was to be incorporated into our new music. Furthermore, the rigorous, hard counterpoint of Beethoven's last quartets anticipated much that was to become necessary in the epoch of a decaying tonality.

Universalism. The Symphony and the Hapsburg Empire

TONAL music culminated in Beethoven, bringing to fruition, in its most widespread and comprehensive form, the dream of Western man to express himself through the medium of music. The "universally human" factor appeared to be as clearly represented in Beethoven's music as in Kantian philosophy, or in that other expression of Germanic idealism, Goethe's "humanity." This meant that the spiritual image had crystallized enough to show the utmost clarity, but not enough to reveal modifications of the image into something special, private, and isolated, that is, something merely "interesting."

While granting that Mozart was a much greater the-

atrical composer than Beethoven, we must admit that
Beethoven's instrumental music is more dramatic because its gesture has a more direct impetus. In Beethoven, expressive directness reached a point beyond which
abstract and independent music could not go without
deteriorating into a genrelike, purely descriptive, par-
ticularistic, and petty individualism. It was this bound-
arylike quality which connected the music of Beethoven
with mankind's eternal dream of freedom; for freedom,
too, involves the notion of "going to a certain point
and no further," since otherwise it destroys itself.
Beethoven's music is completely free of all genrelike
qualities. Even the "German Dances" breathe the full
symphonic spirit, whose universality, however, never
evaporates into a generalized, abstract indifference.

The sonata's emergence into the symphony marked
the completion of the structure of tonality. So far as I
know, little attention has yet been paid to the fact that
the short history of the symphonic form is inescapably
bound up with the Hapsburg Empire and its center;
Vienna. Real symphonies have been composed in no
other city; the names of Haydn, Mozart, Beethoven,
Schubert, Brahms, Bruckner, and Mahler are proof of
this contention. Schumann, Mendelssohn, Tschaikowsky, and Franck can scarcely be called real symphonic
composers; they merely employed the patterns of the
Viennese classics with more or less luck or originality.
Music produced under the title of "symphony" since
Mahler is either imitative or carries the title without
justification. Soon after Mahler was called away from
his unfinished task, the Empire of the Hapsburgs, mis-
understood as no other political entity in the entire
history of mankind had ever been, met with its unde-
served downfall; and this event also marked the end of

the symphonic form. The vital principle of the Empire was, in a sense, "symphonic"; it provided a maximum of freedom within the framework of the patriarchal law, comparable in its essence to the rule of tonality in music. The symphony, too, combined a maximum of freedom of expression with a maximum of order, under tonality's government.

If anything makes music an invaluable art, worthy of the highest rank among the spiritual attainments of mankind, it is its inherent power to present in ever new, straightforward configurations the combination of freedom and order that is the loftiest of social aspirations.

Tonality Becomes Overripe. Franz Schubert

FRANZ SCHUBERT, the greatest master produced by romanticism, was one of its earliest exponents. He went beyond the limits reached by Beethoven, not in the direction of speculative radicalism, but in making the thought still more palpably concrete. Included herein is everything that goes by the name of popularity, "nearness to the soil," "depth of feeling," "emotional warmth," and the like. Sociologically speaking, romanticism instigated the decay of "humanity," of universality in music. Technically, it gave momentum to thematic individuality, shifting the balance of the composition as a whole from its constructive base and stressing inspiration as the compelling original force. We are so accustomed to judge the value of composer and composition by these measurements that we hardly realize that such concepts played no appreciable part in the preclassical epoch. The further back one travels in musical history, the less important the unique, unrepeatable originality becomes. The old masters picked up their subject matter indiscriminately, wherever themes were to be found; they used the same material over and over again, and bartered themes with each other. Before the nineteenth century, composers were not required to write new and original themes. Once the demand for originality was made, the concept of mental ownership followed in due course.

Franz Schubert contributed to the progress of tonality—paradoxically fostering its decay—mostly through his irregular, unsymmetrical periods. Far from emphasizing anew the freely articulated component (to which Beethoven was inclined in his later years), Schubert remained wholeheartedly true to the basic harmonic principle of tonality. By that token he was exceedingly progressive, for he was forced to balance his irregular meters by an enrichment of the harmonic means to an extent but dimly imagined up to that time. In this respect, Monteverdi and Haydn were almost his only precursors.

The Triumphant Return of Chromaticism. Wagner

THE next technical step was the return of chromatics, which could no longer be delayed. Means were provided by an increasing refinement of the harmonic elements and by a constantly mounting determination to foster the expressive tendency. Characteristically enough, the return of this expressive trend was announced in conjunction with *musica ficta*, as had been the case about two hundred years before. Opera and the symphonic poem, its correlated form in the realm of absolute music, took possession of this new means, chiefly through the efforts of Berlioz, Wagner, and Liszt, and for exactly the same reasons that had held sway previously:

they provided a radical intensification of emotional expression. The chromatic four-tone theme, penetrating from the B-A-C-H anagram (according to the German nomenclature) into music and later to emerge in another order in Beethoven's music as an *idée fixe*, at last appeared in Wagner's hands as a consecutive four-tone linear progression radically simplified and therefore radically eloquent. (See the opening of the *Tristan* Prelude.)

Two decisive phenomena were closely bound up with this movement: a spreading national feeling in music and the waning of the art's direct spectacular appeal. The need of extended musical expression, enforced by amputation of so-called "entertainment" music (of which I shall speak again later), once more involved an added interest in the material at hand; and the different national colors of music were discovered with a childish delight in their primitive strangeness, which should have been beneath the dignity of a company that had experienced Mozart and Beethoven. The genius of composers like Moussorgsky and Janáček in reaping an unusual harvest from such a field does not disprove its essential barrenness. It is suggestive enough that both Moussorgsky and Janáček remained dilettanti, if extraordinary ones, up to the last.

A decrease in spectacular appeal was also connected with an active search for original material and fresh effects. The tempo of progress in art, always in advance of the average intelligence, became so rapid that its conflict with the backward times aroused loud protests. Nevertheless, music did not relinquish the spectacular gesture. Contrariwise, the display of musical fireworks increased, as proved by the enormous orchestras of later romanticism. It seemed as if people felt intuitively that the ship was sailing away faster and faster, and wanted to bridge the distance between it and the quickly disappearing coastline by the use of still more sound. Comprehensibility became a crucial problem; but the ingenious instrumental means applied by Wagner to reach the highest degree of plasticity accentuated rather than lessened the ordinary listener's difficulty in absorbing what was heard. Wagner foresaw an ideal of articulation which had no further correspondence with the swift perception of striking operatic gestures.

On the Threshold of Atonality

A PHENOMENON that we encountered in another form before the church modes had definitely changed into the new tonality made itself felt in the late romantic epoch. At that time the fresh and novel effect of the dominant was used more often than was conducive to the ascendancy of a clear key-consciousness. And now the dominant's effects again started to sprout, largely owing to the potency of a fertile chromaticism. Whenever a chromatic passing note was interpolated between two diatonic melody tones, a tendency to slip a dominant chord under it soon became apparent, thus making that passing note the leading tone of the next chord. The result was the same; the clear key-consciousness became more and more blurred until it finally faded into oblivion. This device of the "intermediate dominant" can best be studied in the works of Max Reger; but many other composers, Debussy among them, applied it, too. Debussy frequently used *"ersatz tonalities"* (if one may borrow the term), by which I mean fundamental harmonic elements, valid in one composition or a fragment thereof, but not quite definable as one of the known keys, though plainly referring to the triad harmony and the third-structure of tonal chords. Scales that somehow deviate from the major-minor scale can be derived from such structures; a certain prevalence of fourths may be proved in the composition of chords; and other similar experiments all tend to save this type of music as a sort of appendage to tonality. Claiming the same right, one might cite the later operas of Monteverdi as extraordinary extensions of the church modes; many people may well have done so at the time.

In like manner, a man who wades into the sea until he is up to his neck can, of course, insist that he remains on land for the simple reason that his feet still touch bottom; but in view of the situation he will soon be in if he continues wading, it might be more correct to say that he is in the water. As a matter of fact, the distance from Debussy to atonality is but a step.

Previous steps were consumed in delivering music of the syntax of atonality, of the dominant and the tonal cadence; the last step involved getting rid of major and minor triads, the elements which constituted this syntax and kept it alive. Arnold Schoenberg has taken the final step in his "Three Piano Pieces," Opus 11.

Two conclusive consequences were attached to the ultimate victory of chromatics. The first showed the basic structure of the material to be still unified and simplified; in the place of twelve equal major and minor scales, differentiated solely by their respective timbres, the material now consisted of one homogeneous chromatic scale by which the octave was divided into twelve equal parts. Surely a limit was reached here, since the "half-tone system" could scarcely be more exactly standardized.

Liquidation of the sonata came as the second historical consequence. The entire sonata form was based on contrast between the opposite polar zones of tonic and dominant, and on the harmonic factors of tonality as such; once separated from these root words, the sonata could not very well develop within the confines of a language. And so the new music was brought face to face with an elementary problem of creating intrinsically new ideas of form. In Chapter VII we shall see what has been achieved in that direction.

The outline of a history of musical structures given in this and the previous chapter has, I hope, demonstrated what should be understood by atonality when its inevitable rise from the development of Western music is traced. What can be called tonality, in contrast to atonality, should also be clear. Nevertheless, in the next chapter we shall make a systematic attempt to support this contention by bringing these concepts face to face.

CHAPTER SIX

ATONALITY

Safety First—Through Clear Definitions

IT IS amazing that scarcely another phenomenon in the history of modern art has been the object of such zealous and persistent hatred, even persecution, as atonal music. In the visual arts, to be sure, expressionism and other novel movements have aroused much irritation and opposition. Occasionally we hear of some rabid art lover going to work with a pocketknife on a picture that has annoyed him; but, in general, conservative opposition in the field of the visual arts is trifling compared to the stone wall of silent rejection faced by atonal music. The reason probably is that when music is exhibited as a living organism before masses of people seated in an auditorium, it has a more immediate and a stronger effect on their nervous systems than is produced by a picture in an art gallery, where spectators strolling about at their pleasure receive individual rather than collective impressions. A picture must first attract the eye; the observer must collect his thoughts to look at it consciously; he must concentrate on not looking away. Music in an opera house or concert hall is inescapable; it fills all the space there is; the victims, regimented into orderly rows, haven't the remotest chance of "listening away." (That is why architecture, too, being a much more obtrusive art than painting, is subject to relatively more violent protest from on-lookers.)

Granting all this, it still is amazing to see, after thirty years of atonal music, how much hysterical anger arises when the subject is mentioned. The fact that no one seems to know exactly what constitutes atonality does not appear to cut any ice. Atonality, in the mind of some objectors, has long since become a scapegoat, or a fetish of negative character. Others identify the word with apocalyptic demons bent on driving the world headlong to destruction; to them, atonality is an accessory to various plagues that beset humanity: Bolshevism, the world-wide rule of Jewry, the decadence of the middle classes, capitalist corruption, and such bugbears.

The evil connotations of the atonalist label suggest these potentialities. Not that the word "atonal" was invented by composers who made use of the device; it was, on the contrary, thought up by an enemy. It has been impossible, so far, to establish the identity of this foe; but there is good reason to believe that a critic in Vienna coined the term in his panic and dismay on hearing the first works of Schoenberg that were free of tonality. Today the most accomplished propagandists must regard the verbal invention with admiration, tinged with envy. "Atonality" is at once provoking, mysterious, absurd, and fraught with a fatal efficiency which gives it the effect of a skull and crossbones wherever it may be posted. The word acts as a bogy; yet its absurd mystery goes no deeper than the fact that no one really knows what "tonal" means and so cannot imagine its opposite, "atonality." If the expression "tonal" had ever been familiar, the meaning of its antithesis would be obvious; but it was not until the new catchword came into use that people took an interest in the meanings of "tonal" and "tonality."

In professional terminology, and paraphrasing Webster's definition, tonality means simply the key, C Minor or E Major or whatever it may be, in which a composition is written. If this technical definition were generally accepted by laymen, the critic who invented the word "atonality" could not be considered nearly so malicious as he has been represented. But because the technical interpretation of tonality was little known by the average music lover, people soon adopted another definition which looked very scholarly to them, hinting at the weight of lexicography.

If, according to this latter definition, "tonal" is "whatever belóngs to tone, whatever corresponds to the nature of the tone" and the like, then "atonal," merely on this supposition (whatever it may mean), cannot be applied to anything pertaining to the sphere of music, since music, of any kind, obviously has to do with tones. In this context, the term "atonal" has no sense at all. But meanwhile the development of a hate complex toward new music prevented the only possible conclusion, namely, that acceptance of the foregoing definition of tonal music precluded acceptance of the expression "atonal," in relation either to new or to any other kind of music. The one thing that lingered in the consciousness of the opponents of new music was the conviction that tonal has something to do with the nature of tones, and was indispensable to music simply because music is the art that works with tones. When, somewhere, a type of music called "atonal" became fashionable, these naïve souls jumped to the conclusion that it must be contrary to the very nature of tones, in other words, that, strictly speaking, it could not be music at all. Was not that what they wanted to prove in the first place? The situation was as clear as daylight. In choosing its name, this sort of music demonstrated, beyond the shadow of a doubt, that it must be nonsensical, an unnatural and sacrilegious nuisance!

If we admit the validity of other definitions of tonality (and it is permissible to do so), we must be strict in avoiding the expression "atonality." Since, however, the term does exist and can hardly be exterminated, we should at least be careful that it is correctly used in its grammatical sense. Once concede that "tonality" is synonymous with "key," and "atonality" has the clear and approvable meaning of music without a key. This interpretation applies, to a high degree, to the new music under consideration here. Precisely how far the sphere of tonality extends, whether it takes in the medieval church modes or even the Gregorian chant, is a question of minor importance when we accept the principle that the range of the tonality concept is not necessarily identical with the range of music itself. If it were, a return to the all-inclusive definition of tonality would be forced upon us; and in that case new music, too, would naturally show certain qualities of this all-inclusive kind, whereupon the term "atonal" would again forfeit its sense.

In the light of our historical survey, we can identify atonality by its distinguishing lack of the cadential and dominant functions and the supplementary absence of a definite key-consciousness. Having thus made our position clear, we can proceed to examine serious objections to atonality, that is, disapprovals which rise above the level of vulgar demagogism.

Owing to the lack of unequivocal definitions, these objections have seldom been clearly formulated; thus, we shall try to explain their meaning in the terms of our previous expositions.

Objections to Atonality

ONE objection deals with the origin of atonality. Most of the other unfavorable opinions can be summarized under one heading and are directed against atonality's function in music and its capacity to fulfill the requirements expected of an artistic system.

The first objection is to the effect that atonality has been arbitrarily introduced into music. In its commonest phase the censure declares that atonal composers invented this style when their flagrant inability to write decent music was shown up. "Atonality," it was said, "furnished them with a means of hiding their fiascoes and, in addition, gave them a chance to make more money with their scandalous sensation-mongering than they could have earned had they stuck to their bungling attempts to compose in obedience to tonality." This accusation almost reverses the truth. All atonal composers, without exception, have written music which the public stamped with the seal of "success"; but it was invariably tonal music, never atonal!

A more elegant approach to the point is found in the claim that there was "no necessity" for such a radical change of style. "Perhaps it would have been just as well simply to continue in the old way."

I believe I have outlined here a much more specific concept of "necessity," as involved in the development of music, than is expounded in the foregoing criticism. We have seen in our historical survey how the inner unfolding of the art, in dialectic relation to the social orders during which various kinds of music were produced, proved that changes of style were both inherent in such artistic growth and necessary to it. This also applies to the genesis of atonality.

A more arbitrary action, it seems to me, springs from the subjective conviction voiced by the originator of a work of art that he "just had to do it," an attitude which opponents of atonality are emphatic in endorsing as a necessity. It is hard to understand why a man who claims that he "must" compose tonally should be believed rather than one who can demonstrate by the history of music how he came to atonality—unless one presumes that the "inspired" writer is accepted because his followers are determined to believe in him. This is not the first time that an irrational illusion has been believed in preference to a truth proved a hundred times over.

Even so, the charge of arbitrariness will no more be raised by anyone who is satisfied with the function of atonality than it would occur to the critic to wonder whether Herr Stamitz and his Mannheim colleagues invented the sonata form "arbitrarily" or because they were "divinely inspired." Since this invention has been proved superlatively "right," the question is entirely irrelevant.

Let us, therefore, turn to doubts as to the proper functioning of atonality. These can be summed up in the accusation that atonality is incomparably less intelligible than tonal music. If this meant that atonality was incomprehensible to a number of listeners, the obvious answer would be that such uncertainty or puzzlement has always been engendered by any new kind of music, and that the public can only wait for an adequate lapse of time to catch up with the innovation. But the objection to new music on the ground that it is not so clear as the old is intended to be objective, and can be sketched as follows:

1. The material of atonality is less differentiated than the material used in tonal music; its variegated elements show fewer contrasts and so are harder to distinguish from each other.

2. General rhythmic patterns are less accentuated; the lack of them tends to cloud the forms.

3. The possibilities of expression in atonal music are fewer, by reason of these inherent limitations, than in tonal music.

We may now examine these objections in numerical sequence, in so far as they are based on observation, to determine whether they apply to atonality in principle or perhaps merely to the personal inadequacies of composers who are guilty of errors which others, more gifted or technically better prepared, could avoid.

Is Atonal Music Less Intelligible Than Tonal Music?

1. EVIDENTLY we are dealing here with the question of atonal music in principle. As an inherent characteristic of the material is attacked, we can safely conclude that the quality of the sound language, as such, is under attack, since, as I showed in Chapter One, a sound language is characterized by its material. The reader will remember that by material, or, if you prefer, the wealth of root words of a sound language, we meant primarily the harmonic elements prevalent in it.

We have seen that the dissolution of tonality resulted in a condition where its central fundamental fact, the basic triad (its root word, so to speak), was used with decreasing frequency until at last it was scarcely ever used at all. It is plain, therefore, that these root words will completely vanish in the atonal sound language. In consequence, we see at once a quantitative limitation of the musical vocabulary in certain directions. For an essential group of consonant structures was discarded with the elimination of the triad, and the remaining ones lost much of their importance. When, in conformity with our auditory conventions, we understand the consonants to be not only the unison and the octave, but major and minor thirds, the perfect fifth, and major and minor sixths as well, anyone can easily see that the triad is almost the only harmony of more than two tones which consists exclusively of consonants. Consequently, in atonal writing, three-part consonances disappear simply because the triad disappears. Two-part consonances remain, in principle; but since fully developed music generally consists of more than two voices, the two-part harmonies must be of lesser importance, if only quantitatively. From this it follows that harmonic progressions in atonal music occur preponderantly in the area inhabited by dissonances of a higher degree of tension, and that the lower tensions of consonances have practically no part in the scheme. Nonetheless, an extraordinary variety of nuances is found even within these limits. For example: Experimentation through hearing convinces us that the chord of E Flat-C-D-B reveals a higher degree of tension than the chord of E-C-D-B Flat; but one must admit that the difference is not so spectacular as the distinction between a triad and a diminished seventh chord. One is compelled to acknowledge the validity of this objection to the extent that condensation of the differences in material in a given sector does, in effect, necessitate a sharpening of the listener's ear if he is to identify the various nuances within this narrower range. Certainly the question of whether important gains of one kind compensate for the relinquishment of other elements is worth serious consideration.

Does Atonal Music Lack Rhythm?

2. THE assertion that atonal music is rhythmically un· intelligible does not reflect so much on its principle and has a more personal basis than the first objection. This explains why the charge is generally brought only against the so-called "Vienna school"—the Schoenberg group—and why it underlines the contention that composers like Strawinsky and Hindemith have avoided the mistake. In fact, this is a matter of a gradual difference rather than one of fundamentals.

The freely articulated diction of the Schoenberg group must of necessity sound chaotic to an auditor who cannot realize a rhythmic figure unless, with truly Gargantuan power, it takes the form of elemental pounding, as in the case of Strawinsky, or unless the pattern grows out of a continuous running kinetic chain of some few, easily identifiable formulae, as with Hindemith.

It is easy to imagine that a man who has never listened to any literature save poetry, written in fixed rhythmic patterns, would receive an impression of extravagant and formless babbling on first hearing prose read aloud. Of course it is possible to use fixed rhythmic patterns in atonal music. But when one remembers that the movement leading to atonality was propelled by the need for greater freedom in expression, one cannot forget that the fixed rhythmic pattern was felt as an impediment instead of a help. In removing this impediment, the composer was forced to a further limitation of the spectacular features which had already been reduced by changes in the material.

History teaches us that for long eras music was organized along the lines of linguistic prose, so there can hardly be any fundamental objection to the adoption of the same principle by new music, even after the interval of a few centuries in which tonal music was shaped in the stricter metric forms of poetry.

Does Atonal Music Lack Expressive Force?

3. AN AFFIRMATIVE answer to the above question would entail the supposition that perhaps not all spheres of expression are as widely open to atonal as to tonal music; but the individual point of view would again color such opinion. We know that association of a specified mood with a certain type of music is usually a matter of a very vague judgment indeed. We shall never be able to decide with any degree of certainty whether the first movement of Mozart's G Minor Symphony is gracefully playful, melancholy, or grimly dramatic; different opinions collected during different periods would undoubtedly reveal an incredible variety of emotional reactions to it. And so it is quite possible that although the listener in our age may get an impression of monotonous, gloomy, and disturbing chaos from atonal music, audiences in a later era will find therein a far greater wealth of emotion than is suspected now. Grant, for the sake of argument, the impossibility of proving objectively that atonal music can seldom be made to represent, say, a feeling of naïve joy, we still are without a valid objection to atonality. Perhaps the very inability of atonality to fulfill such a requirement constitutes one of its most characteristic traits; perhaps this alleged

limitation is in reality a sign of sincere emotional expression.

An important English critic recently challenged the imagination to picture a nation burying its heroes to the strains of atonal music. One cannot easily imagine it, for the reason that new music is essentially unsuitable for such a purpose. Funeral marches are, in their inmost nature, the products of handicraft (*Kunstgewerbe*)—decorative, craftsmanlike applications of artistic elements to a eulogy, and thus subordinated to the everyday requirements of life. In Chapter III, I pointed out as one of the characteristics of atonal music that it cannot be used for ornamentation of this or any other sort.

The Absence of Dominant Relationships in Atonality

ALL the foregoing objections fall short of the mark in failing to touch the focal point on which an audience's discontent is concentrated, the issue which atonality forces them to face. It may be that the real cause of auditory discomfort—withdrawal of the dominant's function—is too technical to be immediately formulated even by the more serious critics.

Neither the number nor the sharpness of the dissonances in atonal music accounts for the sensation of strangeness; most of them have been in familiar use since the time of Wagner. Nor does the alleged absence of coherence or order give rise to uneasiness; both are abundantly in evidence, at least in the later atonal music. The fact alone that what is actually coherence in atonal music cannot be realized in the form of the dominant relationship, is the cause of the perplexity which foolish people try to excuse by calling new music "cacophonous." They say that atonal music lacks "balance" (that most dignified shibboleth of Western music) because they are in the habit of recognizing "balance" only in the traditional dominant relation.

In previous chapters I have spoken of the important part played by the dominant relationship in the development of Western music up to the epoch of tonality. From his early youth, Western man has been accustomed exclusively to music organized by the dominant function. No wonder that listening to music of this type becomes second nature to him and that, without further preparation, he is quite unable to understand that music organized along other lines can be music at all—unless, of course, he happens to be a progressive.

It is possible to analyze practically any atonal chord in agreement with the principle of tonality, or, in other words, to associate it with some definite key. For example: The afore-mentioned chord of E Flat-C-D-B, chosen at random, can be interpreted as a suspension of a pure C Minor triad, while the other chord selected, E-C-D-B Flat, clearly belongs to the dominant region of F Major or F Minor, and can easily be resolved into either. This procedure goes so far that talk of "an" atonal chord hardly makes sense. The individual chord is neither atonal nor tonal; whether it can and should be interpreted as either depends solely on the context. The context, however, to which atonality brings its material, speaks against a tonal interpretation because such an arrangement of subject matter cannot be explained by the dominant-tonic principle.

There are those who deny even this, who paradoxically attack the atonality front from the rear by saying that this type of music is not atonal at all (alleging that atonality doesn't exist) but simply a strongly expanded form of tonality. In fact, a quite successful attempt of this sort can be made to interpret not alone the individual chord but its context as well; but such explanations are exceedingly complicated and tenuous. To make use of them, one needs to press into service so many alterations and substitute functions that finally almost nothing remains of the supposedly basic harmonic framework—a method of explanation recalling the epicycles of Ptolemy, who, in order to account for the apparently irregular orbits of the planets, was forced to introduce various auxiliary orbits which were not identified with the movements of any visible celestial body.

The tonal explanation may be ingenious enough to please an analyst; but, granting its success on occasion, it will fail to satisfy the musically gifted listener whose immediate experience convinces him that the composition just heard must have been something different from the manifestation of the key of D Minor, for instance, of which no trace can be found. Many tonal elements, dominant relationships among them, may be latent in atonal music; but surely the vital procedure is to single out those elements which constitute the novel feature, for it is evident enough that something new is happening. For the rest, the end of the tonal epoch was indicated by the fact that as early as in Debussy and Reger one could no longer get at the essential contents of the music by merely ascertaining that the keys shifted continually, although there can only be one opinion about the tonal co-ordination of the single elements and the dominant function inside the separate sections of these masters' compositions.

Thus we can take for granted, at least for the time being, that atonality is a musical language in which elements of a dissonant nature prevail almost exclusively, while the syntactic means of the dominant function are absent.

Attempts to Create a New Order

THE question now arises: What steps have been taken to equip this new language of music with adequate syntactic means? We cannot deny that such means are needed; every language requires a syntax. The problem is one of distinguishing between practical and theoretical efforts to formulate the grammar. The theoretical approach was primarily limited to harmonic research. This is easy to understand, as the most striking innovations seem to have been introduced into the field of the material, the harmonies or chords. The sudden emergence of multitonal and complicated chords, never before heard, drew general attention to what was going on; and many theoretical investigations were devoted to the derivation, classification, and evaluation of chords, from Schoenberg's *Harmonielehre* (Treatise on Harmony) to Hindemith's *Unterweisung im Tonsatz* (Instruction in Composition). I will not tire the reader by going into the details of all these efforts. Nor is it my purpose to write a history of new music, but rather to show its essential characteristics and so open up a fresh view of its significance to our epoch.

It should be sufficient to point out that investigations eventually led to the writing of a "dictionary" of new music, to the compilation of as comprehensive a catalogue of its root words as possible. Attempts were made to build up all sorts of new scales and to itemize every possible kind of harmony. Some tried to systematize the construction of chords—irregular from the orthodox viewpoint—thus initiating, for instance, the endeavor to build harmonies based on fourths similar to those founded on thirds in tonal music. Harmonic rules like those known to tonal music were later formulated to cover the relationships of these chords. (Hindemith's book has this plan as one of its main objects.)

A cardinal mistake lies in the root of these endeavors, which sprang from the idea, more or less clearly defined, that the essential structural elements of tonality could be, and should be, "translated into atonal language" in order to attain a satisfactory working method. The structural elements of one language cannot be transferred to another. The idea which developed into the structure of the old language must be so reformulated that it will provide the new tongue with another framework. To give a parallel illustration: One cannot invent a French grammar along English lines by analyzing, separately, the words contained in a French dictionary. The English student must learn to think in French before he can realize that the character of the French vocabulary corresponds to his thoughts, and that the thought itself produced the grammar. In like manner, the syntax of atonality cannot originate otherwise than in the individual character of atonal thought. A syntax made in the similitude of the tonal grammar can never be adapted to the new material, no matter how accurately its single elements may be vivisected.

It is easy to understand why the first theoretical excursions into the new sound language extended to the harmonic region. For one thing, the most salient change had taken place there; for another, centuries of tonality had taught us to regard harmony as the immovable cornerstone of music, or as the spacious and solidly furnished entrance hall in the edifice of musical forms.

The fact of tonality seemed to have been settled with the creation of the world; and, in much the same manner, the road from harmony to free composition, via counterpoint, had the appearance of a pathway immutably prescribed by a law of the universe. Once atonality had caused a breach in the groundwork of the edifice, there arose the necessity of speedily buttressing the walls; for how could the road to music be trodden if, at the very beginning, a heap of stones obstructed the pilgrim's progress? But many a theory, long venerated as an axiom, has turned out to be open to dispute in the end. Should not, perhaps, the life of a theory as perfectly expounded as the theory of harmony has been for centuries, be ineradicably woven into the existence of a type of music that is predominantly harmonic in its conception?

The prevalence of harmony dates back no further than the prevalence of the major-minor tonality. It could not be otherwise, as the definition of a key is based on harmonic facts. The principle of a theory of harmony teaches first the art of establishing a key by harmonic means, and second, the method of transferring that key into another. When atonal music knows neither keys nor the concept of modulation, is it reasonable to suppose that it needs a theory of harmony, or that it could even develop such a theory at will?

As no valuable results have been gained by theoretical efforts to provide atonality with a harmonic syntax, some students found solace in the claim that a new harmonic theory was followed in atonal compositions (if only unconsciously), even though it could not yet be reduced to definite terms. Certainly the argument is tenable. As verbal grammar was derived from the spoken language instead of vice versa, so the theory of tonal harmony was developed into its full embodiment, as we know it, after more than one hundred years of practical application. It was first evolved, and then obeyed.

Hence it is not impossible that the harmonic laws of atonality may be traced after a corresponding span of time. They are inherent in atonal compositions, but cannot yet be formulated because there is not enough material available for analysis. There is, however, much to be said for the probability that the entire question of harmony (using the word in its tonal sense) will be relegated to the background, making way for an interpretation of atonal music on a wholly different foundation.

For the rest, theoretical attempts to get at the core of atonality can be justified only in that they are combined with the simultaneous practice of composition. This practice has been far more radical than anything engendered by the contemporary theory.

Characteristic Features of Early Atonal Music

IN THE beginning of atonality, compositions were remarkable for their brevity. Schoenberg's "Three Piano Pieces," Opus 11, the first world-famous examples of atonal music, were still relatively long. Works by Schoenberg's pupils, Berg and Webern, appearing at the same time or shortly afterwards, were provocative in their shortness. The re-echoing tumult at a concert in Vienna in 1911 was started by a song by Alban Berg, consisting of no more than eleven measures, though the orchestral apparatus called into play was as large as that used by Mahler for a symphony of more than one hour's length. Such conspicuous brevity is explainable by the circumstance that a language which has not had time to develop a syntax must confine itself to exceedingly short sentences. When the constructive means to connect the various thoughts have not yet taken shape, it is necessary to put a full stop after each thought and start again from scratch. Yet it would be wrong to conclude that the first atonal compositions were primitive. Their brevity was not merely a phenomenon forced on them by the lack of connecting lines: it was also the outcome of extreme concentration. The single element of atonality is, at least at the beginning, much more pregnant with significance than that of tonality. In the later tonal music, the triad expressed so little that triads were scarcely ever used any more. The opposite is true of the new chords. They are freed from all shackles—the relationships of the old system—and stand isolated in their novel environment. Thus they are far more expressive than were the old chords, which depended on their surroundings. Terrific concentration on the part of the atonalists is necessary to express as much as possible at one stroke and is tied up with the extremely radical nature of atonality. It cannot be denied that atonality is founded on a decidedly destructive tendency. The first atonal compositions often give one the impression of watching a cataclysm through reversed opera glasses.

Lacking the constructive equipment, endeavors to proceed to more extensive forms did not immediately lead to a really new order, but to emphasis on seeming confusion. A really constructive technique was replaced by the method of using contrasting extremes to delineate the form.

Tonality's main form, the sonata, also depended on the concept of extremes. The basic contrast, as planned in the structure of the tonal language and executed in the sonata, was that of the opposite harmonic polar zones of tonic and dominant. Contrast between the main themes in the exposition part of the sonata movement became increasingly accentuated; and the development section, the focal point of the composition, grew into nothing more than an actualization of that contrast in the idea of struggle, the dramatic sharpening of an antithesis. And so the use of this principle in the formation of atonal music was obvious. Since the material basis, the contrast of tonic and dominant, was lacking, the development of contrasts in the details of the form had to be all the sharper. This suggested an emphasis on extremes of every kind—concentrated dynamics in *fff* and *ppp*, placing the instruments and the human voice in the most extravagant positions and taking them over terrifying jumps, violent action alternating with complete standstills, etc. All this was perfectly in line with the psychic force animating the entire atonal movement, the need for a stronger and more intensive technique of emotional expression.

At first, these extremes stressed the chaos. The suspension of metrical balance, the transition to musical "prose," was not at all arbitrary but a necessary corollary of the process as a whole. The regular meters of tonal music had been part of the structure of tonality from the beginning; and whenever this structure disappeared, there was not only no necessity, but scarcely a possibility, of metric regularity. Of course it is technically possible to build eight-measure periods in one way or another, even with atonal means; but this would hardly justify the introduction of a new sound language. The radical tendency that is implicit in the new movement repeatedly breeds the need to delve to the root of fresh possibilities, instead of trying to adjust the new methods to an imitation of the old forms.

The "chaotic" tendency of atonality culminated in Schoenberg's *Erwartung* (Expectation), a sort of one-act opera called a "monodrama," as one character alone appears in it. A considerable length of time is filled with music that has no apparent thematic relationships and that, in a sense, is molded in a "formless" fashion. The music goes on and on in a continuous flow of new material, without repetition or reference to anything that has previously been expressed. In its own way, *Erwartung* has remained a unique example; whether necessarily so, it is hard to say. Unity, an indispensable factor in any work of art, has been secured to a large extent by the text, while the music follows the libretto much as a railing serves as a support across a footbridge. Whether it is possible to write music like *Erwartung* without a "railing" remains an open question.

New Rhythms and Polytonality

IN ANY case, Schoenberg's opera indicated a turning point in the expansion of atonality in the sense that from then on Schoenberg himself, as well as atonal composers who were independent of him, started to look for untrod ways which, to a certain extent, tended to decrease the tempo and the radical quality of the crusade. We must not think of atonality as a local invention of the Vienna school. Time has helped us conveniently to forget that, by the end of the first World War, atonality had become a fairly general movement. Two tendencies in western Europe aimed to dispel the chaos. One tried to attain its end by the use of rhythm, the other with so-called polytonality.

It was Strawinsky who initiated the attempt to give
atonality a new form through the application of elemental rhythmic forces. His rhythms are novel in so far
as they are not an outgrowth of simple symmetrical
dance patterns (decisive in tonal music) but introduce
complicated Oriental meters having an organization
which had been very little exploited. Some progress
then became possible; freedom from the rhythmic tie of
tonality, inherent in atonality, could be dovetailed into
the complicated new rhythmic designs. Destruction of
the last bond with cults and crafts, and progress to a
free type of speech, articulated like prose, can be
credited to the Vienna school. The western European
school of atonality, however, has tried to preserve these
ties. It is by no means accidental that atonal music in
western Europe has grouped itself around the Russian
ballet. Nor can there be any doubt that the ballet's
ostentatious performances of archaic rituals, given with
the most elaborate *raffinement,* border on the zone of
handicraft, whether the presentation be that of a fan-
tastic "rite of spring," an ancient Russian "peasant wed-
ding," or a cosmogonic Negro myth. It is characteristic
of recent capitalism to find recreation in the reproduction of primitive, barbarian, grandiose directness.

Another effort to subdue atonality is seen in the device known as *polytonality.* Polytonality, as cultivated
chiefly by some French and British composers, signifies
technically that the musical structure consists of the
simultaneous unfolding of several elements, each in a
different key. (In practice, not more than two keys are
usually employed.) One can imagine the effect by thinking of two bands playing independently but at the same
time. The single components of the structure are in-
disputably tonal, mostly even extremely simple. To

call the result polytonal indicates its origin, not its character. The character can be either tonal or atonal, since whatever is not tonal must be defined as atonal. If analysis of such a dual composition shows the total effect to be tonal (which is not impossible when one key drowns the other), atonal reasoning is not concerned with it. And if the effect is summarized as atonal, it is subject to the criteria of all atonal music, in which case the question of its origin (whatever that may be) has no primary importance. Therefore, "polytonality" should never be listed in an equal category with "atonality," as is often done. Anyway, history proves that most composers who occupied themselves with polytonality later returned to the safe haven of good old "monotonality." No important contribution to the growth of atonality has come from this side.

The "Athematic" Style

WHILE western Europeans were engaged in purifying atonality and curbing its chaotic impulses, the same impulses attracted a group of Slavic musicians who, led by Alois Hába in Prague, refused to take part in Schoenberg's endeavors to found a new order. They will be discussed in detail in the next chapter. Suffice it here to say that they had nothing in common with the restorative tendencies current in western Europe. Hába felt that composers should continue from the point at which Schoenberg had stopped in *Erwartung*, and founded the "athematic" style. "Athematic" means a kind of music which does not exhibit themes as objects of its development, which does not concern itself with elaborating such themes, but is free at any instant to go on as it pleases without referring back to what it has set forth before, and without being bound to a planned progress indicated by thematic landmarks. In this concept we find a curious mixture of promise and doubt, prophecy and whimsy. True, the concept of a freely articulated utterance has been logically thought out to the end, and there is nothing alarming in the suggestion of developing a musical idea without tying it to any prescribed form. And yet the freest possible speech has *some* subject which it treats and examines from various angles, and to which it refers from time to time. There is grave danger in the likelihood that "independence," elevated to a password in the name of unbounded liberty, may become as tyrannical as the dogma which it is to replace. Even in those athematic compositions which have been most carefully cleansed of all thematic or motivic relationships, it is almost impossible not to stumble over such impediments. If the auditor is not required to listen atomistically (and obviously one could not well be so compelled, else it would not matter whether an opus ran for ten seconds or thirty minutes) he will automatically and involuntarily establish relationships between the single elements. While taking the position that our ears are perhaps guilty of more prejudice than any other organ of the body, I still am of the opinion that we are not concerned with an atavistic way of hearing, but rather with one which must be applied as long as music progresses in time. Even athematic music cannot escape that eventuality.

Hába has also occupied himself in large measure with quarter- and sixth-tones. Though he has not been the first nor the only composer to do so, his works in this vein are the only ones that can be taken seriously.

Quarter-tones are formed by halving once more the

interval of the half-tone; for instance, by interpolating between C and C Sharp a tone which is equidistant in pitch from both. Sixth-tones are formed analogously, by dividing the half-tone into three parts. While the available material is multiplied in this way, no new-fangled methods of composition are involved as yet. Naturally no tonal music will be written with this material, since the major and minor modes have no place for these additional tones. Whether, for purposes of atonal music, the octave is divided into twelve, twenty-four, or thirty-six parts, is, however, more a detail of quantitative importance than a matter of principle. To be sure, this experiment, too, stems from the need for more subtle and refined expression. But in practice, the result is that the acoustical nuances are drawn so close to each other that the untrained listener, or the listener who is not particularly gifted, has great difficulty in distinguishing them; and so this method defeats its own purpose. Therefore it is questionable if the technique of such a multitonal system is suitable for the presentation of musical ideas, at least today, when we have not yet come to the end of the twelve-tone atonal-ity—in fact, when we have just begun to tap its resources.

Hába enjoys quite a vogue among the younger composers in eastern Europe. His adherence to what may be called the "anarchistic" tendencies of atonality is connected with a certain mystical concept of a particular Slavic freedom. This also applies to many of his followers. The fanatical and rambling instinct, so well known as a typical Russian trait, is peculiarly combined, in Hába's case, with his anthroposophic ideas. I believe this nationalistic and spiritual fixation accounts for the failure of the progressive features of the athematic style to stand out in sharper relief.

In contrast to Hába's concept, atonality as practiced by the Vienna school has attained to a degree of supernationality rarely reached, perhaps not aspired to, since Beethoven. This comparison is not intended to put Beethoven and atonality on the same level of values, but is meant to be merely an objective presentation of their respective characters. It is impossible to find any kind of folkloristic ingredients in the atonal music of central Europe. Atonality has always aimed straight at the substance, the gist, of musical expression, eliminating intervening associations, all nonessential elements, and all the ornaments of handicraft. Perhaps the artistic worth of atonal music is uneven; I do not wish to propagandize in any way; but its human and historico-cultural value is definitely in the open and can be clearly ascertained. Atonality has given speech to the individual, liberating him from delusive chains and seductive illusions. By intensifying the expression of personal emotion to the utmost, it has demonstrated the loneliness and alienation of humanity as clearly as possible. The most intense emotional expression has created chaos in music; and as this is the true picture of the chaos experienced beyond the realm of music, it stirs up fright or vexation among people who are interested in preserving the chaotic state. Atonality, however, has not hesitated to raise the issue of a new type of musical order.

CHAPTER   SEVEN

MUSIC UNDER CON-STRUCTION

Atonality Has Destroyed "Balance"

A STRONG inner similarity exists between the transition from the medieval sound language to tonality, and the present mutation from tonality to atonality. But in their exterior forms these changes show an essential difference. The rule of the major and minor scales prevailed slowly but irresistibly through a generally recognized victory. Atonality, on the other hand, seems scarcely to have gained ground after an existence of more than thirty years, constantly struggling against renewed reactionary opposition. Can it be that atonality is unfit to live? Benevolent reactionaries are quite willing to concede that we owe many valuable "stimuli" to atonality; but they point with gratitude to the younger generation which, they say, is returning from its erring ways and exchanging its foolish experiments for a "healthy modernism." Can they be right?

We regard that "healthy modernism" with suspicion, with less sympathy than we feel for a reactionary trend that is frankly endorsed, as we have said again and again. Nothing is proved against atonality by extreme opposition when the opposition can easily be explained. We must remember that the victory of tonality coincided with the rise of spectacular and appealing musical forms. Tonality signified an extreme simplification and popularization of the sound language. The new forms —opera and concerto—demanded such a vehicle of expression, and tonality was created to make them possible. The way to atonality runs in exactly the opposite direction.

I showed in the last chapter how confinement to the sphere of dissonances and renunciation of the extensive and popular vocabulary of the consonant triads mean a tightening of the nuances and a refinement of the sound language. The effect of the transition of the symmetrical-scanning style of tonality to the free, prose-like diction of atonality is of the same order. Furthermore, it is seen that an impressive distinction between melody and accompaniment is thrust into the background to make room for a closer texture of independent voices. All these peculiar qualities show that atonality will not attain facile and quantitatively measurable superficial successes; for while tonality carried music from the enclosed territory of the church to unexpectedly large masses of people, atonality seems to move the art backward out of their reach and to shroud it in an atmosphere of exclusiveness.

The unwilling listener is not likely to realize this. He only knows that atonality does not please him. He even feels somehow cheated when he hears it, expressing his annoyance by saying that it sounds as if his three-year-old son were trying to play the piano, or as if the cat were walking on the keys. What he would say if he could express himself more articulately is that atonality lacks the quality of "balance." Balance is brought about by an orderly relationship between the two dimensions of Western music: the horizontal or melodic, and the vertical or harmonic. Everyone taking part in Western culture is certain (unconsciously, if not consciously) that the balanced relationship between these two dimensions is the vital achievement of Western music and the root of its dignity. Western man is sure that music is good, indeed, that it *is* music, only if it manifests the principle of balance in one way or another. He is insulted when he is offered something which does not seem to comply with this most primitive requirement.

As a matter of fact, atonality has radically posed the question of "balance" anew. Tonality was an unbelievably rich and perfect system for the concordant presentation of the two dimensions. I shall not repeat how and by what unavoidable processes this system came to an end. But doubtless circumstances set the task of finding fresh means latent in the new field, of establishing another "balance," that is, a still newer and satisfactory relationship between the dimensions already in use. The "balance" ensured by tonality stems from the harmonic facts presented in the intricate and ingenious fabric of tonal harmony; and it is this texture which has been torn by atonality. Are we not driven to a condition in which there is no balanced systematic order of harmonic relations, a condition which reminds us of the beginnings of polyphonic music? Granting this supposition, it would then appear sensible to look for the center of the new "balance" exactly where the ancients looked for it when they began to submit disorderly harmonies to an organized principle, namely, in the sphere of polyphony and counterpoint.

And indeed, many progressive composers of our time have been attracted by contrapuntal problems, even before systematic efforts of this sort were made.

The Twelve-tone Technique Revives the Iteration Concept

ACTUALLY, the twelve-tone technique which we shall presently discuss is nothing more than an attempt to produce a new "balance" by contrapuntal methods. It is merely one more tie between our atonal music and music of the pretonal, ecclesiastical kind, as if a circle has been completed, bringing us around to the starting point of a spiral where ideas of the pretonal epoch are again strongly asserted. Naturally the new music has many aspects that differ from those of the medieval age, since the enormous experience of the past centuries has been garnered and turned to good account. But whoever looks beneath the surface of the material will soon recognize the vital resemblance of music in the twentieth century to scholastic music.

According to our theory, this means that, after the indigenous European, symmetrical-scanning concept had held undisputed sway in the era of tonality, the ancient Oriental features have come again to the fore in the fateful interlacing of the two basic components of Western music. It further signifies that the concepts of free articulation and iteration will regain their influential position. Free articulation has acquired great importance in atonality; one may even say that it has actively co-operated in bringing atonal music into existence, for repression of the symmetrical period formation was one of the leading actions involved in the disintegration of tonality. The concept of iteration, however, did not appear until after the twelve-tone technique had been evolved, taking on a new aspect and a novel significance.

It is probable that Schoenberg was unconscious of this historical association when he started to perfect his technique. But the existence of the association proves the method's pregnant import in the whole picture of contemporary music. The twelve-tone technique appeared exactly at the point where, on the basis of historical deduction, we had to expect something of that sort. We therefore imitated the tactics of an astronomer who defines the position of a star before he proceeds to discover its presence in a precise location. Twelve-tone technique appears as so urgent a necessity that we can readily conjecture that if Schoenberg had not performed this task, someone else would sooner or later have evolved a theory to provide for the principle of iteration within the framework of atonality.

How is the concept of iteration manifested in the twelve-tone technique? The answer is simpler than one might expect. The fundamental principle of the twelve-tone technique is that all the elements in a musical composition, whatever they may be, are developed from a single germ cell consisting of a succession of twelve different tones, stipulated in advance. Why twelve? Because we have neither more nor less than this number of half-tones within the compass of an octave, and because the stipulated succession thus presents the complete range of available material in a characteristic manner. Peculiarly enough, the erroneous notion that all atonal music is based on a single series of twelve tones has received wide circulation. According to authorities on the permutation theory (dealing with the change or combination of any number of qualities), there are 479,001,600 different twelve-tone successions in existence; and only one is chosen for the particular extension of the musical sphere within which a composer, aided by such a succession, wishes to create a structural unity. In general, that will be in the sphere of a single composition; but a composer may also wish to combine a group of pieces as a unit, in which case he can either use the same succession for all the items or make another distribution.

"Series" and the "Scale"

THE misconception that there is but a single fundamental succession for all the atonal music is probably due to erroneous use of the expression "twelve-tone *scale*." Many people have the vague impression that Schoenberg invented some new scale. He did not. As I said in Chapter V, tonal music utilized the twelve existing tones from its beginning; and neither atonality nor the twelve-tone technique has added quantitatively to this material in any way. He who would insist on talking about the "twelve-tone scale" must clearly understand that nothing but the chromatic scale, long since known, is identified by that term.

Meanwhile, the twelve-tone series which forms the groundwork of composition in twelve-tone technique has nothing to do with scales. We can best understand its nature and function by thinking of repetition in the old iterative style of the Gregorian chant. Remember that repetition and variation of single melodic elements in the Gregorian chant served to give that type of music coherence and form. The single melodic elements which were thus varied and repeated were not scales at all, but rather "patterns," or, as we would say today, "basic figures." A scale results only when the atoms which constitute such a melodic feature, namely, the single tones, are isolated and schematically arranged according to their pitch. To give an example: When the tones of the melody C-G-B-A-F-D-E are arranged according to their pitch, the result will be C-D-E-F-G-A-B, or the scale of C Major. Likewise the tones appearing in all kinds of twelve-tone series can be arranged in accordance with their pitch, and the result will be C-C Sharp-D-D Sharp-E-F-F Sharp-G-G Sharp-A-A Sharp-B, that is, the chromatic scale. But obviously the successions themselves are not scales.

What do we mean when we say that the succession is a "basic figure" in the sense of the old "patterns"? Just this: that the succession is used, as the patterns were, to give coherence and formal unity to a musical progression. Literal repetition is the most primitive method of combining elements which have to be brought into relationship. If the element X-Y-Z is followed by the element X-Y-Z, the two are obviously related, since the second is a repetition of the first.

Basic Features of the Twelve-tone Technique

THE Gregorian chant knew several other forms of relationship—above all, inversion and retrogression. As an example: When a melodic section reads A-B-D, the section A-G-E has the relationship of an inversion; the ascending interval A-B corresponds to its descending equivalent, A-G; and the ascending third, B-D, to the descending third, G-E. The relationship of a retrogression exists, however, between the elements A-B-D and D-B-A, the second element containing the same constituents as the first, but in retrograde order.

Twelve-tone technique utilizes the same basic forms of relationship in order to build its system of fundamental structures. In addition to the original form of the series, its inversion and its retrograde form are also used. The latter can again be turned upside down; or, to phrase it differently, the direction of the intervals can be changed into its opposite. There are, then, four different fundamental forms of the same series, comparable to pictures of a geometrical curve in the four fields of a plane co-ordinate system. Each picture originates from one of the others through 180-degree revolutions around one of the co-ordinate axes.

This system of fundamental forms can be further expanded without touching the fundamental structure of the first series, and without encountering figures already known. It is possible to shift every one of the four fundamental forms twelve times, keeping them parallel to each other; or, in other words, to transpose them on the twelve separate steps of the chromatic scale. From this it follows that we have always had forty-eight different fundamental forms of the same kind, but interrelated in conformity with a distinct law.

If our music were merely single-voiced, like the Gregorian chant, a composition could originate only through continuous repetition of these fundamental figures. The difference would simply be that the treatment of the chant in the twelve-tone technique would be highly rationalized and unified. Our "patterns," however, would be far richer than the old ones, for they would always contain twelve tones, whereas the chant's basic figures rarely exceed four. In the idiom of a new terminology, we can say in this case that the twelve-tone series fulfills approximately the function filled in tonal music by the so-called "motifs." In view of the prevailing confusion concerning the use of the terms "motif" and "theme," we shall try to define them.

Series, Motif, Theme

By "MOTIF" one generally understands a concise and preponderantly melodic element, easily recognizable by its characteristic figure, in contradistinction to the more complex and individually outlined features of a *theme,* which includes melodic, harmonic, and rhythmic elements. "Motivic development" is the core, as well as the alpha and omega, of composition; and the treatment of "patterns" in the Gregorian chant was nothing but the first stage of such development. Eventually, the concept of contrapuntal imitation transferred motivic relationships from the limited orbit of the single voice to the wider range of polyphony, the characteristic motivic elements of one voice reappearing in another. The contrast, modification, and expansion of motifs provided the chief material for the development technique in the later sonata form.

But if the twelve-tone series has only the function of motifs, and if we have been familiar with these motifs for a long time, what factor is really responsible for bringing the twelve-tone technique into prominence? Here is the answer: The twelve-tone motifs—as we shall call the series for the time being —have taken on a more vital significance in the structure than the old motifs ever had.

The substructure of the tonal forms is found in the plan of their harmonic groundwork. If, for instance, one were to remove the entire individual superstructure of motifs and themes from a sonata, a clearly definable layer of harmonic data would still remain at the base. This does not prove that the motivic work in tonal music is merely ornamental or accidental in character.

One can say, though, that a certain division between the static *harmonic* scaffolding and the mobile *thematic* equipment in this music engenders its real life. In this sense, the tonal style can be likened to a type of architecture in which the basic arrangements of supporting columns appear again and again without detriment to the variable and fanciful execution of the building founded on them. The bipartition of function disappears in atonality, since there is no plan of a harmonic groundwork to provide for the general binding force inherent in tonality. The architect is no longer able, while using a more or less specified design of columns as a basis, to let his pictorial fantasy run away with him; on the contrary, what previously happened in the airy regions of the superstructure, founded on secure tonal supports, now must answer for the stability of the entire edifice. The motivic labor which once raised the individual life of a composition above the level of its inert harmonic foundation is called into play for cooperation in building a consistent structure with the new material.

I said just now that if our music were single-voiced like the Gregorian chant, the twelve-tone series would have motivic functions similar to the Gregorian "patterns." But our music is polyphonic, and no one entertains the thought of robbing it of this attribute. From a practical point of view this means, first of all, that the twelve-tone series will appear in several voices at the same time. For, as we will remember, the basic idea of this technique is that all elements of a composition must be developed from the basic twelve-tone series. But we are immediately confronted with a phenomenon which weakens and modifies the motif functions of the series to a considerable extent.

By its very nature, the twelve-tone series is not particularly suitable for the purpose of functioning as a
motif in the old sense of the word. Such a series is
simply too long and contains too many elements—
precisely twelve in number—to form a significant, easily
grasped figure. In polyphonic arrangements, the twelve-
tone series gradually disappears from the obvious melodic surface; but it acquires, in inverse ratio, the nature of a material element which gives character to the
whole texture, much as a slender red thread will lend
color to a woven fabric.

These fade-outs can only benefit a composition; for,
because of them, the region of the superstructure (the
region of individual thematic elaboration), where the
real life of the musical piece flourishes, is saved from
the danger of being too closely tied up to basic figures.
Themes which give a work its unique figure and really
carry the emotional expression are in no sense identical with the twelve-tone series; they are created just
as freely and are as much due to "inspiration" as in
any other type of music—with the reservation, of course,
that they employ the motivic elements represented in
the twelve-tone series and are limited to these elements.

Thus music has again reached a certain bipartition
of its functions, whose interdependence, however, is
to some extent the opposite of conditions existing in
tonal music. For the harmonic facts in tonal music—
in other words, the basic structure of the material—
are decisive and determine the arrangement of the
superstructure. Atonality, on the other hand, in so far
as it is organized according to the twelve-tone technique, takes its first cue from an element belonging
to the superstructure, namely, the motivic function of
the twelve-tone series; and this element influences the

basic structure only when it is elevated to what may be called a "totalitarian" principle.

When we speak of "influence" we must not think that the twelve-tone series' penetration of atonal material would in any way lead to the kind of construction that is used in tonality, that is to say, to a harmonic system equivalent, or even comparable, to that of tonality. The entire twelve-tone technique is built on the assumption that such a harmonic organization would no longer be possible.

What Was the Gain for "Balance"?

THE question arises as to what, after all, has been gained in regard to "balance," since it appears that balance is based on a systematic organization of harmonies. Was not the balance of medieval polyphony founded on an extremely limited choice of harmonies from all those available? When now, in atonality, *all* possible harmonies are equally permissible, the chaos is obviously not dispelled despite the fact that the twelve-tone series has penetrated the whole musical texture.

May I remind the reader that I have formulated the intellectual premises of the old choice of permissible harmonies in a slightly different manner? I wrote in my historical survey that this choice was not made according to an absolute superiority of certain harmonies —for instance, because of their nature-given beauty— but rather because a sensible intertwining of freely articulated single voices, presenting a melodic material based on the Gregorian elements, proved most effective when this selection and no other was made from the available harmonies. It is evident that the intermingling of *our* single voices, in the presentation of melodic material which is essentially chromatic, requires a totally different choice of harmonies. (There is no necessity again to discuss the historical justification for this statement.) Apparently the selection could first be more easily, if not exclusively, formulated in a negative fashion: "Almost no pure consonances, and never any triads." The impression created would be that of having simply adopted an attitude contrary to the rules enforced by the old counterpoint, which generally demanded precisely the opposite.

This explanation may not go far toward satisfying someone who is unaware of "balance" unless this balance appears in the shape of a fully developed harmonic system. Yet it would be wrong to make any other assertion, under the circumstances. It is not unthinkable that a new order of harmonies is being germinated in atonality; but it is not yet in conscious use. Yet there is little reason to give the matter much thought now, as the new order cannot be deduced until more traits, common to most atonal compositions and covering a longer period of time, are available for analysis. Still, it is quite probable that our new harmonic entity will never show more than certain primitive basic facts, as was the case with the harmonic system which could be deduced from medieval compositions. For atonal music, like the latter, has a primary leaning toward polyphony.

The pivotal achievement of the twelve-tone technique in reference to "balance" is embodied in the unification of the structure which it established. All the elements of the composition, down to the remotest ramifications of its less important voices, have been fabricated from one and the same texture; and all the details of the concrete forms lead back to the elements of a single basic figure. The result is a stylistic purity, scarcely attainable by any other proceeding, and a really astronomical orderliness of the whole thing, recognizable by the listener—provided the composer's technique is correspondingly perfect.

Of course no listener is expected to recognize all the numerous entries and thousandfold variations of the twelve-tone series; not even a trained musician can do that. The auditor should let this music come to him as naturally as music of any other sort. When he listens to Mozart he does not take in all the intricate modulations, metrical shiftings, and contrapuntal combinations, either. But the more thoroughly a work is infused with a unifying principle, the more intense will be the listener's impression of expressive force and spiritual power. Under radically different conditions, it is the same higher degree of articulation and mental strength —in a word, of greater "balance"—which causes a symphony by Mozart to create a deeper impression than can be made by the conventionally inarticulate, perfunctory, and superficial writing of many of his contemporaries.

Here is another reason why atonality has greater difficulty in making its way than tonality did. The step from tonality to atonality is considerably longer than the step from the medieval church modes to tonality. The choice of harmonies made by medieval polyphony, that is, its preference for consonant triads, prepared the ground for the fundamentals which were to support the harmonic system. Owing to that fact, the harmonic world of tonality seemed to be little more than an organic development of the field. On the other hand, the respective harmonic facts of tonality and atonality are as contrasted as black and white, or as positive and negative. For in atonal music the triads are eliminated as fundamentals and are replaced by dissonances.

If the concept of "balance" in the atonal sphere is manifested at all through harmonic factors, the manifestation will probably be effected by means of the twelve-tone technique. The central principle of this technique causes the continual recurrence of elements pre-established in the individual twelve-tone series. This simple fact gives prominence to certain characteristic intervals which are seen in the series and which can easily be used to develop typical harmonies.

Special Forms of the Twelve-tone Series

THE reflection that intervals represented in the series will have primary importance in the harmonic atmosphere of the opus, because they are repeated again and again, is one of the agents leading to an attempt to find a series containing all the eleven possible intervals between the twelve different tones. It is clear that such a series, under favorable circumstances, could least affect the composition's harmonic color, as no one interval would outweigh another. Naturally this does not imply that a series including, for example, two fifths and two thirds, should necessarily lead to an obvious preponderance of triad formations. Whether such a preponderance may appear, still depends on the position of the intervals within the series, and, last but not least, on the way in which the series is treated. However that may be, an examination of the all-interval-series (of which there are many more than one might imagine) opens up a large number of fascinating problems.

The puzzling question of how many series of this

kind can be formed is, of course, negligible for musical purposes, and interesting only from a mathematical point of view. I have presented the problem to numerous mathematicians; so far, none of them have found a general and satisfactory solution. Nicolas Slonimsky, who has gone into the matter a little more deeply from a musical viewpoint, partly at my suggestion, has made interesting discoveries along this line.

In addition, there are qualified successions of another kind: for instance, those whose second half is identical with the inversion or the retrograde form of the first half, transposed only by a certain interval. Further interesting relationships can also be established. How they are used in composing will always depend on the specific artistic task which the composer has set for himself. As in other types of music, the theory supplies only the tools. Mischievous people who slyly suggest that the twelve-tone technique is nothing but a convenient formula enabling any shoemaker to produce "correct" if horrible music would be flabbergasted if they made even a modest effort to put the theory into practice. And even if they succeeded in manipulating the series and the possible combinations in the manner of jugglers, the argument would lose none of its validity.

One thing is certain: the composer's ability to compose in the twelve-tone technique will be commensurate with his intimacy with the series and his efficiency in handling it. The same statement applies to tonality; a composition will not be one whit the better for being tonal if the composer does not master the technique of tonality. And he will not accomplish anything in either system if he is not a musician. By that I mean if he has no fantasy and no resources of expression, but has merely learned the rules by rote.

The Necessity of Elaborating New Forms

THE achievements of the twelve-tone technique include more than supplying the material with a new, homogeneous, and unified structure. The technique also opens up possibilities for ideas that are applicable to the development of the new *forms;* and this is an extremely important consideration in the field of atonality.

We have seen that the sonata is the standard form of tonality. Understandably enough, many efforts have been made to save the sonata form for atonality, and to mold it in conformity with atonal rules. The sonata and the symphony are such marvelous organisms that one hates to give them up. Yet we are forced to realize that the sonata, in its classical guise, cannot thrive in atonal soil. The premise of the sonata is the broadly lined, but pithy, harmonic formation alluded to previously. It is only in the dramatically intensified development section that the motivic idea, raised on the foundation, turns and penetrates so deeply into the subsoil that it attacks the foundation itself by the application of extended, bold modulations. Since atonality lacks this harmonic basis, the motivic idea delves the more deeply under the structure, touching all the strata of the musical organism.

This means that the development character prevails in the composition from the start; and by "development character" we mean that perforated, contrapuntally resolved type of music making which predominates in the central section of the sonata. The fact, however, shows an essential formal principle of the sonata to be shaken, because the development, an obvious contrast to the static parts—the exposition and the recapitulation—in-

creasingly absorbs the entire formal organism. Naturally it is possible, having the means of atonality and
the twelve-tone technique at hand, to build forms which
in their general outlines imitate the appearance of the
sonata; or, to put it differently, to show contrasting
groups following the well-known course with an increased emphasis on a midway development section and
a sort of recapitulation. But certainly it is questionable
whether such procedure would be in line with the real
nature of the new musical language.

The sonata gained at least part of its formative power
from the attributes of the material's basic structure.
This fact suggests an examination of the new, atonal
structure to determine whether it includes any hints for
the elaboration of new forms.

We could not talk about a new atonal structure until
the twelve-tone technique was actively used in atonality.
In its beginnings, approximately in 1908, atonal music
was notorious for its lack of structure, a lack that almost
amounted to a definition of atonality. And here, we
must repeatedly underline the distinction between
atonality and the twelve-tone technique; they do not
even belong to the same order.

Atonality covers a far larger territory and indicates
a sound language—a condition of the musical means
necessitated by its historical development.

The *twelve-tone technique* signifies a *grammatical
style* of the language, *a method of composing* within its
range.

Although the grammar will doubtless have a strong
influence on the eventual nature and potentialities of
the new tongue, the composition of atonal music without using the twelve-tone technique is not only con-
ceivable but was actually done almost exclusively for

many years, before Schoenberg published his first twelve-tone work in 1923. Compositions similar to the first were also produced after 1923, and are still forthcoming, since not all atonal composers take advantage of the twelve-tone method.

It is likewise possible to use the twelve-tone technique in composing tonal music. Alban Berg occupied himself with experiments in that direction in his last period, writing exceedingly impressive music in his Violin Concerto and in his unfinished opera *Lulu,* which for long stretches can be characterized as tonal yet corresponds to the twelve-tone technical method. In practice, no exception should be taken to such experiments, in so far as they are successful; but theoretically one can raise the objection that application of the twelve-tone technique to the creation of tonal music is neither necessary nor sufficient in itself, so that the result is somewhat analogous to an overdetermined equation in mathematics.

New Form Ideas

INHERENT traits in the new structure, imposed on the material by the twelve-tone technique, stem from an extensive correspondence between the single musical elements, owing to the fact that they originate in the series' four fundamental forms. It is as if a complicated system of mirrors were placed across the whole building. Wherever inversions occur, one can imagine a horizontal mirror reflecting the original material downward or upward. Retrogressive forms can be imagined as reflections in vertical mirrors. An extraordinary richness of local symmetrical forms is shown; and it is far more reasonable to consider them as real symmetri-

cal forms than to regard the pseudosymmetries of the
tonal periods as real. A systematic distribution of these
manifold "reflections" is conducive to a broad stimulation in the development of new forms. The same purpose is furthered by including in the formal concept
a corresponding distribution of the forty-eight transpositions of the fundamental forms.

I should like to illustrate, by explaining the formal
scheme of one of my latest compositions, *Variations for
Piano,* Opus 79, how a composer can execute a new formal design by exploiting the relationships and correspondences existing between the forty-eight basic patterns.

This relatively extensive work, lasting about twenty-
five minutes, consists of twelve variations divided into
three sections. The first section, a sort of dramatic *al-
legro,* includes five variations; the second, a broadly
constructed *adagio,* has two; and the third, again of a
slightly agitated character on the whole, contains five.
The forty-eight basic figures of the series are divided
in such a way that the first variation employs but two
transpositions of the original series; the second and the
third variations have each two other transpositions, and
so on until, with the sixth variation, all twelve original
forms have been exhausted. Two transpositions of the
inversion are added to the two original forms in the
third variation, and two different ones in the fourth,
and so on. Thus, a total of four forms of the series is
called into play from the third variation to the sixth,
two being original and two inverted. From the fifth
variation on, two transpositions of the retrograde inversion are added each time, so that, in the fifth and
sixth variations, three different forms are simultaneously
active. In consequence, the two first transpositions of

the retrograde form appear in the seventh variation. Owing to the fact that the two central variations (the sixth and the seventh) are welded together to strengthen a unified whole, all four fundamental forms are simultaneously represented at the center by a total of twelve different transpositions. From this point on, the structure becomes less compact until, at the end of the final variation, there remain only two transpositions of the retrograde form, corresponding to the two original forms of the first variation. The entire structure of the piece is symmetrical, built around an axis situated in the middle between the sixth and seventh variations. This is why the central part, the *adagio*, has been developed as a canon which returns to its beginning; in other words, starting from a certain turning point, the forms employed are retrogressions of those employed previously. The eventual development of this formal idea, down to the minutest detail, is reinforced by the circumstance that the composition is based on a series which is symmetrical in itself, and in which the second half corresponds to the retrograde form of the first half.

New Light on the Concepts of Variation and Repetition

IT IS an intrinsic quality of the twelve-tone technique that the *variation*, in the fullest sense of the word, becomes a formal basic principle. No matter what the particular form of the composition may be, it will always develop from an endless chain of countless variations on one and the same fundamental element, namely, the twelve-tone series. The circumstance that the factor of *repetition* will play a part entirely different from the role it played in tonality is thus explained. Twelve-tone music is an extraordinarily intensified spiritualization of the primitive iteration principle. Through the dominating importance of the variation concept—alteration and transformation of the given material—the repetition loses the character of restoration which it had in tonality, owing to a point of view based on natural philosophy. The first section of a sonata revealed a landscape; the development section covered it with a thunderstorm which distorted the outline of the scenery, partly hid it, and showed it in a menacing light; but the recapitulation consoled the listener with the assurance that nothing was actually changed and that he could again view the old picture, confirmed and embellished in its static quality.

A twelve-tone composition, contrariwise, passes before us like a portion of the starry sky seen through a telescope—a kaleidoscopic, inexhaustible round dance of perpetually moving elements that suggest a fragmentary sector of eternity; innumerable unknown combinations may precede what we see, and countless different clusters may follow its apparent end. The return to the beginning, always near at hand through the twenty-four retrograde forms, has nothing to do with the positive and confirmatory nature of the recapitulation. Everything is literally repeated; but it is almost unrecognizable in the repetition because the order of succession is reversed. The inference rather plays with the idea that time can even be turned back. I shall discuss this further in the next chapter, when I examine the relation of music to mathematics.

The analysis of the twelve tone technique has furnished ample evidence that this method has generated more genuinely new musical phenomena than other contemporary endeavors. Nonetheless, some objections against the technique are made which we shall not hesitate to discuss.

Is the Twelve-tone Technique Necessary? Is It Desirable or Dangerous?

AN OBJECTION to the twelve-tone technique raised by serious and progressively-minded musicians is embodied in the argument that composing with the aid of all the mirrored reflections and strict motivic correspondences is merely exceptional, and that the composer who may occasionally want such relationships can very well produce them without chaining himself to the twelve-tone method. It is an objection that may be allowed to stand in principle. But the experience of composers who have been the most thoughtful and energetic in accepting the challenge of atonal music proves that the richness and compactness of motivic correspondences do not constitute a special case, but a principle that is highly beneficial in the development of extensive, logical, and coherent forms. This is indeed plausible, because the new style (as we have insisted again and again) is essentially contrapuntal in its orientation. Always, in such a style, relationships of the kind under discussion constitute a formative means of the first rank; medieval polyphony and Bach's style are striking examples. Now, if one is inclined to compose in such a manner, there seems to be no reason why one should not make use of the method in which these relationships are fundamental. And if one decides to do so, the method ceases to be an impediment and becomes a help.

The most popular objection to twelve-tone technique is that it makes music dependent on mathematics and destroys the highly valued action of inspiration. I shall soon go further into the alleged relation of music to mathematics; here I shall merely point out the cardinal

difference between them. The objection can be interpreted as follows: Everything in the twelve-tone technique is prearranged, as in science; imagination no
longer has full sway; and composition henceforth will
consist of filling in diagrams formed by abstract calculations. But the essence of the mathematical process
is that a unique solution must be traced for each problem. The elementary equation (which is all that the
layman has in mind) consists of finding a single value
for the unknown factor which alone fulfills the conditions. But the *theorem* is in no sense applicable to the
twelve-tone technique. The musician can not only de-
vise a thousand completely different compositions in
using the same twelve-tone series; he can, in addition,
proceed from any point of a given opus in an entirely
new direction, and that without breaking the rules.
The question of how to proceed is not predetermined,
but depends exclusively on the composer's artistic intention, controlled here, as in any other method of composing, by his imagination, and by nothing else.

Inspiration is no more limited by the twelve-tone
technique than by any other system of musical rules.
That music is subject to rules is a fact not even doubted
by those reactionaries who become excited over the
"dictatorship" of the method, after decades spent in re-
proaching new music for being "anarchistic" simply because it destroyed the old rules.

It is, however, not only imaginable but to be expected
that the twelve-tone technique will eventually become
more flexible. In the future, one will no longer use
the whole series continuously, but will choose characteristic groups from it; one will allow certain variations
within that chosen series in specified situations, and
the like. A tendency toward free treatment can already

be found occasionally in Schoenberg's twelve-tone compositions. In brief, it can be taken for granted that atonality, after the strict training to which it is being subjected in the twelve-tone technique, will graduate to a condition where it will no longer need this tight apparatus. What atonality has learned from the twelve-tone technique—the richness and compactness of close symmetrical relationships and the use of them in building logical forms—will in time become second nature to it. Although the twelve-tone technique is neither the only nor the last word in new music, it probably will always remain the best pedagogical method of learning and practicing the art of atonal composition. In this respect, it will be the exact correlative and natural continuation of the so-called "strict" counterpoint, which has been derived from the medieval style and is still used—and rightly so—for contrapuntal training.

Another and purely demagogic objection to the new method is that atonality and the twelve-tone technique are symbolic of a communistic conviction. There are people who, apparently in all seriousness, claim that the "twelve-tone *system*" (as they call it) corresponds to Bolshevism because it is supposed to eliminate the patriarchal hierarchy of the steps subordinated to a single fundamental tone, and to proclaim equal rights for all twelve tones. It does not seem either especially profitable or pertinent to carry on a controversy dealing with such barroom arguments, although one should be careful not to take them too lightly after seeing how successfully certain barroom occupants have set out to conquer half the world. I only want to indicate that it is just as easy, and much more plausible, to associate the twelve-tone technique with the Catholic philosophical thoughts of the Middle Ages, with Thomas Aquinas and the *philosophia perennis*. I shall not go so far as to assert that the many parallels between our music and that of medieval times must bring out a new close connection with a definite religious credo. But the retreat from the crass, spectacular attitude of which we have been speaking is doubtless related to a strong spiritual tendency, and to a turn in the direction of problems and substances which are akin to religious thoughts and sentiments. It is interesting, if not surprising, to note that atonality and the twelve-tone technique, which the fascists threaten with extermination as *Kulturbolschewismus*, have lately been rejected by the Soviets as decadent and unsocial "formalism." One can hardly imagine a stronger proof that they are on the right road.

A real danger to the twelve-tone technique would arise if it were allowed to degenerate into a new kind of fetish. In that case it would have a kinship with every sort of rabid totalitarianism. The way to escape lies in using the method as a means, not as an end. Twelve-tone technique, like any other technical process, is sensible in so far as it increases the mastery of the human mind over natural resources; or, to phrase it differently, in so far as it enlarges the region of spiritual freedom. Without technique, man would still roam the primeval forest like an animal. But if progress should make him a slave to technique, his fate would be hardly more enviable.

It depends on us to produce technique and to remain its masters—in life as well as in art.

CHAPTER   EIGHT

MUSIC AND MATHEMATICS

Tones and Figures

AFTER the twelve-tone technique has been explained
to the average man, he is likely to exclaim, "But that
is pure mathematics! Anyhow, I've always known that
this kind of music is computed, not inspired. One can
tell that by listening—and now you have proved it to
me."

Because he is unwilling to believe that emotional
and imaginative forces can animate modern music, the
man in the street has sized it up as a purely intellectual
pursuit. His reaction is negative because his own imagination and emotions may be less stimulated by what is
new than by what is old. The average person will never
realize that this is no fault of the music. Moreover,
when he sees that, to simplify procedure and analysis,
sounds are designated by figures, and intervals by numbers, he will boast of having tracked down our mathematical vices.

What would the average person say if he were familiar with the formulae of our good old thorough
bass, studied by all the recognized masters of imagination and emotional expression—Bach, Mozart, Schubert, *et al.?* No one can deny that the following formula looks dangerously like an involved mathematical combination:

$$\text{e IV} \begin{smallmatrix}9\\7\\6-\end{smallmatrix} 6 \qquad \text{C III} \qquad \text{IV} \begin{smallmatrix}9\\4\end{smallmatrix} 3 \text{ I} \begin{smallmatrix}6\\4\end{smallmatrix} \qquad \text{V } 4 \; 3 \text{ I}$$

Yet it merely represents an absolutely innocent final cadence following a simple modulation from E Minor to C Major.

The mere fact that something can be expressed in figures does not prove that it is "mathematical" by nature. Let us suppose that we have set up a tabulation in which we express, in measurements of twelve inches to the foot, the heights of various mountains in a range. Now, the discovery or establishment of certain relationships between the figures will not explain why the peaks are famous for their beauty. But it would be foolish to contend that measurement of the Alps robs them of their splendor.

Average persons will readily agree that music has, indeed, some connection with mathematics through physics. Probably we all have heard, at one time or another, about Pythagoras's "music of the spheres" and about vibration ratios and overtones. It is easy to see that the length of strings or pipes used in the production of tones is related to the pitch of the tones thus produced. Certainly this is very interesting, and something which instrument makers need to know; but one can hardly call the knowledge a decisive factor in the art of composition.

When we learn that the special nature of the octave interval is the result of the vibration ratio 1:2 of the two tones which constitute the octave—a very simple relationship—we are quite impressed; but the ear needs no such scientific instruction to find out that the octave is the purest form of consonance. When I am composing, it is enough for me to bear in mind what my ear tells me. Yet, how I shall use the octave, whether I prefer it or even avoid it, must depend on my artistic intention and not on the interval's physico-mathematical nature.

On the contrary, stressing of this natural condition could create the danger that the intervals and interval relations determined by physics might be set up as fetishes. Suppose a composer writes something which is not in keeping with the predominance of the octave. If he does, one can criticize him out of loyalty to the octave and on the ground that it is an absolutely superior interval by reason of its "beauty," though this is only an aesthetic judgment and is subject to dispute. Yet, in adopting the viewpoint of physics, one can further argue that the octave's matchless proportions 1:2, established by physical science, prove a magical recommendation on the part of nature; and that a meddlesome and intellectually willful composer should not sin against a natural law. The objection brings the reply that certainly the relationship 1:2 is simple and beautiful, but that calculations with π are not less lovely or satisfying because the number happens to be more complicated. To place the multiplication table above logarithms in an aesthetic valuation would be, of course, utter nonsense.

Overtones and Scales

OVERTONES have recently been given the status of a musico-mathematical god. Overtones, partial tones, or harmonic series are, as we know, a series of tones heard simultaneously, but without being actually played, over a tone which is really produced. If we were to represent the series in a graph, it would develop somewhat like a parabola; the lower overtones, those nearest to the tone actually produced, would have the greatest distance between them, while increasingly smaller distances would be seen between the higher ones. The first overtone is the octave of the fundamental or "generating" tone; the next is the fifth of the first overtone; the third, the fourth of the second overtone; the fourth, the major third of the third overtone, etc.

These overtones, together with vibration numbers, have served as an inexhaustible mine for musical theorists. Every second book of musical instruction starts with the familiar picture of a well-manicured phantom hand dividing the strings of a mysterious, archaic-looking instrument into sections, and then moves on to imposing columns of overtones surrounded by more or less substantial tabulations. This is completely in line with the materialistic fetishism of the nineteenth century. A new theory is not accepted as authentic, and so cannot possibly be taken seriously, until it bears the label of a scientific analysis of its material premises. We see this in commercial advertising as well as in music; a campaign to publicize a new brand of chewing gum, for instance, is likely to be carried on with the aid of elaborate and flamboyant "scientific" certificates relative to vitamin content and calories.

Overtones had first to prove that the major and minor scales stemmed from them, for this would also prove that the diatonic scales had their roots in nature and were obviously safe from any human caprice. If this were true, any attempt to write music without using these scales would be about as sensible as trying to make water flow uphill. How splendid it would be if one could expose atonality not only as Bolshevism but even as a childish prank! Yet this would not be so easy as some people think.

Under favorable conditions you can pretend to yourself that you do hear the first two or three overtones, if you are prepared for the exact moment when they should come out and are on the alert for their appearance. I do not mean to cast any doubt on the presence of the other overtones. Their existence has been sufficiently established by experiments, and is even indirectly quite evident, since they determine the timbres of various instruments and voices. The timbre of a tone played on the oboe is wholly unlike that of the same note produced on a violin, owing to dissimilar groups of overtones standing out in each case. The distinction can be accurately analyzed by physical means. We now have mechanical equipment to separate groups of partials from a tone received through the microphone in such a way that, when heard through the loud-speaker, the tone seems to be completely assimilated with the tone of an entirely different musical instrument. (The distortion of sound to which music is still subject when heard through the medium of the radio or the sound-film camera can be traced back to the uneven transmission quotient of that particular apparatus for a certain group of partials.)

In saying that we *experience* overtones as timbres, or sound colors, we present proof that we do not *hear* them as such. No person alive is in a position to say, apropos of listening to music, that the fifth to the ninth overtones in the case of one instrument have greater weight than the twelfth to the seventeenth overtones in another instance, or vice versa. Since the partials are responsible for the characteristic sound of an instrument, their contribution is heard as a whole.

That is why it was a mistake for musicians to suppose that by hearing overtones directly they could range them in the form of a major or a minor scale. Even if the theorists had heard them, this kind of disposition would have been arbitrary; for the overtones have been strung "by nature" in a curve like a parabola. The scale, however, is a linear arrangement. Besides, in all the history of tonality there is not the slightest indication of acoustical observations or experiments which might have led to the establishment of tonal scales.

But we can dismiss the issue. Perhaps it is possible that a marvelous intuition was at work when the diatonic scales were laid down; and perhaps it is only today that we are able to prove scientifically how well they agree with natural conditions. But this supposition contradicts the serious consideration that both the succession and the single elements of the tonal scale fail to correspond to acoustical theories. Up to the fifth overtone, only two of the occurring tones differ from the fundamental tone—its major third and its fifth. The major triad, at least, is thus accounted for, but four tones in the seven of the major scale remain to be placed. These do not oblige us by appearing in a semblance of rank and order after the fifth overtone. On the contrary; from the sixth partial on, tones which persist in turning up have not only no place in the scale based on the fundamental tone but are alien to our entire tonal scheme. They lie between the half-tones used in our musical system and need all sorts of irregular fractures for their correct placement. And so the relation of the tonal scales to the harmonic series includes a complete change of the succession as well as a change of their constituent parts. We cannot complain of any lack of arbitrary action here.

Instead of trying to figure out how all this business is related to overtones, would it not be simpler to say that the major-minor system was produced by creative minds because it was better suited than any other to the expression of their thoughts? It would not only be simpler but also more correct. At the same time, this interpretation would automatically involve the idea that other creative minds could produce a different system, which is the inference to be avoided at all costs.

"Functional Modes" and "Combination Tones"

HINDEMITH has undertaken in his *Instruction in Composition* to trace the chromatic scale also to the harmonic series. He has no wish to perpetuate the major-minor tonality as the only explicit possibility for music. He tries to pave the way to a slightly more liberal interpretation of musical means. Yet both in theory and in practice Hindemith's progressive orientation is subject to doubt. He is not quite progressive enough to break away altogether from traditional methods, and compromises by trying merely to enlarge the field of what can be legalized with overtones. Since today we need more than just the major and minor scales, Hindemith suggests that the chromatic scale be given an honorary role in the drama of natural resources. The suggestion seems impractical; the chromatic scale is hardly more suitable for this purpose than the major scale, and hence a variety of new interpretations and exceptions must be introduced.

Nonetheless, we must acknowledge that Hindemith has at least *not* tried to prove that the *linear* order of the chromatic scale is natural. His twelve-tone succession, derived from the (arbitrarily adapted) harmonic series, reminds one of the "functional modes" originated by Richard S. Hill (*Musical Quarterly*, 1934). Instead of the mechanical linear scale arrangement, Hill suggests a succession of the tones which would express their special functions in the compositions. For example, Hill arranges the C Major scale as follows: C-G-E-F-A-B-D-C, to demonstrate certain relations often found in tonal music. The idea is good, though of course it can only be used analytically and not as a means for establishing rules. We can deduce the Hill succession, as a functional mode, from tonality because a great deal of tonal music can be traced back to it. No such mode can be set up now for real atonality. There simply is not enough atonal music in existence to provide the necessary statistical data. And one can hardly make any chromatic "functional mode" into a norm by insisting on its alleged conformity to nature-given overtones; conformity is purely fictitious in view of the fact that partials comprise a physical and not a musical reality.

Anyhow, Hindemith's theory is distinguished by its coherence. By it he was induced to add to his melodic hierarchy—allegedly based on physically determinable facts—a harmonic authority founded on the same data; and he believes that he has found such justification in the so-called *combination tones.*

Combination tones are a type of acoustic specter of secondary rank, distinguishable from overtones by being supposedly heard when two real tones are played simultaneously. (As we know, overtones accompany the sounding of a single tone.) Furthermore, they appear not over, but under the real tone, and so can be referred to as "undertones." They are believed to be responsible for the tension degree of the interval that is actually heard. Besides being even less audible than overtones, the "undertones" can at best furnish only a physical explanation of the quality of a harmony; in no case can they tell us how that harmony should be applied in composition. That, again, depends exclusively on creative imagination or artistic intention, never on the physical nature of the material. In spite of Hindemith's wish to pave the way to a progressive type of music, his theory necessarily results in favoring the basic facts of tonality—the major triad and simple harmonic relationships—exactly as in the old tonal music.

I do not wish to examine the extent to which Hindemith's theoretical reflections may have been prompted by a desire to use apparently unassailable scientific arguments as an explanation of his evident return from a radical method of composing to a more moderate manner.

Tones Are Not Raw Material

THE legitimacy of musical mutation, especially the transition from tonality to atonality, can be seen only by ascertaining the independence of the sound language from nature's system, and by recognizing the status of music as a humane, spiritual creation. In discussing this concept we find unexpected support in mathematics and physics, the very sciences which we have just banned from the musical field; but the support has a totally different sense from the interpretation we have dealt with so far.

When we conceive of music as a spiritual sphere, and composing as the art of producing spiritual realities by musical means, we are unlikely to succeed if we try to discover the principle of composition by investigating natural qualities. The tones at our disposal are not raw materials like oil and cotton. Oil and cotton are natural products, and examination of their inherent qualities must precede their technical exploitation. Our tones are not natural products in this sense. There are no tone plantations or mines. Tones must be produced by artificial means. Natural laws laid down in the science of acoustics are obeyed in production, to be sure, but otherwise it is an arbitrary procedure. The tone of a violin or a piano has no precedent in nature.

Our choice of tones for use in composition is likewise wholly artificial. In my historical survey I referred to the importance of tempered pitch. The device was responsible for a decisive material change in a stratum far below the level of artistic creation. Since then, the musical material has had little in common with the natural tones and their relationships as described by elementary acoustics. The material has been transformed to meet the needs of creative minds. Such a transformation was necessary to enable the creative mind to manifest itself through this material in the only form possible at that period of musical development. Yet attempts are constantly made to perpetuate the form as if it were bestowed by nature. Many people go a step further in trying to prove even that the style first developed in dealing with the material (the tonal style) is the only "natural" one.

The main difference between music and raw materials is that the former has a history. Cotton that grows in the fields and oil that rests in the bowels of the earth have no history, or at best one in which hundreds of thousands, or even millions, of years are necessary to bring about a transformation. Man's *use* of oil and cotton, however, has a history comparable to the use of musical tones. But the use of tones involves their production. That is why the history of musical material is coincident with the history of mankind.

The Relativity of Scientific Systems

PHYSICISTS and mathematicians are far in advance of musicians in realizing that their respective sciences do not serve to establish a concept of the universe conforming to an objectively existent nature. They are fully cognizant of the fact that, conversely, their task is to make an existing conception of the universe conform to the largest possible number of observations demonstrable by scientific experiments. And by an existing conception of the universe, we mean one that is postulated on the historical situation.

No doubt the statement that the sun revolves around the earth was objectively just as correct as the later assertion that the earth revolves around the sun. But the historical situation—and by this we mean the development of man's spiritual structure—forced humanity in a certain epoch to abandon the geocentric concept of the universe in favor of another. Physical science then undertook the task of evolving a corresponding theory and supporting it with suitable experiments. Of course, a subsequent view of the situation gives the impression that observations led the scientists to expose the inadequacy of the old theory. But a new attitude, a modified spiritual structure, and a new type of mind were prerequisites in anticipating the results and the interpretation of the observations. The new discoveries are made possible through the mutations in the general state of mind.

The Significance of Axioms

PHYSICAL and, above all, mathematical theories owe their independence from so-called reality to their logical coherence. We know that experiments in non-Euclidean geometric systems were made as early as the beginning of the nineteenth century. A comprehensive systematization of these experiments is furnished by the science of axioms. All the facts and operations of ordinary or Euclidean geometry can be reduced to a series of first principles called axioms; as, for instance, a straight line is the shortest distance between two points, or, only one parallel can be drawn to a straight line through any given point outside it, and the like. By axiom, one understands a proposition which cannot be reduced to another by logical deductions, or, in other words, which cannot be "proved." The *theorem* of Pythagoras is no axiom; for not only can it be proved, but it must be proved to be credible. The theory that only one straight line can run through two points cannot be more definitely proved. Such assertions have acquired the character of "eternal truths." It has seemed as if they expressed an objective and irrevocable conclusion which man was forced to accept, as if we must be glad that we are gifted with an immediate insight into original truths without which we would be unable further to develop our powers of perception.

The study of axioms tells us about a different character of axioms. It does not recognize axioms as occult facts, but enquires into their why and wherefore, to reach the conclusion that axioms are free statements of our minds, enunciated for the purpose of making geometry possible. Can one perhaps formulate other axioms than the Euclidean ones? One can. Does that mean complete anarchy? Not quite. If a given group of axioms is to fulfill its purpose, namely, the production of a geometric system, its constituent axioms must be independent and compatible. Independent, in that none of them can be deduced by logical reasoning from one or more other axioms (because in that case it would cease to be an axiom); compatible, in that not one of them includes anything, and nothing can be deduced from any of them, which would be incompatible with the remaining axioms or with facts to be deduced from them. For example: If an axiomatic system postulates that the sum total of the angles of a triangle is 180 degrees, then no chain of syllogisms of any kind based on the same system can yield a different result. But if the two conditions previously mentioned are fulfilled, nothing stands in the way of constructing non-Euclidean systems. If the operations described in general geometry are carried out in such systems, the result is non-Euclidean geometry.

Geometric systems of this kind have frequently been worked out. If, for instance, we should apply to one of these systems the proposition that an infinite number of parallels can be drawn through any given point outside a straight line, or that the sum total of the angles of a triangle belonging to such geometry is less or more than 180 degrees, we would appear nonsensical to an inhabitant of a Euclidean world. But who can tell whether our world really is a hundred per cent Euclidean? Have we not learned from the development of physics that the sphere which was sufficient for classical mechanics, and which coincides to some extent with everyday physics, is a relatively minute section of what is physically possible? Euclidean axioms were laid down to enable us to practice geometry in our natural sphere. Whatever we deduce from these axioms can be successfully applied to our observations, or rather, *could* be so applied until recently. New observations in the macrocosm of the universe and in the microcosm of the atoms, photons, and electrons demand other mathematical-geometric principles. Yet, according to what I suggested before, we should rather say that man first chanced on the creation of new theoretical principles, and that only then was he enabled to make external observations, the interpretation of which was already anticipated ,in the principles themselves.

Axioms in Music

WHAT has all this to do with music? I believe the comparison is sufficiently clear. Musical systems, languages of sound, or sound languages as we call them in our terminology, have not been created by nature or by some mystical Supreme Being, but have been produced by man to render music possible within a certain sphere. The fundamental facts of a sound language may have many formal points of similarity with the axiomatic system. In his *Foundations of Geometry,* David Hilbert introduced a discussion of Euclidean axioms with the following monumental propositions:

"We imagine three distinct categories of things. The things in the first category we shall call points and designate by A, B, C . . . ; the things in the second category we shall call straight lines and designate by a, b, c . . . ; the things in the third category we shall call planes and designate by α, β, γ. . . . We conceive of these points, straight lines, and planes as having certain mutual relations which we indicate by means of such words as 'are situated,' 'between,' 'parallel,' 'congruent,' 'continuous.' The exact, and for mathematical purposes complete, description of these relationships is achieved through the axioms of geometry."

The importance of these propositions lies in the fact that Hilbert did not write, "There *are* points, straight lines, and planes which one can handle thus and so if one has explored their natural qualities, which proceedings can be called geometry." Instead, he characterizes the points, straight lines, and planes as thought-concepts, as products of the mind; and whatever we can do with these thought-concepts depends on the definitions which we impose on them.

One can very well imagine a general theoretical interpretation of music which would start with the following proposition:

"We *imagine* three different categories of things. The things in the first category we shall *call* tones, the things in the second category chords, and the things in the third category melodies. We *conceive* of the tones, chords, and melodies as having certain mutual relationships which we *indicate* by means of such words as 'high,' 'low,' 'interval,' 'consonance,' 'dissonance,' 'contrary motion,' 'inversion,' and so forth."

These propositions would form the basis of a musical theory including all sound languages of whatever nature. As the study of axioms eliminates the idea that axioms are something absolute, conceiving them instead as free propositions of the human mind, just so would this musical theory free us from the concept of major-minor tonality (or any other systematized form of musical material) as an irrevocable law of nature. The theory would make way for the concept that the facts of a sound language, too, are products of the human mind, created freely by musical thought.

Another case of thorough anarchy? Or rather, of utter arbitrariness? For we cannot take the bare logical coherence of a musical "axiomatic" system as the sole criterion of its soundness! This would indeed be impossible, as directly contradicting our reflections in Chapter I, where we showed the outstanding characteristic of music to be its independence from the linguistic limitations of general logic.

Naturally the propositions of a musical theory are also subject to general logic, since they are expressed in words and must make sense. But it is obvious that propositions about dissonances, inversions, and retrogressions need not necessarily express anything of service to music, even if they are unobjectionable from the standpoint of logic.

Musical Theory and Musical Practice

YET that is the point at issue. Here the parallels of musical and axiomatic theories come to an end. Whereas geometric axioms are sufficiently justified if their combinations prove them to be both independent of and compatible with each other, the accuracy of musical axioms can be proved exclusively by their fitness for practical use. Propositions circumscribing a musical sphere are correct only if real music can be produced on the basis of facts presented by them. That is why a concrete theory which is valid for a particular sphere cannot be constructed until a corresponding consolidated practice in the sphere is available.

A system of musical axioms can never be established in theory until it has been demonstrated in practice.

This applies to both tonality and atonality. Before the former was completely formulated it had one hundred years of practice behind it; the latter has been practiced for only thirty years, and so its thorough theoretical formulation is not yet possible.

If I see a clear advantage in the axiomatic method of presentation, that does not imply that I wish to endorse promiscuous inventions of musical systems. I merely want to prove that there is no cause for alarm in any necessity to face whatever facts may deviate from a recognized axiomatic system. Of course such facts are not entitled to any consideration if they are not products of a musical practice.

In using words like "consonance," "dissonance," and "contrary motion" to define the relationships of our musical thought-concepts, we obviously mean that these relationships are not inherent in the material, but that we add them to it. Their significance depends on *how* we define them. Anyone will probably agree that this interpretation applies to such "artificial" concepts as "inversion" and "retrogression." Elementary concepts like "melody," "dissonance," and "consonance," however, apparently are allied to the very nature of the material, no matter what names we give them. In regard to this objection, I want to re-emphasize that the record of dissonance, a fascinating chapter in the history of music, demonstrates that not even such "elementary" concepts should be taken for granted.

Of course there is something to this objection. The material has idiosyncrasies of one kind or another; otherwise we could not take up the difference between consonance and dissonance at all. Yet, if we were so inclined, we should be free to call all harmonies dissonances, with the exception of the octave (as was done in early medieval times); or we could limit dissonances to the minor second and the major seventh. (As a matter of fact, we are today not far from this situation. For though orthodox critics will not admit it, we have only to turn to "swing" music to see that the ear of the masses has gradually adjusted itself to the most "unorthodox" harmonies.)

The fact that we notice tension differentials in harmonies at all is based on objective qualities in the material. But we must not allow ourselves to be overimpressed by this circumstance. It was on the basis of some objectively existent quality in space that the theory of relativity suggested a curvature returning to itself. Although no one is able to imagine this condition as plastic, the abstract thought tallies with certain observations. Naturally it is not possible to observe the curvature as such without entering the fourth dimension; and thus far the idea remains an intellectual construction, a scientific "inspiration." At the same time, observations made within the three-dimensional space accessible to us speak for the accuracy of the "inspiration."

If the ideas set forth in the theory of relativity, in that of wave mechanics, and in the quantum theory are to be accepted as characteristic of the intellectual attitude of our time, it should be interesting to study analogous expressions in atonality. The first and most striking example is found in the concept of twelve-tone music, which shows interesting relations to the thoughts active in modern physical science. This does not mean that twelve-tone music has assimilated physics, or has turned into a new kind of mathematical operation. The example merely connotes similarities in habits of feeling, viewing, and thinking.

"Abstractness"

THE paramount issue involved is the gradual disappearance of our inhibitions with regard to abstract procedures. The new physics has "mathematized" its subjects —motion, matter, energy, etc.—to such an extent that its methods scarcely remind us of the real happenings in which these concepts play a tangible part. The question of relating time to the co-ordinate system of space, developed by the theory of relativity, is an especially conspicuous detail in the diffuseness of the process.

When the figures deduced from time are mixed in a calculation with those deduced from space to form part of an unforeseen mathematical species, we are left without the remotest possibility of imagining what really happens. Yet one would expect to imagine this, since we have to deal, not with abstract calculations, but with calculations which are supposed to tell us something about the universe. Still, the result of abstractly constructed calculations can be retransformed into images of the actual relationships of natural phenomena, and later tested in experiments. Can it be that, viewed objectively, the universe has "been designed by a pure mathematician" (as Sir James Jeans indicates in *The Mysterious Universe*), so that a mathematical interpretation would, in a certain measure, correspond to the world of facts?

However that may be, the twelve-tone technique, too, seems to be based on a quite diffuse and abstract method of thinking, miles away from the nature of music. When, for instance, I decide to build a movement in a string quartet, using the inversions of all the series found in the preceding movement, I may appear to have embarked on an absurd mechanistic project, to be guilty of pretentious caprice. But suppose my mind is "structured twelve-tonelike," analogous to Sir James's "mathematically designed" universe, or suppose that thinking in series relations is a natural habit of mine; one could then well imagine that this "abstract" method would aid me in getting results susceptible of being smoothly retransformed into the "nature of music."

Dealing with the Time Factor

ANOTHER analogy concerns the use of the time factor. The concept of retrogression in new music has had a lasting effect on its entire formal development, the concept of time being interpreted in a new sense. In tonal music, with its metric apparatus, a measurement of time is divided into virtually equal sections. A composition has a general tempo, exactly as it has a general key; everything in it is deduced from and related to these basic facts. Metric units regulated by the tempo are mute, so to speak, and in evidence under the music, like the woof of cloth which is decorated with embroidery. The musical piece rests on a metrical scheme; and the metrical scheme, in turn, is based on the concept that time progresses in one irreversible direction.

Atonality discarded this scheme; and the action, undertaken with full realization of its importance, marks one of the most significant innovations achieved by atonal music, as well as one of its greatest difficulties. It is of little help to us that Bach foreshadowed some of these problems in his contrapuntal experiments, which seem to us familiar in material, though they remain enigmatic in essence.

Every freely articulated single phrase in atonality must first produce its own meter. The meter is not founded on a filling-in of a rhythmic scheme which would continue to pulsate in silence underneath the music; it is based on a free distribution of weights in a continuity that is indefinite in its direction. No abstractly progressing ¼ or ⅚ time signature is thus presupposed; instead, the metric figure is created simultaneously with the musical idea. Time is divested of the character which tonality has agreed on, and becomes, instead, a spacelike continuity. When there is no longer a steadily pulsating meter to suggest the familiar "one-way street" of time, the time measurement to be filled with music seemingly assumes the quality of space through which we can move in many directions, *even in opposite directions*. Thus, a musical retrogression could well create the impression of time moving backward. It appears as though the time quantity consumed by the forward-moving musical unit would be "repaid" by its retrograde statement. It must be understood, however, that this impression is merely imaginary and that in reality a retrograde motion progresses forward in time just as its prototype, the progressive motion, does.

Solidity and Motion

A SLIGHTLY more obvious analogy is provided by a comparison between tonal and atonal music on the one hand, and classical mechanics and modern physics on the other. The whole idea of tonal music, including its concept of the fundamental tone, the hierarchy of steps, and dependence of the formal structure on relation to the key, has an evident connection with the method of reasoning used in gravitation mechanics, having a clearly arranged concept of masses whose relationships are uniformly regulated. The method is based on the assumption of relatively firm, substantial, and corporeal matter. Physicists have labored tirelessly to find a new interpretation of matter and to destroy its corporeality. They split and examine the once "indivisible" atom, finding therein phantomlike electrons which they interpret ambiguously, now as minute particles, now as mere movements of waves. Nothing remains of the physical character of matter; it has been dissolved into myriads of diminutive systems of indefinite limits, moving continuously and with inconceivable rapidity.

In the same way, atonality has destroyed the solidity of the tonal structure, replacing it with a more fluid method of presentation. The structure of tonality, symmetrical in principle, is arched over the firm columns of triad harmony; atonal compositions, especially those built up on the twelve-tone technique, originate from a long chain of movable cells that are homogeneous in their nature and yet transformable, and that constantly influence each other.

The theme in tonal music is a solid structure, something one can transport to different places without danger to its life. (The basic idea of tonal form even results from the transportation of such solid complexes to different planes, that is, different keys.) In atonality the figures are far less solid, being boneless, much more elastic, flexible, and variable. It is not a matter of chance that transposition has lost its old significance in atonality and is no longer an acute question. But surely there is no reason why music should not join the other arts and the sciences in ridding itself of its excess and obsolete appendages.

New Music Is Simpler

THESE arguments may sound complicated and esoteric, as sophisticated and intellectualized as new music itself. Yet we can apply to our art what Einstein says in *The Evolution of Physics* about the apparently increased abstractness and complication in his field:

"To clear the way leading from theory to experiment of unnecessary and artificial assumptions, to embrace an ever-wider region of facts, we must make the chain longer and longer. The simpler and more fundamental our assumptions become, the more intricate is our mathematical tool of reasoning; the way from theory to observation becomes longer, more subtle and more complicated. Although it sounds paradoxical, we could say: 'Modern physics is simpler than the old physics and seems, therefore, more difficult and intricate. The simpler our picture of the external world and the more facts it embraces, the stronger it reflects in our mind the harmony of the universe.'"

New music can well envy modern physics its possession of an interpreter who expresses his opinions with such intelligence and calm self-confidence. In this case, the man who originated the theory provided also its interpretation; and the composer who starts out to interpret the new music analytically may derive hope and courage from Einstein's example. There is not much else he can do but explain the music himself, after he has composed it.

I should add that this task is reserved for the composer without too much protest. Regrettably enough, when someone else talks about the tasks, experiments, and problems of new music, he usually exhibits a stag-

gering ignorance of the simplest and most available
pragmatic facts. A well-nigh incredible number of mis-
conceptions in analysis and interpretation, and—even
worse—a superior unconcern, complete the equipment
of such "experts."

Excellent books are written on the interpretation of
musical notation in the thirteenth century and on similar academic subjects—tomes that show an imposing
amount of tireless scientific research. Nor are these
efforts altogether superfluous; I would be the last to
question the value of knowing as much as possible
about such matters. And yet I feel I can truthfully say
that no one reference work or encyclopedia of music
contains a halfway pertinent or intelligible interpretation of new music, unless it quotes from modern composers. For, curiously enough, although composers
should not be called on to supply perfect analyses, it is
they who talk most intelligently about their job. When
the opponent finds himself involved in a discussion of
new music, he will lightly touch on it, using impressive
technical terms which are neither understood by his
listeners nor explained to them. Generally he will give
the impression of having been forced against his will
to waste a few carefully chosen words on a rather pain-
ful subject—an indelicate subject that is not fit for discussion in genteel society, as if he were a doctor who
had been asked to discuss venereal diseases at a fashionable five-o'clock tea.

Notwithstanding all this, Einstein's train of thought
does apply to the musical field as well as to his own.
The more music frees itself from the magic bonds by
which it has been confined since the days of its origin,
the more the art realizes spiritual dominion over material laws, the more it integrates itself with the suprem-

acy of the spirit, the more truth it contains and the simpler it becomes in its essence, the more complicated will its structure seem to become and the more difficult will be our analysis of the art. Yet this analysis must be undertaken, and honestly and diligently carried on. In no other way can we come to an understanding of new music and to an immediate appreciation of its innate values.

The Journey to the Truth

WHEN I said that if the creative spirit were formed "twelve-tonelike" the application of the twelve-tone axioms would correspond more closely to the "nature of music" than is the case in any other method, I meant to speak objectively. Did I perhaps give the impression of advocating an absolutism of twelve-tone music as a "dictatorship of the twelve"? I did not mean to do that. My argument is that *every* musical method is relative and subject to changes imposed by its own dialectics. Atonality is no exception; it, too, is exposed to change, to disintegration, and to transformation into a different sound language. To help in bringing recognition to atonality means at the same time to witness its disintegration. That breaking-up is rooted in the general law of history, and can neither be accelerated nor delayed by any method of practice or analysis.

Granted that all languages of sound, and the activities within them, are relative to each other, they are nonetheless all oriented to one absolute quality—truth. This is why they are mutually relative. History can be compared to a long journey, in the course of which we constantly try to see truth as fully as possible; but each time we look, we see it from a different angle. Whether we consider this journey as desultory or methodical depends on our equipment. The man who carries the compass of religious faith is convinced that the ultimate objective is a point from which man will be able to see the whole truth. Then history will have come to an end. He who does not share this faith must needs realize that man will at least always continue his search for the truth. And so, these two types have a common desire to keep moving onward. But the traveler who believes the journey can be halted at any specified place becomes unfaithful to the ideal set before him. Since art forms one of the most dignified efforts of man to attain to the truth, we must neither deny nor delay its motion and changes, but must rather promote them and pay attention to their development.

Art may tell us more about the direction of our journey and the adventures that await us than we can learn from any other facts of so-called real life.

CHAPTER NINE

NEW MEDIA

Composition and Performance

THE long road that leads from the composer's hand to the ear of the listener has grown more winding in the course of centuries. A musical work, unlike literature or the plastic arts, has not yet achieved the final form in which it can be made available to the public, once its creator has laid down his tools. For a musical composition needs a middleman—the performer—who alone can make it audible and thus accessible to its potential audience. (That this performer may be at the same time its creator is beside the point.) The fact that a work of literature needs to be printed in order to become accessible to a larger number of readers does not alter these basic conditions, the printed copy being merely a replica of the original manuscript. The performance, however, without which the original, the ultimate, purpose of a musical work would not be fulfilled, "translates" the score into a new medium, by transforming the silent, timeless, two-dimensional, graphic symbols into a manifestation of sound, progressing in time and pervading the three-dimensional space.

This condition, however, is undergoing a marked change, almost a reversal. In primitive times, music was what one heard; its existence was bound to the moment of its performance. How much of the music was written down, if, indeed, any of it was written, was a detail of minor importance. Musical notation was a mere auxiliary for the convenience of singers or players, and its use was limited to their singing and playing. I would remind the reader that as late as the beginning of tonal music, when a highly developed sound language was current, relatively perfunctory notations were deemed good enough to ensure satisfactory performances.

We have studied the transformation of music into literature from various angles, and have found the development justified by history. This process caused the general shift of emphasis from the moment of performance to the field of notation—the durable substratum of the opus—making the notation an independent survivor of the act of hearing. Obviously this tendency interfered with the spontaneity of the performance; but it was not forced on music by the composer's desire for immortality. As time went on, and more was demanded of performers, casual notation was no longer adequate. What people wanted to hear was so full and complicated that it had to be stabilized in advance in increasingly permanent and unequivocal form. Little by little the performance lost the character of a spontaneous, momentary accomplishment, and became literally a reproduction of something cast previously in a fixed mold.

By and large, the public still is chiefly and necessarily interested in impressions created by singers and players through their vital presence. Your musician, however, and with him a large number of the laity in an audience, wants to know the relation of this accomplishment to the composition on which it is based—the relation of the reproducing artist to the composer's purpose as clarified in written symbols.

The struggle between the performer, who depends (or who appears to depend) on spontaneity, and the composer, who insists on a literal interpretation of his score, had its origin in this shift of balance from rendition to notation. The battle raged practically during the whole epoch of tonality and today seems to have been decided in the composer's favor. As late as in the nineteenth century, momentary vitality in the performance brought triumphs to the virtuoso who used the score chiefly as material for his brilliant and soulful exhibitions. Once more the task was to create the impression that the music had originated at the moment it was heard, that it was an inspired improvisation on the part of a genius.

Today, faithfulness to the music, or "work-fidelity" as we may call it, is recognized as the highest qualification for a performing musician. He is not averse to appearing as demoniac as Paganini or as fascinating as Liszt; but he does not legalize his achievement by personal *bravura*, preferring to demonstrate his artistry by punctiliously following the composer's instructions.

Sporting interest played an obvious part in the hero worship accorded the nineteenth-century virtuoso. Recently this public interest has been transferred to physical sports. I do not think that even the Italians, with their well-known love of *bel canto*, get as excited as they used to over which tenor can sing the most sensational High C. Formerly such men became national heroes. Today they have been replaced in the hearts of nations by transatlantic aviators, football halfbacks, and boxers. Probably the general enthusiasm for sports is stimulated by the fact that an athletic feat can be measured to the fraction of an inch or a split second; and modern man, in general, does not even tolerate the modest and purely superficial claim on his imagination made by the musical virtuoso's accomplishment. If it were only a matter of who could play the piano faster—an accomplishment which one could check with a stop watch—there is no doubt that pianists would be as important as champion swimmers.

Meanwhile, the increasing infiltration of both music and life by technique has moved another type of reproducing artist to the center of attention, and has reserved for him at least some of the old hero worship. We refer to the conductor. In the nineteenth century the orchestral apparatus became more complicated and hard to survey, like the industrial machinery. The achievements of individual musicians were gradually absorbed into a richly interlaced texture. In our day the listener no longer knows what the third clarinet or the fifth horn is playing; and orchestra players at their desks are in a position similar to that occupied by workers in a factory who turn screws on the assembly line. All the more reason, then, for public interest in the "leader" who co-ordinates the functions of all the players and illuminates the meaning of the whole arrangement.

The Development of Orchestration

THE tendency to gloss over the working process in the reproduction of music has a parallel in the development of orchestration. Contrasting colors in the classical orchestra were relatively pure and unmixed. The string instruments sounded like string instruments; the woodwinds provided a choirlike contrast, or reinforced the strings without "denaturalizing" the string tone as such. Brass instruments were unsuitable for purposes of color because they were limited to natural tones and were used almost exclusively for dynamic effects, to suggest power. That is why *tutti* passages in the classics took on their characteristic rigidity. The horn received soloistic treatment only occasionally, particularly in Beethoven's works.

Innovations following the romanticists' discovery that sound had an individual value were limited. A feeling for rich and bright effects had already become apparent in the critical transitional period from the church modes to tonality. Instrumental suggestions in Monteverdi's *Orfeo,* often quite peculiar, pointed to a colorful orchestra and to a deliberate consideration of contrasts for the purpose of dramatic characterization. But most of the curious instruments used in the Middle Ages died out with the standardization of the sound language introduced by tonality. In this field, too, progress in the improvement of tonality was made at the expense of other resources.

Romanticism was responsible for reviving color, not so much by introducing new instruments as by new methods of orchestration. Essential innovations in the tonal period were the introduction of the clarinet in the eighteenth century and of valve brass instruments in the nineteenth. These two important acquisitions marked the only changes made, except for variety and improvement in the percussion section. No other new instruments were accepted as permanent members of the orchestral family. The use of Wagnerian tubas remained in the hands of Wagner and Bruckner; the basset horn or alto clarinet, heckelphone or baritone oboe, the bass clarinet and English horn, retained more or less the character of curiosities. Not even the saxophone, the instrument which conquered the field of entertainment music, has been given a chair by the fireside in the modern symphony orchestra.

Sound color acquired a distinctly eloquent and symbolic value during the romantic period, taking its place as a means of expression alongside the thematic pattern, based on melodic elements, and the key color, supplied by harmony. Composers began to balance the various registers of the instruments against each other and to mix values with increasing subtlety. The deep clarinet passage in Weber's *Freischuetz* Overture has frequently been described as the birth of the new color. The heavenly soaring of the high divided strings at the start of the Prelude to *Lohengrin* and the foaming in the first chord of *Rheingold* clearly prove the value of color in symbolic expression. Since then, the principle of descriptive sound pictures has reached its peak in the sophisticated and subtle miracles wrought by such composers as Debussy and Ravel.

The effect, and to a certain extent the meaning of the process, was a growing alienation of sound from the machinery of its production. Henceforth the listener neither could nor should determine how the magic phenomenon was produced.

Wagner went so far as to lower his orchestra into a cavity below the audience's line of vision to emphasize the illusionary character of his *Gesamtkunstwerk,* or "symbiosis of the arts." Experiments have proved that ideological rather than acoustical reasons must have been responsible for this innovation, the Wagnerian orchestra (as well as every other type of orchestra) sounding better in the normal pit than in the deep Wagnerian trench. The welding of all the complicated activities involved in Wagner's operas was intended to produce a new medium, an all-embracing synthesis whose component parts should not stand out individually. Later we shall see that the development of opera in our time has followed an entirely different direction.

The Role of the Conductor

CONDITIONS in the latter part of the nineteenth century led to the gradual emergence of the conductor as the central figure in a performance. His function gained importance because the intricate activities in the orchestra could be surveyed only from a conning tower. There was also a psychological reason why the man who took the place of the unpretentious *Kapellmeister* came to the fore; the whole process of the production seemed to be concentrated in him, the mysterious phenomenon of music apparently radiating from him in some miraculous fashion.

The outstanding accomplishment of these new heroes of the musical world consisted of their assembling and training magnificent orchestral bodies. We have today in America and in western Europe several marvelous orchestras whose precision and beauty of tone are a source of unending wonder and delight. And the standard is astonishingly high among the many orchestral ensembles which strive to emulate the first-rate organizations. We owe this gratifying situation to the labors of a few star conductors who are eminent because of their intensely keen sense of hearing, their special knowledge of players and instruments, their wide experience, and their great pedagogic talents.

Unfortunately their indisputable merits are somewhat dimmed by a halo of more than mere technical authority, an attribute to which they do not hesitate to subscribe. No reflection on their significance or on their

merits is intended by saying that they are masters of the
orchestra, as Paganini and Sarasate were masters of the
violin, without their having an intimate relation to the
central problems of music. As in former cases, the attitude of these conductors toward new music is the touch-
stone of their relation to the focal problems of music in
general; and as this relation is usually one of perplexed
rejection, one is likely to presume that their understanding of old music does not penetrate to the essen-
tials, either.

To be sure, patrons of orchestras, boards of directors,
and similar controlling forces often prevent a conductor
from featuring new music. But if that were the only
reason, there would be no need for many conductors to
shoulder the responsibility for such a negative attitude;
nor would they need to continue their protests, in public as well as in private, that they simply do not understand new music and have a very low opinion of it
anyhow. The truth is that they often reveal their shocking ignorance when they produce modern novelties.

I distinctly remember the dismal impression made by
a performance of Schoenberg's *Orchestral Variations*
under a European star conductor a few years ago. The
rendition was disappointing although the star, by using
a score that was ostensibly read to shreds, apparently
wanted to show how intensely he had studied the work.
Some time afterwards a less pretentious but thoroughly
musical conductor performed the same opus (from an
uninjured copy, by the way), and suddenly the music
proved to be comparatively simple, absolutely clear,
and most impressive.

Thus it would be advisable for prima-donna conductors to be cautious in claiming a sovereign ignorance
of new music. Their haughty attitude is less an evidence

of intellectual greatness and admirable conservatism than of a lack of any conviction at all, likewise showing a lax association with the art as a whole. When a musician assures me, whether arrogantly or in desperation, that he does not understand the new music, I cannot make myself believe that he is a high priest of Beethoven.

For the rest, the musical uncertainty of some of the star conductors is often apparent in the ineffable programs they build. Even when the matter is merely one of old music, symphonic programs frequently remind me of the kaleidoscopic miscellanies presented at cheap outdoor "proms."

"Work-Fidelity"

THE halo of authority finds its origin in and is stimulated by the work-fidelity mentioned before, a principle generally adopted by the stars of today. Should not one expect a musician who protests with great solemnity that his holy rages help him to realize the composer's directions, down to the last staccato dot, to have an intimate association with music? Does not this attitude distinguish him favorably from the superficial and erratic virtuoso of a former period who treated masterworks flippantly? How, then, can it come to pass that, in spite of declared work-fidelity, the "Seventh" as read by Furtwaengler will differ considerably from . the "Seventh" when Toscanini conducts it? How can it happen that this difference is intentional, when each claims to be an infallible executor of the composer's will?

In reality, work-fidelity is turned into a verbal lash with which music is chastised in the name of abstract liberalism. It is inadmissible to eradicate the last touches of the human element in music, and then justify this action by quoting chapter and verse. It merely shows a distressing cynicism and distrust. Outside the field of music, this attitude has resulted in the rise of those dictators against whom the venerable taskmaster of the world's great orchestras takes such a resolute stand.

No one knows better than the composer that work-fidelity which sticks to the letter of the score leads to an unbearable caricature of his composition. But does not this same composer insist that the least of his directions is of cardinal importance? Will he not fume and rage if an interpreter neglects a single accent, a tiny crescendo sign? Certainly. The answer to the seeming contradiction is quite simple. Naturally the composer demands that the performer observe all the directions of the score with the greatest care. Yet he expects more, asking the performer to read those symbols with an insight which transcends their literal meaning. Under such circumstances, where does the detestable "caprice," the so-called "interpretation," begin? Would it not be desirable, to guarantee indubitable certainty, for the composer so to perfect his system of notation that strict obedience to the signs would result in a performance exactly in accordance with his intentions?

In theory, there could be no objection to such explicit notation. But from a practical point of view it is impossible of accomplishment with the means now at our disposal, regardless of the fact that nc music composed up to the present time, and above all no classical music, would benefit by such a technical improvement in writing.

Articulation and phrasing, the fields of reproduction in which our methods of notation fail most dismally, constitute its most important terrain. There can be no doubt that the constant use of symmetrical-scanning tonal music is largely responsible for the present decay of speaking articulation.

Though the symmetry of periods in a Mozart sonata or a simple song by Schubert is heard with machinelike importunity when some insensitive player or singer hammers out the meters with deadly regularity, we still get a recognizable and quantitatively complete picture, tedious and distorted as it inevitably must be. Yet it would be hard to substantiate objections to this kind of a performance on the ground that it was not faithful to the work. For there is nothing in the score to indicate breathing spaces, agogic preparation of high lights, nuances in the treatment of repeats, the distribution of light and shade in chord groups, or similar "subjective tricks," as autocrats of work-fidelity call them.

However, if one follows comfortable pedantry in *new* music, the outcome will be not only insufficient but simply catastrophic. It is sad enough when "work-faithful" performers content themselves with rattling off the classics because they lack musicianship. New music, having neither regular meters nor symmetric period formation which comes off by itself, cannot be performed in that manner. I have repeatedly heard honest and talented musicians make a sorry caricature of a work in the modern idiom, despite the fact that they reproduced it literally and, from a technical viewpoint, unobjectionably. When I have called their attention to faults of omission or commission, they have asked, in surprise, almost in reproach, "But isn't that what is written? Do you expect me, a conscientious artist, to play something that isn't in the score?"

My answer is: "What I expect on a given point can no more be written than a dramatist can indicate in his dialogue how long the caesura after one comma should last as compared to the break after another, or how high the voice should rise on a question mark over the pitch touched on the strongest accent in the sentence." An attempt to include such directions in the script of a play would be unspeakably pedantic, and a playwright guilty of it could justly be reproached with a crushing pessimism, since he would imply that he could not depend on the actor to bring out the difference between two commas, or between accent and question mark, on his own initiative.

The trouble is that we are bound to be disappointed when we expect performing musicians to exhibit the combination of technique and intelligence that we look for in actors. The condition is partially caused by the discipline forced on the former in ensemble playing. The member of an orchestra or a chamber music group is not free to interpret according to his own lights.

In most cases, however, your musician has not learned to read music as if it were speech, nor to phrase it intelligently. No one has ever explained to him the importance of doing so. The reason is that these concepts gradually vanished in the period of symmetrical-scanning tonality. Doubtless an articulation similar to that of speech was a matter of course at the time of Palestrina and Monteverdi, because music then was indissolubly connected with the spoken language, and free articulation was one of its constructive principles.

The Schooling of Interpreters

IT IS clear that a thorough schooling is necessary to familiarize performers with their new task. We can be sure that, in addition to many intrinsic reasons, the extraneous fact of inadequate performances contributes to the unpopularity of new music. Technical difficulties are repeatedly quoted as a cause of faulty reproduction. In reality these difficulties are not exceptional, especially in view of the exceedingly high executive standard maintained by the average musician of today in comparison to that of his predecessors.

Mutilated performances must be traced to intrinsic difficulties. But whatever the cause, we have to face the fact that teachers and students seldom bother with new music because it is unpopular. A vicious circle is closed and it is extremely hard to break. At best one can but try to prove that these conditions are also at the root of poor performances of old music.

Richard Wagner, the last composer to realize how vitally the fate of a new style depends on a convincing reproduction, set out, with his customary thoroughness and energy, to solve the problem by founding the Bayreuth organization. The "Wagner conductor" and the "Wagner singer," who dominated the opera house for decades, are products of a training originated and led by the master himself. It was these specialists who made the relatively fast distribution of Wagner's works possible. Without the Wagner disciples, his music dramas would probably have made their way more gradually; certainly they would not have been spread with the same sectarian furore.

It is much harder for new music to build a comparable organization, since it is not concentrated in such a spectacular center. The most successful effort along this line was made by Arnold Schoenberg when, after the first World War, he founded The Society for Private Musical Performances in Vienna. The idea was to establish an independent forum where worthy contemporary works of every kind, not confined to the output of the Schoenberg circle, would receive the best possible performances before instructed and receptive listeners.

The atmosphere was that of a students' forum, applause being forbidden. Music was supposed to create concentration and insight, instead of amusement and absent-mindedness. After a general program had been outlined, the audience never knew in advance which items would be presented at a specified meeting. In this way, auditors who might have stayed away had they expected to hear the repetition of a difficult work were forced to listen to it several times. On the other hand, they were allowed to attend rehearsals, which were extensive in number and duration. In some cases rehearsals of a piece ran into months, to guarantee a satisfactory rendition. All the participants, even if only one or two were needed for a particular piece, worked under a supervisor, usually one of Schoenberg's pupils. Ample proof of the excellence of the method is found in the fame of interpreters, the Kolisch Quartet among them, who were trained in this intimate community before appearing in public. It is regrettable that the Society's activities came to an end after a few years and have never been revived in the same spirit.

A similar enterprise, but on a large scale, can be recommended for the United States. It could include courses to prepare artists for the authentic presentation of contemporary music under the guidance of the composers.

One might also suggest that the larger schools of music incorporate in their curricula courses of this sort for the advanced students, and present the results of such studies in local music festivals.

Gramophone and Radio

ANYTHING that can be done to train interpreters for their new assignments and, at the same time, open a new access to old tasks, should be approved. Apart from this, while we are occupied with the problem of giving notation a clearer and more definite form, we receive a surprising hint from an unexpected source.

Almost side by side with the rise of new music, the electro-mechanical forms of musical reproduction have experienced an extraordinary impetus. We refer to the gramophone and the radio. These two mechanical devices do not belong to the same category. A gramophone record embodies a performance which may be heard an unlimited number of times in separate places numerically corresponding to the existing copies of it, while performances emanating through the radio are limited to the exact time of their rendition, though audible in a theoretically unlimited number of places.

Both types of reproduction are of a secondary order, the first reproduction being the performance of the work by living musicians in the radio or gramophone studio. From a social point of view, the gramophone is the more aristocratic. Curt Sachs once handsomely compared these mechanisms to the automobile and the railroad. The man owning an exhaustive library of disks can decide the time and destination of his excursion into the land of music, while he who depends on a relatively cheap radio receiving set must adapt himself to the timetable provided by the management.

Productive and interesting research in analyzing the sociological functions and effects of these mechanisms has been done and is still in progress, instigated by the fact that, by unprecedented and ⸱quick methods, the radio and the gramophone have increased the amount of musical reproductions and the number of listeners to an extent never before imagined.

Without losing our way in this subject, little explored as yet, we want to emphasize, as the most evident result of those investigations, that the radio has induced innumerable people to listen simultaneously to the same composition.

But in contrast to the old way of listening to music, a radio audience is not assembled in one place; it is separated into small groups, since people mostly hear the programs in their homes. Thus the character of enjoyment is intensified, but at the expense of its social value. Conditions formerly associated with the pleasure of hearing music, such as freedom from other preoccupations, the wearing of special clothes if the auditor sat in the more expensive seats, and the journey to the auditorium, have been eliminated. The radio listener remains within his own four walls, he does not "dress up," and he can engage in other occupations while the music gushes forth through the loud-speaker.

Radio programs in most countries seem to be based on an assumption on the part of the managements that the average person wants to listen in only when that music is offered which will permit of a desultory, intermittent attention, that is, a type of music in which the spiritual and intellectual demands made in the concert hall are whittled down to match the narrower environment. The sorry picture is lightened a little if we remember that the enormous masses of people brought into contact with music through the radio must contain a percentage who are thus aroused to a real interest in music, and who would never hear so much in any other way. It is perhaps more a matter of temperament than of research whether one is to stress the positive or the negative side of the situation.

One thing is certain; under present circumstances, new music has only an infinitesimal representation on the radio. If the radio audiences were rightly educated, and if the program makers took the proper attitude, broadcasting could be made a singularly appropriate medium for the dissemination of new music. The intimate atmosphere, the lack of diverting formalities and of distracting impressions should help to stimulate the necessary concentration and to engender the attitude of mental and emotional participation which is essential in understanding music of this kind. The listener can smoke, drink, follow the score or walk around, or do other things which may aid his concentration and which he could not do in the concert hall.

To be sure, it would be better not to read the newspaper, play bridge, cook, and chatter—all those interfering occupations which often are carried on when the members of a household listen in. Abuses will be eliminated when the majority of listeners no longer look on radio music as merely a pleasant background for homely affairs. But that will not come to pass for many years.

How Does Music Survive the Ether?

FROM a purely musical standpoint, we are less interested in the sociological considerations raised in profusion by the radio than in the condition of music after it has passed through the ether.

Not only is the production of sound again made invisible, but the sound itself is disguised. At first, musicians and radio technicians were disturbed because the "sound picture" transmitted by the radio deviated greatly from that received in the concert hall. Since then, the machinery has been improved to a remarkable degree; but even today no one with a fairly keen ear will be apt to confuse live music with what comes to him through the loud-speaker. All electro-technical methods of musical reproduction, whether by means of the radio, gramophone, or sound film, have a neutralizing tendency, a uniformity of color, a common dullness of tone. We can easily distinguish the timbres of the various instruments, but differences are drawn closer together, and shades of tones fade into a mist. The listener will know, for instance, that a trumpet is being played; but the radiant, individual, and brilliant quality of its tone, so marked in the concert hall, no longer stands out. The trumpet sound in the loud-speaker symbolizes, so to speak, the trumpet element foreseen in the score, without being itself any more. Moreover, there is a shrinkage of dynamic nuances. No man can release the full force of a symphony orchestra in his room, no matter how inconsiderate of his neighbors he may be. The picture is a more or less blurred miniature of the original. In a peculiar way, the radio withdraws music from the listener after bringing it nearer to him than it was ever brought before.

One of the two tendencies of this metamorphosis promotes the intentions of modern music, while the second runs counter to the new idea. The alienation of tone from its source results naturally from the development followed by orchestration since the romantic period. It was thus a progressive move. The renewed exposition of natural sound elements in the revival of the archaic *concerto grosso* style, and in other "neoclassical" efforts, is as reactionary as stylistic endeavors of this sort must always be.

In so far as the electro-mechanical transmission of music veils the sources of sound, it does not interfere with corresponding tendencies in genuinely new music. On the other hand, the neutralization and withering of nuances and contrasts connected with the transmission run counter to the new movement. The fact that tone colors become symbolic of themselves is not harmful. For new music can and will stand an objectivity, in which instrumental qualities would not be unduly obtruded. But a reduction of nuances and a blurring of their lines of demarcation seem suspicious to those of us who place a high value on clear and incisive articulation.

It might seem easy to evade these detriments by allowing for them in the composition. When writing a string quartet, a composer cannot entertain thoughts he would utilize in a symphony. Similarly, he apparently must consider the limitations of electro-mechanical reproduction if he composes with that medium in mind. Efforts to produce radiogenic music were made years ago in Germany, and have since been carried on elsewhere.

These experiments will be unsuccessful so long as they are based on the idea that the distortion of the tone picture in radio, experienced as disturbing, can be redeemed by special instrumentation. In other words, the plan would so adapt itself to the distortion that the effect would be normal. The basic error here has its roots in the fact that the composer would deliberately accept creative limitations in his work in order to avoid limitations imposed by the machine. No compromise would be possible if the composer refused to tolerate the violence inflicted on his writing. All he would have to do would be to avoid using the machine which causes this violence. At any rate, it is a matter of taste whether the radio composer considers the limitations of radiogenic music compensated by the advantage of avoiding the distortions mentioned above. Be that as it may, the idea of a special type of radio music has miscarried because the public is not worried by distortions. The public would rather hear old, well-known pieces in a twisted form than listen to new works in which the contortion is avoided.

Records "On the Air"

THE acoustical effect of gramophone records played "on the air" is not dissimilar to the impression made by living artists in the broadcasting studio, though there is an obvious psychological difference. One can easily tell whether a pianist is playing in the next room or whether his solo is heard from there through a loudspeaker. It is harder to guess whether the sonata is being performed in the studio or comes from a disk made by the same artist a long time ago. We have three orders of reproduction: 1, Performance; 2, Reproduction of the performance on a gramophone record, or by broadcasting; 3, Radio transmission of the recorded reproduction. The third differs only slightly from the second.

To the chagrin of interpretive artists, radio stations, profiting by this state of affairs, often save money by broadcasting disks in the place of living performances. Few radio experts have given the matter sufficient thought to conclude that only records should be broadcast, not because the procedure is inexpensive, but because the best performances could thus be ensured. As it is musically immaterial to radio listeners whether they hear a live orchestra or a gramophone record of it, test recordings could be made and the best chosen (a procedure similar to the production of a film). The latter idea has not proved acceptable, owing to the extra expense involved.

Identity of the Script and the Sound Picture

THIS train of thought, however, leads to another, newer idea. Could the composition be transferred directly to the mechanical apparatus without the intervention of a human interpreter? The mechanical possibilities of disks have occasionally been tested in experiments along this line, although involving a previous human reproduction of the music. There are, for instance, gramophone records presenting a composition played at normal speed and reproduced at a breath-taking, abnormal pace that cannot be achieved by ordinary means. Sometimes music has been perforated directly into rolls for a mechanical piano without first playing it into the mechanism. Strawinsky and Hindemith have made such experiments. But the notion of composing on a gramophone record still seems preposterous. For who could so engrave the microscopic grooves and notches that a complex tone picture would emerge?

The sound track of moving pictures appears to offer more hope. In this case, the indentations of the disk are represented by a curve in the oscillations of which all the elements of the music played into the microphone are fixed. Development of the process would call for an apparatus which the composer could use to design the curve on a light-sensitive track. The prospect looks adventurous, but not impossible. Film technicians have already experimented with the idea and are reportedly able to distinguish spoken words from music, and orchestral music from the singing of a choir, by looking at the sound track. Experts declare that theoretically the problem is solved. There is nothing, they say, to prevent the production of synthetic sounds of any sort by means of corresponding curves. The one thing lacking is the necessary contrivance to transfer the composer's complex thoughts into the required lines. One cannot imagine drawing the curves with a pencil, no matter how sharply pointed, and then photographing the result. Perhaps experts will work with light rays of varying strength and changing circumference; possibly one might copy superimposed curves and the like; but suppositions like these come from the dreams of an amateur. At any rate, the idea has fascinating ramifications. Who would dare, for instance, to compose an instrumental work in which, perhaps only for a few seconds, the tone of a thousand-voice choir suddenly appeared? The modern composer guilty of such an enormity might be labeled as more of a madman than he is considered anyhow. Yet if the dream comes true, similar and even more startling effects would be no more difficult to produce than a pizzicato on the violin.

The Final Integration of Music into "Literature"

BUT that would be more an achievement than a mere perfecting of a technical operation, for it would complete a gigantic historical process, rounding out the return of notation to sound. The performance of the composition would at the same time constitute its "original," in a sense never dreamed of before. No longer would the script be just a dead symbol of the sound picture, needing the life-giving intervention of an interpreter; it would be identical with the sound picture. A sound track in the library would be as original as a painting on the wall. To hear precisely what the composer wanted people to hear, one would only need to slip the work into a recording machine. The age-long process of identifying music with literature, in its larger sense, would reach its consummation. Although on a different level, the new composition would be as direct a musical utterance as a singer's improvisation in primeval times, before man had thought of notation. The essential difference would consist in the modern version's being disciplined by experience and the rationalization produced by thousands of years of thought. The material of nature would become subject to the creative spirit, to an extent hitherto unimagined.

It is undeniable that there is something horrifying in the prospect. But the element of terror is latent in all technical achievements. As advancing technique subjugates the apparently disorganized and hostile material of nature, the technique itself rises to the height of a new apocalyptic figure; and we have no choice but to strive for the retention of a mastery over powers we have evoked. Once called into action, these powers cannot be arrested or driven back by any pious wish or reactionary moderation, like so many creatures summoned by a "Sorcerer's Apprentice."

Is it not discouraging to fear that the very breath of humanity, man's freedom of subjective interpretation (no matter how restricted by the composer's demand for work-fidelity in a performance), might be stifled in music? Since it is not in my power to carry out the final mechanization, my opinion that it would not prevent living interpretations may have little weight. In the early days of broadcasting, we heard jeremiads about the probable consequent destruction of amateur music making; but if current signs are true, the opposite is coming to pass. Amateurs seem to be encouraged by radio. One is therefore prompted to conjecture that composers' sound-track records of music not otherwise subject to presentation would in no wise retard the performance of other works in the old way. Nor would the procedure dampen the ambition of amateurs to play and sing.

Composers like myself dream of sound-track composition, but not because we seek a further subjugation of expression by rigid mechanical principles. On the contrary (and herein lies the paradox), our goal is complete freedom, united to a clear and significant articulation. One needs no mechanical means of transmission to rattle off music in kinetic-mechanistic fashion. All that is needed for that purpose is the feeling and imagination possessed by the average interpreter. It is rather the complete freedom of expression, so rare today, which would be secured by the definite identification of the score with the sound picture.

CHAPTER   TEN

FROM MINUET TO SWING

A Perpetual Conflict

ONE of the most peculiar phenomena in the present
musical situation is the chasm separating serious music
from products of the so-called "popular," "light," or
"entertainment" variety. That chasm is not so wide in
the United States as it is in Europe, or at least Americans are less conscious of the separation. In Europe,
the distance between the two fields is so marked that
use of the same technical means in each case almost
strikes the observer as strangely coincidental. Yet a
serious composer and a composer of operettas have less
in common than an astronomer and a bootblack; an
atmosphere of somewhat strained courtesy is likely to
be engendered if they meet. The "song writer" admires
the erudition to which he cannot lay claim, and feels
inferior; but, in order to preserve his self-esteem, he
calls attention to the money he makes. The serious composer gazes in astonishment at the other's ill-gotten
gains, envying his colleague's financial success as keenly
as he criticizes the cause of it.

Actually, the distinction between the two trends is
found rather in convictions regarding the social functions of the art than in the approach to music as such.
We cannot deny that the production of music has become as clearly a factor in the capitalistic system as any

other kind of production; the composer depends on the laws governing the system as surely as does the manufacturer of material goods. But at least the serious composer tries to stick to certain immanent principles, even though his loyalty to them blocks his access to the public ear. How long he can manage to live if he persists in maintaining such an unpopular attitude is an incidental question, to be answered individually.

The "popular" composer is released from adherence to the principle which animates his colleague. To him, composition is reasonable only if the largest possible number of persons can be converted into customers willing to spend money on what he writes; and he stands ready to alter his style day by day if the market indicates the advisability of so doing.

Numerous song writers and operetta composers view their craft with a charming kind of melancholy. Nearly every one of them hugs an ambition to write "better" music; this is especially true of creative musicians in Europe, where most composers of operettas began in the serious vein. Memories of prematurely interrupted contrapuntal studies and of frustrated efforts to compose symphonies or operas have not faded from their minds. Many a symphonic fragment reposes in desk drawers; many odd moments are spent in dreams of finishing the incompleted work, as your newspaperman will brood over his unwritten novel or play; and not a few composers allege they are impatient to find an opera libretto that suits their taste. But alas! the right libretto never does appear because the man who waits for it has cast his lot with travelers on a road which does not permit of a return journey. The case of *The Tales of Hoffmann,* composed in Offenbach's old age after his operettas were written, proves nothing; this exception to the general rule was barely made possible by a unique combination of circumstances.

Pathetic excursions made by operetta composers into the higher regions are comparable to the less condonable escapades of serious writers in the nether regions, traceable to an understandable if less elegant desire for money. But in these lower realms the serious composer is destined to be as unsuccessful as his low-brow brother is in higher altitudes. For it is an immutable law that no one can produce below his own level. If he succeeds ostensibly, that merely proves that the lower plane was always the one on which he belonged, and that he never again will rise above it. When a "serious" composer begins to write popular hits, we soon see that in reality he never was a serious composer and that he belongs in the place to which his adventures have led him. It is a mistake for serious composers to suppose, as many do, that it should be easy for them, because of their incomparably more developed technical knowledge, to produce cheap goods by the dozen (like so many neckties) after the manner of the popular song manufacturers. A song in the popular vein is not a success unless it represents the highest plane which its originator can reach, and has cost in proportion as much subjective intensity as a profound string quartet. The man who grinds out banal verses for a popular song text probably struggles as arduously over his rhymes as Goethe did over his immortal poems. If this were not the case, millions of persons would not sing, play, and whistle the hit resulting, in part, from his labor. And indeed, it is puzzling to watch the naïve enthusiasm with which some song-writers go about their low-brow business, as compared with the disappointingly strained attitude of serious composers toward their creative tasks.

Folk Music and Entertainment Music

WAS there always a gulf between serious and entertainment music?

Before answering this question, we must realize that entertainment music, in the present sense of the word, did not exist prior to the industrialization of our civilization, when it replaced the so-called "folk" music. By folk music we mean a type that was supposedly originated and nourished by a socially inferior stratum of the population. One likes to wrap its beginnings in a mystic veil of anonymity; it is believed to have gushed spontaneously from the lips of unnamed and untutored singers, to have spread from mouth to mouth until it gradually took on the unique and magical shape we prize so highly. This assumption is probably largely influenced by the mythological element introduced by elderly civilizations to give them the touch of authenticity and immortality; though it is highly probable that there is some truth in the assumption of anonymity in the origin of folk art. It is undoubtedly true that most of the individuals who have produced folk music are anonymous today, yet it is likely that they were at one time identifiable musicians of special talent. "The people" cannot compose music; the term stands for an abstraction. Composing must be done by an individual. If his melody has undergone various changes in being handed down to posterity, if it has remained consistently racial in character, we still should not deceive ourselves as to its personal origin.

In general, medieval art music showed little respect for the folk music of its day, considering it both vulgar and profane in contrast to works which were exclusively sacred. A more significant reason for this attitude certainly was the fact that the indigenous European, symmetrical-scanning concept prominent in folk music was a source of danger to the freely articulated polyphony of art music. The point is still important, for all "light" music, including the type used for modern entertainment, has always embraced this component. Freely articulating entertainment music organized as prose has never existed. Popular music is thoroughly identified with social dancing, which demands the simplest possible metrical relations, realized in four- or eight-bar periods.

Art Music Absorbs Folklore Elements

IT IS evident that the chasm was narrowed when the symmetrical-scanning concept gained the upper hand, that is, in the epoch of tonality. Composers of the Renaissance, whose sacred vocal music was still connected with the freely articulated style of the Middle Ages, left an extensive collection of secular choral works in which they made use of the song and dance structures developed by folk music. The first characteristic instrumental form produced by tonality—the suite —came about in such a way. Composers of that day were lucky in their ability to express vital (and progressive) ideas in a popular and intelligible form. Bach's suites, numbered among his most personal and expressive works, are sublimated presentations of relatively primitive and folklike architecture. But anyone who imagines the situation to have been ideal should remember that these works were not generally liked, as we are inclined to believe a folkloristic type of music must be. With all their crystal clarity, Bach's suites did not penetrate beyond a strictly limited circle. In the end, the personal sublimation probably proved stronger than the folkloristic quality, which is what one would naturally expect. It is not the latter element that gives such music its imperishable nature, but the personal note which the master introduces in his conscious aloofness from the material on which he builds.

However desirable we imagine these conditions to have been, we must remember that the inevitable changes in history brought them to an end. The minuet was the only dance form to be retained in the sonata, that higher development of the suite. And, in common with other suite dances, the minuet had already become less folklike music than entertainment music, composed by skilled musicians for the social needs of a special class. The minuet could not long maintain its position in the sonata; soon it was stylized into the scherzo, in which the dance idea was presented in various imaginative forms. In so far as elements of real folk dances appear in the symphonic music of the nineteenth century, they increasingly show the character of exotic quotations from remote materials. This was in line with the disintegration of the universal music of classicism into national divisions.

Entertainment Music Absorbs Art Elements

FROM then on, we find alterations in the character of folk music within the sphere of Western civilization. Art music of the tonal epoch approached it so closely that folk music could not escape the cultured influence. The extensive absorption and sublimation of folkloristic elements by art music generated a process·that led in the opposite direction. Music that was now to be accepted by classes of society who did not participate in the consumption of art music was nourished less by new and original forces from beneath than by deposits seeping down from the stratum of deliberate art. Folk songs of the nineteenth century are mostly art songs in imitation of the folk type, while still drawing on those art elements of the preceding period which had been most acceptable to "simple people." This reabsorption of art elements by folk music banalized these elements and thus urged art music to increase the speed of its progress.

At that point, folk music became entertainment music. A quasi-spontaneous production of music by the social class intending to use it was replaced by a systematic manufacture by professionals, who held a position analogous to agents selling merchandise to the masses. The transaction is similar to the peasants' purchase of cloth, factory made instead of, as formerly, woven by themselves, for the garments they wear on their farms. The same phenomenon is visible in the character of the picturesque country costumes whose conservation is exploited as a national interest by soil-minded fanatics. Usually the origin of such apparel is remote from the mystic imagination of the rustics themselves. A stylistic analysis of European peasant costumes shows them to be chiefly simplified imitations of what was worn at eighteenth-century courts.

The birth of modern entertainment music is also related to the fact that the class known as "the people" was supplemented in the nineteenth century by a type which had been of less importance, namely, the urban proletariat. From the first, the proletarian cared little for the old kind of folk music, preferring to be entertained by music which suggested the pastimes of the rich but was easier to understand and less expensive. One of the reasons why entertainment music follows hard on the heels of art music is thus made clear. Even if the "jitterbug" or "alligator" has never heard a composition by Debussy, he will instinctively notice that an especially delectable morsel is being served up to him when in fact the swing arranger has despoiled the lovely arsenal of Debussy's harmony.

It was approximately in the time of Johann Strauss the First that folk music changed definitely into entertainment music. Many of his compositions differed but little in form or manner from the dance movements of Franz Schubert. A number of Strauss waltzes might easily have been written by Schubert, but not one of Schubert's symphonies or sonatas could have been composed by Strauss. By using all the root words of classical and early romantic music to suit his purpose, Strauss was able to exploit the product on a large commercial scale.

Wagner and Offenbach

THE real break started in the days of Richard Wagner. When he spoke of *Zukunftsmusik* ("music of the future"), he consciously laid down the rule that henceforth the evolution of art music would be in advance of the average audience's capacity to understand it. In this way, art music received a pseudosacred ordination; its creators demanded that it be lifted above the profane sphere, that it be reserved exclusively for the initiated as the hallowed emanation of an exalted spirit. The newly developed and disdainful attitude of art musicians toward the entertainment of the *profanum vulgus* had its origin in this state of mind.

Wagner's counterpart in the field of entertainment music was Jacques Offenbach, a musico-dramatist of a totally different sort but one who equaled him as a theatrical composer. Offenbach's sound language was simple almost to the point of being reactionary. In a way, it was an apotheosis of tonal basic facts and square periodicity. He used the plainest harmonic relationships and metrical proportions. Despite technical limitations (which make the dreaded handcuffs of twelve-tone writing look very harmless indeed), Offenbach's work is sparkling and vivacious because he happens to have been one of the most inspired composers of all times. The restriction of his music to the fundamental, venerable elements of the tonal order, at the time of its impending dissolution, was made possible only by its association with the merry disorder of the operetta. The result was an extraordinary dialectic mixture. A smooth, masterly surface of unsurpassable simplicity masked Offenbach's recognition of the fact that the "old" sense could not be saved except by the utter nonsense of a feather-light stage world where normal logic led to absurdities. One cannot imagine chamber music or symphonies written by Offenbach in the sound language of his operettas, or rather, one can picture them only as empty salon music animated by a somewhat tedious wit.

When Offenbach's music was heard in conjunction with the silly but profound fantasies which his librettists conjured up in the theater, it showed the trickiness of a magic box with a false bottom. The composer's public, compelled to restrain its political dislike of dictatorship under Napoleon III to innocuous laughter, was forced to take what Offenbach gave them as harmless entertainment, as we can also. At the same time, to those "in the know," the Offenbach operettas constitute a *mene tekel* inscribed on the tottering foundations of a crumbling order and turning the elements of artistic order into a laughing, anarchical means of expression. Offenbach is an early and rare case of *montage* in music, in whose works we find the superimposed blending and combination of heterogeneous elements belonging to different stages of history. When surrealists look to the atmosphere of the Second Empire for inspiration, their preference for the period may, in part, be accounted for by the circumstance that Offenbach belonged to it.

His *opera seria, The Tales of Hoffmann,* is a unique, inimitable opus. At that time, it was still possible to write a real opera with his restricted musical means, enlarged to an insignificant extent for the purpose. These means permitted the creation, on the basis of the old musical comedy and the *opéra comique,* of a serious opera showing many traits of an operetta. Bizet's *Carmen* and some of Verdi's early operas were along the same line; but Offenbach's accomplishments in the field of the true operetta are incomparably more important. He confronted an order that was intact with its own inevitable suspension, its progressive decay.

The Viennese Operetta

OFFENBACH has had no successors. It was impossible for anyone to succeed him. Though his style appeared to be poised, it was rather the product and symbol of a catastrophic crisis. Composers of Viennese operettas who came after him took over the leadership in the realm of musical entertainment, but soon branched out on a different path. The Offenbach tradition did not outlive a few products of the sixties and seventies (en-

chanting to this day), developing instead the pernicious
ambition to give operettas the likeness of operas. It is
true that Johann Strauss the Second wrote many de-
lightful waltzes; but if he had been a true dramatist he
never would have tried to carry the profound nonsense
of the Offenbach scores into the saltless stupidity of *The
Bat* and *The Gypsy Baron*. To be sure, the light music
of the latter part of the nineteenth century sounds
graceful and genteel compared to what gushed over the
world through the Viennese operetta of the twentieth
century; but already Strauss was at home among the
ruins. The operetta as Offenbach had perfected it, the
elegant beacon in a crisis, had ceased to exist. Instead,
there remained only its victim, unworthy of pity.

Circumstances which finally caused the downfall of
the Viennese operetta were tragi-comical. The question
was one of somehow keeping pace with the steady and
rapid progress of the sound language used in serious
music. Neither subjectively nor objectively was it possible for composers of operettas to imbue the old material with the freshness, elegance, and incisive power
of an Offenbach. They had less imagination and fewer
ideas. Moreover, the decay of tonality had progressed
too far. But, above all, the liking for theatrical irony,
responsible for Offenbach's music, had died out. People
began to think of his heavenly nonsense as stupid and
old-fashioned. They wanted the operetta to show some
of that "dignity" which the *petite bourgeoisie* deemed
an indispensable ingredient of everyday life. Thus
began the era of a brutish seriousness, tying the entire
world to that horrible discipline which deadens the
sense of humor.

At the same time, it seemed necessary to retard musical progress as much as possible, since its progressive

tendency had rendered serious music unpopular and unsuitable for industrial purposes. By the turn of the century, light music had clearly become an appendage of big business. Stockholders of large publishing houses, allied with widely branching theatrical concerns, dictated its production.

Before long, the operetta composer had ceased to be enthusiastic over his job. In addition to suffering embarrassment as the slave of his subjective craving for money, he was also, *de facto*, caught in the apparatus of production. There remained gratifying exceptions, as, for instance, Oscar Straus in his earlier days, and Leo Fall with his fine taste, whose compositions were often technically quite clever. But, by and large, the Viennese operetta after the last war slumped into an unspeakable desolation. The music became jellyfishy, bombastic, shapeless, and uninspired. It was over-orchestrated, while its substance shriveled. A kind of entertainment music arose in Vienna that infected even the backward serious music in that city; both became empty and ornate. The light music of Europe had been brought to bay exactly where the most radical transformation of serious music had taken place, namely, in Vienna.

Jazz

In its death struggle, the Viennese operetta had occasionally administered to itself mild injections of a tonic imported after the war under the name of *jazz*—naturally without success. The treatment, probably considered homeopathic by the incurably naïve patient, was bound to have a bad ending. Jazz was not a medicine to stimulate an exhausted invalid; its effect was what the photographers call "too contrasty."

This contrast could best be observed in the attitude of jazz composers to the progress of serious music. Unlike the timid and sentimental old-style composers of operettas who longed for higher regions, they took a cynical view of their "serious" contemporaries.

Your jazz arranger is "ready, willing, and able" at the drop of a hat to adopt any daring harmony conquered by art music. No Schoenberg chord, no matter how passionately stigmatized in the concert hall as a diabolical cacophony, is safe from quotation in the variation chorus of a popular song orchestration. The musical significance of the "crazy" chords invented by his serious colleague does not interest the jazz arranger for a second; all that concerns him is their momentary effect as a stimulant. If and how these harmonic "extravaganzas" can be made a part of the tonal order, or whether they tend to explode it, is no affair of jazz.

The mad eccentricities of jazz music, and the fanatical effect this music has had on a large section of humanity, have set many pens in motion in an effort to trace the grandiose character of this demiart. Legends of its origin and the miracles it has worked are legion. To those of us who are concerned only with the purely musical aspects of jazz, it should not be too difficult to explain the phenomenon, though the result of our meditations may not exactly be in the nature of a dithyramb.

Let us grant, for the moment, that jazz generally takes an unscrupulous attitude toward the traditional choice of musical elements, and of harmonic elements in particular, since the latter are the most direct characteristics of the sound language. How, then, does jazz manufacture the element of "balance," discussed at length in these pages and recognized as indispensable to the music of Western man? If special care were not taken to embody an obvious "balance" in jazz, this type of composition would not differ greatly from real atonal music and would be as unpopular as atonality. We know that the increase in the arsenal of harmonic means, brought about by atonal music, was not prompted by cynicism, and that atonality has developed new forms of "balance"; but the unfamiliar aspect worn by atonality is due to the fact that these new forms, no matter how articulate they may become, are not easily understood by the average listener.

Attempts made by jazz to keep a palpable "balance" in its idiom—an idiom extended to extreme limits—are realized in an unswerving adherence to the eight-measure, periodic, symmetrical-scanning meter. Regardless of what happens between the regularly distributed caesuras of jazz music, the listener can always depend on a clearly defined break after four or eight bars, emphasized by a safe landing on a harmonic step belonging to the fundamental key, or at least belonging to a key that is close to it. By this means his orientation in the exciting harmonic terrain between the periods is ascertained.

The excitement is not due to harmonic boldness alone, but rather—and here we find the mainspring of the jazz extravaganzas—to apparently unrestrained disturbances of the meter, the so-called syncopations. Accents within the two breaks which ensure the regular period are quite freely distributed, without regard to the constant meter underlying the composition as a whole.

Extravaganza and Normality in Jazz

AT THE outset, jazz used real syncopes. In each case the accents were shifted from the strong beat of the underlying meter to the contiguous weak beat. But the meter, generally a normal quadruple rhythm, was invariably carried through, mostly by the piano, the bass drum, or the banjo, no matter how far the other instruments might have gone astray in the syncopation. The dull, heavy, unobtrusive throbbing of this central mechanism vibrated with a soothing regularity throughout the piece like a ship's engine, unaffected by raging gales above. Subsequently the technique of syncopation in jazz underwent extension and refinement. I am not in a position to verify and interpret the findings of many detailed and learned investigations into the fine distinctions between "hot," "sweet," "swing," "boogie woogie" and similar nuances. It seems to me that these gradations, in addition to having certain sound characteristics, are chiefly differentiated by the way in which the thoroughly primitive metrical proportions of the basic arrangement can be screened and ostensibly suspended.

The essential feature of jazz, however, is the *fictitious* suspension of the simple metrical fundamental scheme. Harmonic and rhythmic happenings within the individual sections may be arbitrary; the music may move without restraint between points that are fixed at regular distances; but under all circumstances the tonal coordination of the harmonic caesuras and the subterranean meter are imperturbably maintained.

When we interpret jazz in relation to the present condition of Western music, we find it a logical conse-

quence of efforts to retain tonality in entertainment
music, while also including as many of the new elements as possible. In respect to the latter detail, jazz
can go much further than it was possible for the Viennese operetta to travel. For jazz can, with impunity,
make use of many more elements of the later tonality,
and can even employ numerous elements unavailable
before the advent of atonality. Jazz is able to neutralize
these ingredients within its extremely primitive but
mechanically exact metrical framework.

The machinelike frame is America's contribution to
later tonality. Every example of "progress," every refinement of compositional means in the realm of the
Viennese operetta, pointed to the disintegration of
tonality as caused by the progressive tendencies in
serious music. The fate of the Viennese operetta was
sealed when it had to shun progress or face destruction
of the conditions under which it had existed.

Jazz and "Serious" Modern Music

HOWEVER, in the elementary simplicity of the basic
metrical conditions established by jazz, entertainment
music found a last chance to participate, if only partially, in the progress being made in the new material.
Inherent audacities were domesticated by a rhythmical
arrangement of a hitherto unknown rigidity and precision. The attentive reader may detect the close affinity
between this principle and that represented by Strawinsky. It is no accident that Strawinsky was one of the first
to apply the intonation of jazz to the new art music.

Many composers who worried over the salvation or
re-establishment of tonality have resorted to jazz as a
method of regeneration. For a time I was one of them.

Jazz is progressive as to material, but conservative so far as its ultimate attitude and effect are concerned. If the propagandists of certain current political ideologies prohibit the use of jazz, they have in mind its progressive leanings, and hope to strike through it at a concept of Americanism and democracy which, in their minds, is bound up with arbitrariness, immorality, debauchery, and the supremacy of an "inferior race"—the Negro. When a few experimental musicians resorted to jazz some fifteen years ago, they likewise interpreted the new movement as progressive and American, but associated it with ideas of youth, power, originality, directness, and vitality. The fact that jazz represents the last grandiose attempt of tonality to hide its disintegration was overlooked by erstwhile proponents of the popular novelty and has since been unrecognized by its opponents.

According to the dialectics governing antithetic concepts, such as "progress" and "reaction," jazz performs a progressive task in spite of its reactionary trend. There can be no doubt that the fanatical partisans of jazz will automatically show more tolerance toward serious modern music than is entertained by persons who occupy themselves with "semiclassical" salon music or with diluted or adulterated performances of poorly chosen classical works. Condensation of heterogeneous elements, abrupt changes in color, and rhythmic complications that elude exact notation, all call for an uncommon receptivity and presence of mind on the listener's part. Even though the finesses of jazz can be reduced to a number of formulae, constantly repeated, a very precise aural refinement, hitherto unnecessary in listening to entertainment music, is required to grasp them promptly and properly.

It is interesting to note that even the difference

between the powerful leading melody and the subordinated accompaniment has been cut down in the latest jazz. I have noticed in many new swing arrangements a lack of perspective and comprehensibility which, though apparently no hindrance to their popularity, would doubtless be criticized in a serious composition. One may therefore assume that the jazz fans of today have acquired a keener ear and a quicker intelligence than those professional critics who still insist that a modern score is "rhythmically amorphous," that it disintegrates into fragments of motifs, and that it is short-winded and disconnected whenever its melodies fail to rest on simple harmonic foundations and are not served up to the auditor by a solid brigade of string players.

Add to this, as a second pedagogical principle, the indescribable and amazing technical perfection of the jazz bands. They have developed a proficiency far in excess of anything previously believed possible in instrumental ensemble playing. If Europe's contribution to twentieth-century musical history has been atonality, we can say that the contribution of the United States, equally important, is jazz and the upsurge of instrumental technique. Yet, just as a jazz audience, despite its mental alertness and its intelligent auditory development, is still unprepared when facing atonality, so are the most marvelous jazz musicians generally helpless if asked to play atonal music, although its problems are, in the main, not unlike those presented by jazz, and often technically simpler. The difficulty is caused by the interference of the conservative element in jazz—its adherence to the tonal cadence and the regular meter. It must be stated that, in the final analysis, this conservative element obliterates the progressive tendencies of jazz.

The Factor of Improvisation

ANOTHER handicap can be traced to the fact that jazz musicians have perfected much of their incredible dexterity through improvisation. Their technical faculties would be contradicted as well as the character of the "liberties" they take if they were to indulge in these "liberties" according to fixed notations. Here the dialectics common to atonality and to jazz are seen in a nutshell. In order to guarantee the everlasting freedom of music, atonality has turned the art into the apparently inflexible image of literature, using the magic symbols of exact notation. Jazz, bent on preserving the shackles of tonal relationships, has revived the art of improvisation to an extent unknown by serious musicians since the days of the *super librum cantare,* the contrapuntal extemporization of the fifteenth century. This factor, too, indicates an essential difference between jazz and the earlier types of entertainment music in which improvisation had no part. In the era of truce, when serious music absorbed many traits of folklore, entertainment music, as a sort of equivalent, also came in for a share of the literary unction which serious music poured out in ever increasing measure. Meanwhile, entertainment music fell by the wayside. Betrayed by serious music, it appealed to improvisation for help.

When I discuss Schoenberg and atonality with Americans, I am often asked: "And what about Gershwin?" "What do you think about swing music?" Such questions are hard to answer, showing an amazing naïveté on the part of the questioners, who seem to take the equality of these phenomena for granted. It is as if an eighteenth-century musician who talked about Mozart had been asked what he thought of Haydn. But even if (probably wrongly) one supposes the questioner to be as sophisticated as the intricate dialectics of the problem demand, the answer will hardly be easier to supply.

I have here attempted to offer such a reply.

CHAPTER   ELEVEN

WHAT MUST WE DO?

Music and Politics

THE circle is closed.

Reflections recorded in these pages began with a survey of the general music situation, bringing to light many contradictory and problematic phenomena. The survey led to a thorough analysis of the contemporary production of music, a production which is the essence and soul of musical life. Next came an examination of new methods of composition to prove their relation to the history of Western music and to the evolution of modern society. The road leading from the composer's hand to the ear of the listener, and many new issues, have been examined. Finally, we discussed the function of entertainment music, the focal point of public interest. It remains to deal with the question of how to eliminate, or at least how to reduce, obstacles that stand in the way of a real and productive contact with the essential values of music, and of new music in particular.

The central problem is to raise the listener to a higher state of consciousness. This idea has been carried through my later arguments as a leading motif. I pointed out the obstacles to such an interpretation of music, also indicating the reason (partly intrinsic and partly extraneous) why the most progressive type of new music encounters special difficulties in fulfilling its mission of intensifying spiritual clarity. Before discussing ways and means of suitably expanding this function, I should like to present an essential idea, namely, that attempts to give new music its proper recognition can succeed only in an atmosphere of political liberalism. I will even go so far as to say that this atmosphere is essential for such attempts.

Like all other terms of the same kind, the expression "political liberalism" has been made so ambiguous by its use as a slogan that it calls for comment in the present case. The word "liberal" has different meanings in America and in Europe. In Europe, a man is "liberal" when he believes in the free interplay of economic forces within the capitalistic system, in representative government, and in the rights of man. In the United States, the label often hints at subversion, revolution, and socialism. Americans frequently give the word the connotation it had in Europe in 1848, when it was on the tongue of alarmed aristocrats. While "liberalism" in Europe today is an old-fashioned creed, in America the word still is tinged with insinuations of a veiled menace.

Causes of this divergence are not pertinent here; but the distinction must be understood when the word is inevitably used. When I say that new music has a chance of success only in an atmosphere of "political liberalism," I interpret the term as applying neither to an old-fashioned social condition (as in the European sense) nor to revolutionary and subversive plots (according to the American interpretation). All I have in mind is a social order in which the individual's spiritual freedom has no barriers except those imposed by the frailty of human nature; an order in which man is not hampered by barriers other than those separating the field of knowledge from the realm of faith, and the natural world from the sphere of the supernatural.

It is not for me to judge whether the free interplay of economic forces and the principles of representative government—capitalism and democracy—are insepara- bly related. Nor am I in a position to determine whether these principles furnish the best or the only guarantee of the spiritual attitude just mentioned. It is easy enough to refer to the terrible offenses against human dignity and spiritual liberty which have oc- curred in history under the colors of democracy and in the name of capitalism. But until now no proof has been forthcoming that mankind has fared better under any other political and economic conditions. Even if one were to agree with the opponents of capitalism and democracy that high ideals are used as excuses for exploitation and licentiousness (and no valid argu- ments are available to support this claim), that agree- ment would not prove that human dignity and spiritual freedom would be better served in a politico-economic order under administrators who consider both these concepts of secondary importance at best, if, indeed, they do not spurn them with cynical sneers—as they have repeatedly done.

No; these values are not created or guaranteed by political systems, though such systems can destroy them, as we know only too well. On the other hand, the secu- rity of political democracy seems to rest on a recogni- tion of the moral and intellectual ideals under consid- eration. Abandon the ideals, and democracy would expire, to be succeeded by a regime which would annihilate them. In so far as cognizance of moral and intellectual values is intimately connected with man's spiritual clarity and independence, the art of music,

creating the highest degree of consciousness, is a means
of promoting it. Music will be apprehended in proportion to a comprehension of freedom and order, attributes which are found in the good music of all times
and styles. Totalitarian enemies of liberty, profiting by
the teachings of a liberalism that has grown weary, have
no need to persecute the old music, since these teachings tear every type of music from its ethical setting and
exhibit it as a mere museum piece. Music that is really
new must be prohibited by such an attitude, because
its spiritual implication is still too vigorous to be
silenced or reinterpreted for reactionary purposes.

New music does not oppose democracy and capitalism or champion either fascism or communism. It has
nothing to do with any of these creeds. Instead, as an
expression of freedom and dignity, new music is related
to democracy to the extent that democracy promotes
the ambition to be and do right.

. The values which democracy exists to preserve do
not subsist by themselves; they are not guaranteed by
the abstract letter of the law. The public must be educated to a conviction of their importance if the best
constitutional provisions are to have sense and power.
From this it follows that new music, in its very nature,
will be an effective pedagogical means in the long
array of methods to be employed in improving the
education of humanity. But this is a long-range project.

Organizations for New Music

WHAT can be done in the meantime to bring those who
have outgrown the current educational processes to a
better understanding of new music, and to a more
thorough preoccupation with it? As the larger peda-

gogical ideas have not been carried out to any great extent and cannot take effect without the passage of time, many future generations will need to strive for contact with new music. For this reason, the problem of an immediate, practical mode of operation is as important as the pedagogical question itself. The first and most obvious suggestion that comes to mind is to provide opportunities for listening to works by the new composers. It is clear that the constant hearing of new music, under the most unconstrained circumstances, trains the ear and the spirit, and leads to an appreciation on which public demand can be based. We know that ordinary "official" music institutions are inadequate for the task. For this reason, special organizations have been dedicated to the propagation and cultivation of the new art.

Associations of this sort all suffer from a common fate—the steady battle against economic hardships which is involved in the nature of such enterprises. If wealthy people who like to spend money on music were sufficiently interested in new music, it would be given in the "official" concerts they support, and special organizations would then be unnecessary. Under the pressure of economic and political crises, a situation has developed in Europe which I once jokingly described as follows: The man who organizes concerts of modern music expects to get the hall and the music gratis; he expects the performers to contribute their services free of charge; and the public expects free tickets of admission.

Unfortunately this picture is not greatly exaggerated. The landlord can rent the hall for more lucrative programs, the music dealer can sell music that is more popular, and the performer can reproduce music that

is in greater demand. The one person who has no re-
dress is the composer, for if he is honest in his aim, he
can write nothing but "modern" music. And yet, the
composer is the only one who is not allowed to complain. He is reminded that the landlord, the music
dealer, and the interpreter can never receive enough
praise for their sacrifices on his behalf; and if he ac-
cepts the conditions as less than heavenly, he is given
to understand that he should offer heartfelt thanks to
those who have condescended to bring his absurd
production to performance. What! Has this ungrateful
wretch forgotten the advertising value of the performance? He should make a virtue of necessity, and not try
to reap the fruits of his labor before seedtime.

The unfortunate soul will only make matters worse
if he tries to point out that for many years he has enjoyed the unquestionable privilege of unpaid performances, hoping thereby to spread propaganda for the
future. He will then acquire the reputation of a
troublemaker and a querulous fellow, and further
chances for free performances will be nullified by the
opprobrium.

To the honor of those who organize special performances of new music, it must be said that they do not
allow the composer to go away empty-handed while
they fill their own pockets. American societies which
busy themselves with new music are in a more comfortable position than their companions in Europe,
where, in spite of the depression prevailing here, economic conditions are considerably less favorable. For
all that, it is deplorable that societies for new music in
the United States are outnumbered by those in the Old
World. It is more to be regretted that chapters of Pro
Musica, which have rendered valiant service and still

try to keep up the good work, have shrunk to an evanescent quota.

The danger in all organisms set in motion for missionary purposes is that their number is increased mostly through procreation by cleavage. When a society for the propagation of modern music is formed, one can generally assume that two or three similar bodies will soon spring into being, owing to disagreements between the original members over aesthetic and personal matters. One is sure to find energetic committee members who will secede and form a new association to prove to the "rump" organization "how it really should be done." It is just as certain that within a short time in the town or city which was the scene of the movement, opportunities to hear new music will be fewer than ever, though the originators of the split may cling tenaciously to their position and hold agitated, if sterile, executive sessions—with precious little advantage to modern music.

Up to now, associations that have best stood the test of time have been those directed by individuals or by a small group of enthusiasts sharing the same convictions and united by mutual confidence. Such a group may undertake exactly as much as it can account for. It does not need bureaucratic committees who are in the habit of diluting results as well as responsibilities.

I have hinted so little in these pages at sympathy with any kind of dictatorship that I may now venture the opinion that the wisest artistic decisions are rarely made through democratic methods. Compromise is undoubtedly the elixir of life in political democracies. When representatives elected by taxpayers cannot agree on how the tax money is to be spent—whether on armaments or on housing—a middle course offers not only

the one possibility for the continuance of that democratic society, but, in a sense, a fair solution of the
question. But the compromise which democracy must
adopt in politics should be the price paid by that
democracy for promoting intransigence in the field of
spiritual efforts.

In Europe, reactionary opponents of radically new
music continually bring the charge that it belongs to a
"clique" or a "party" who would force it down the
throat of an innocent public by terroristic methods.
Unfortunately, the accusation is false. It is difficult to
imagine how, with weapons no more formidable than
pencil and music paper, one could terrorize the adherents of century-old institutions that appear unshakable,
and it is to be lamented that new music is not the
cement of indissoluble cliques. Its reputation and the
fate of works wrought in its name have not benefited
from the tolerant and correct deportment of its representatives; but they do not regret their decent conduct.
Certainly, in the long run, the enemies of new music
will have profited even less by their contrary behavior.

The "I.S.C.M."

THE one noteworthy organization in the service of
modern music is The International Society for Contemporary Music, founded in Salzburg on the initiative of
a few Austrian musicians, soon after the first World
War. The Society's original aim was to re-establish between musicians of different countries the contacts
which had been interrupted by the war; but the first
session, featuring notable performances of contemporary music, was not accomplished without arousing
palpable, if muted, displeasure in some local circles.

In this connection, it is not uninteresting to look into the mentality which had cost new music its right to live in certain countries where the art was labeled "Jewish" and "Bolshevistic." We have already dealt with the question of Bolshevism and new music. So far as the position of Jews in the first rank of new music is concerned, I know only two, Schoenberg and Milhaud, the majority of their confreres being as "Aryan" as the most rigorous Board of Racial Examiners could wish.

It was decided, at that first meeting in Salzburg, to continue the sessions at yearly intervals; but, for the reasons just mentioned, to alter the original plan of always assembling in the Austrian city to one of congregating in different countries in rotation. The object of a flexible organization was to absorb, as national sections, both the existing local associations and those yet to be formed. To Professor Edward J. Dent, of Cambridge, England, the eminent musical historian, was entrusted the presidency of a conference, made up of delegates from all sections, to be held in connection with yearly festivals. The act of localizing the central bureau in England introduced a method of democratic compromise which has, perhaps, enabled the Society to exist until today but which certainly has narrowed its function in the cause of new music.

Following the practice of democratic procedure, the delegates elected a jury to build programs for the festival. When the jurymen endeavored to bring out the phenomena of new music, they were bitterly accused of partisanship; and when they tried to please everyone, they pleased no one, since everyone complained that the fare was inferior.

A witness of the sessions over a period of several years could gain therefrom an aesthetic pleasure, though his enjoyment might be colored with melancholy thoughts as he saw how minutely, in details of internal politics, the musicians reflected simultaneous phases of the League of Nations. The German section disappeared even before Germany withdrew from Geneva. A section from Soviet Russia, which had existed at the time of the Society's organization, was forever on the point of being reorganized; so far, this plan has miscarried because at first no really serious expression of intention was procurable from Moscow, and because later participation involved ideological demands which the English bureau viewed with suspicion. The most vital activity was found in the sections representing smaller countries. Austria provided the strongest spiritual impetus, while Czecho-Slovakia furnished the greatest organizational energy. A solid block of musicians held together in the smaller countries and might have constituted a majority in decisive polls had they not, on the actual field of battle, and after many wild speeches, chosen discretion as the better part of valor and followed the lead of the "big ones," England, France, and Italy, in favoring an adjournment of decisions *sine die*—again, just like their political confreres.

In the years of apparent "stabilization," that is, until about 1931, the Society declined into apathy. It seemed to lack an objective as soon as modern music had acquired the rights of citizenship in most official institutions. Many serious musicians lost interest in having their works performed at the Society's festivals, feeling that the programs were often insufficiently prepared and that better performances could be obtained elsewhere.

The passive stand taken by progressive composers of central Europe toward the Society was abandoned from

1933 on, owing to vehement reactions in their countries which ended all illusions of "stabilization." The western European sections watched the turnabout of the "radicals" with rather mixed feelings. The former had settled down into a comfortable *juste milieu* with "healthy modernism," and objected to being berated for developing the Society into an association *against* new music. Professor Dent spent many anxious hours in trying to ward off, with his figurative umbrella, the deluge of criticism pouring in from all sides.

The "Conseil Permanent"

THE entire Society finally achieved a slightly firmer position by the alarming organization in Germany of the so-called *"Conseil Permanent pour la Collaboration Internationale des Compositeurs,"* which owed its genesis to Richard Strauss and was established according to the principles of its country. Every section in the I.S.C.M. is completely independent and sends elected delegates to the Society's yearly plenary meetings. Representatives of the *Conseil* in various countries, on the other hand, are appointed by the central bureau—in other words, by Richard Strauss and certainly not against the will of the authorities to whom he must kowtow; and these representatives, in turn, choose the music for the *Conseil* festivals.

Since it was impossible for many sections of the I.S.C.M. to take part in the festivals without the support of their respective governments, there arose the fear that in certain countries only personal or political considerations on the part of *Conseil* representatives, taking orders from Berlin, would ensure official endorsement and that only music approved by the central bureau of the *Conseil* could penetrate abroad.

Not much has been heard from the *Conseil* since it organized a few festivals, which were more notable for the enormous amount of music performed than for the quality of it. Apparently the *Conseil* later concentrated its energies on an interchange of concerts based on a transfer of the economic barter system to the cultural field. After German music was played in foreign countries, a corresponding amount from those countries was given in Germany.

The salutary effect of the alarm caused by the *Conseil* in the rank of the I.S.C.M. was immediately seen in the marked improvement of the latter's festivals, with a few fluctuations, from 1934 on. People realized that new music and the I.S.C.M. were together struggling for existence and that a "sound modernism" was no longer sufficient.

The Festivals of the I.S.C.M.

NORMAL objections to the festivals may be enumerated as follows:

1. The overwhelming majority of the works given are bad.
2. The concerts are too long.
3. The various nations represented do not receive equal consideration, the works from different countries being unevenly distributed.

We grant all that. But the first two objections are based on the false premise that a music festival is an entertainment. Many a man who buys a concert ticket mistakes it for an insurance policy for enjoyment; and if most people feel cheated at isolated concerts, audiences at a festival must have much the same reaction. Characteristically enough, those who get in free as "also musicians," critics, colleagues, or "friends" express the bitterest disappointment.

Naturally it is not always a pleasure to listen to several difficult new works presented often by mediocre performers. But musicians, irrespective of whether or not they happen to be named on the program, should appreciate the fact that festivals of the kind under discussion provide the only opportunities of hearing such music. Therefore it should not be too much to ask that they spend a few days in studying a problem which so vitally concerns them.

The third objection—that not all nations involved have equal representation—can be advanced only by a critic who forgets that music is not produced by groups, by races or classes, but by individuals. A commentator who is ruled by such a quantitative sense of justice is forced to turn for justification to the barter system in which artistic values are relegated to the background to make way for an indulgence in national inferiority complexes. It is clear that the cause of music cannot be furthered by these arguments.

Numerous complaints have been to the effect that the American section of the I.S.C.M. has not taken so active a part in the Society's affairs as would be commensurate with the size of the country and the importance of its composers. Two causes contribute to this state of things: the geographical distance separating the United States from Europe, and the American isolationist creed as evidenced in political as well as in artistic attitudes. The interest of many American delegates to festivals has been limited to perplexed head-shakings over the endless and (to them) unintelligible, embittered quarrels of their European colleagues. I have no wish to prophesy or to advise, but I believe that the Society's future rests to a great extent in the hands of the American section. Since the influence of progressive members in central and eastern Europe has been reduced (if not wiped out) by political developments, the function of production is inherited by the United States; and much will depend on this country in the realization and solution of the problems involved.

Must Opera Perish?

IT IS in the nature of things that organizations like the I.S C.M. and its branches can most easily devote themselves to chamber music. It is more difficult to handle orchestral works, and almost impossible to produce opera. I have already discussed the trend of operatic management. Repertory opera houses forming a compact network in central Europe were the only ones concerned to an appreciable degree with modern productions, and now that they have been eliminated the new opera has practically no home. The few stages that might be available—those in New York, Paris, Brussels, and Stockholm, for instance—belong to the representative social type. Their use for new works is prohibited by psychological, traditional, financial, and organizational reasons, no matter how keenly interested some of the leading officials may be.

Under these circumstances, one might be tempted to consider the development of opera as a dead issue for the time being. With no rich operatic life continuing outside central Europe, we see that no need of it is felt elsewhere—and we are forced to accept the situation.

It seems indeed hopeless to try to transfer the old European repertory opera house system to the Anglo-Saxon world, the only field now worthy of consideration. In England, persistent and extended efforts to replace the short and purely social season at Covent Garden by an established national opera house have failed so far. The United States, with its hundred and thirty million inhabitants, can point to no more than a few conventional seasons (as, for instance, those in Chicago, San Francisco, Philadelphia, and St. Louis) apart from the Metropolitan Opera in New York. But the situation is less discouraging than appears on the surface.

The production of new operas is little suited to the old repertory system, and the progressive opera composer is not interested in seeing such a scheme established in the United States. Neither is he worried because attempts to found operatic associations in America seldom succeed. Your progressive composer will rather be convinced that the failure of the plans is due to an approach to the question that is not sufficiently thorough. The situation is understandable, particularly when we remember that promoters who undertake such ventures either view the case from a purely commercial angle or are intent on finding leading roles for unemployed singers.

The New Way

No ONE seems to realize that there cannot be progressive opera in the United States until a new start is made from the production end. Once the problem is efficiently attacked, something which can rightly be called "American opera" will come into being. I do not mean

that it must deal, above all, with the American scene
or with Americans characters—an idea which has, regrettably enough, been taken for granted by most composers having the cause of American opera at heart.
Italian opera of the seventeenth century dealt almost
exclusively with affairs of Greek mythology; but it was
no less Italian for all that, since it created its own style.

A new American style would be the spontaneous
outcome of the practical situation confronting us. One
can hardly expect to see this country dotted with opera
houses in the typical central European manner, each
with its own important orchestra, efficient chorus and
accomplished staff of soloists, and each capable of giving weeks of rehearsal to the preparation of a new
work. The need here is to create different conditions.
A repertory opera house is not feasible in the smaller
American towns, which lack opera-going audiences of
sufficient size to fill the theater consistently. On the
other hand, a new operatic work requires many rehearsals, and many performances are needed to liqui-
date the considerable expense of this preparatory work.
When numerous repetitions in one place are impossible, all that can be done is to divide the presentations
among as many places as possible.

This principle of the *Wanderoper* (traveling opera
or road company) is, of course, not unfamiliar; it has
been practiced in the United States, as in other countries. But my proposal to apply the principle consistently is novel. The traditional traveling company is
useless for the introduction of new works, because it
imitates the aspects of the big city theaters. The road
show tries to console its audiences for the absence of
elephants in *Aïda,* but does not help to correct the fal-
lacy that elephants are a necessary adjunct of fashion-

able grand opera as patronized in the big town during festival days.

The solution I have in mind is based on a different concept of the essence of opera. When performances are to be given in various cities or towns, it is a prime requisite that the entire apparatus and personnel be easily and cheaply transportable. There should be no economy in rehearsals, since the artistic excellence, which is difficult to obtain, should be a *sine qua non.* We should try to manage with few and simple settings, and a staff not exceeding fifteen persons, including singers, players, and stagehands. The usual repertory would be discarded. At most, only a few of the seventeenth- and eighteenth-century operas would be given, such as Mozart's *Bastien et Bastienne;* and these should certainly not be the worst of their genre. But I would urgently advise against making this type of opus the nucleus of the projected program. Revivals of old works never fail to fascinate anyone occupied with them. Unfortunately, the attraction is usually limited to professional musicians—performers and musicologists —and is much less felt by audiences. The kind of traveling troupe I have in mind could not exist if it were confined to historical programs.

The greater part of the road company's repertory would have to consist of new works composed especially for it. And why not? We started with the idea of discovering new possibilities for production. Here they are. Impressive dramas can be (and have been) written for casts of four or five persons. Extremely novel effects can be obtained by the use of gramophone records made for the purpose by orchestras, solo singers, and choruses. By engaging players capable of doubling on various instruments, the color of the miniature orchestra could be enriched to a considerable extent. It is also possible to compose for five instruments in such a way that varied and powerful effects can be realized. Operas so presented need not be merely witty, or bear the stamp of the cabaret, the musical comedy, or the operetta, as one might suppose at first thought. On the contrary, the aim should be the creation of entirely new musico-dramatic works, including all the possibilities of the musical theater.

As is the case in many operatic works on a larger scale, the spoken word would take on a fresh significance. The new opera no longer follows the tendency of the Wagnerian *Gesamtkunstwerk* to produce, by a mystical marriage of heterogeneous materials, the illusion of an unfamiliar, all-comprehensive medium. The new opera poses its own problems for *discussion*. It is its own interpreter, destroying the deceptive appearance of the closed form and believing no longer in the theory of a final philosophy of life. It employs whatever heterogeneous means lie at its disposal for a systematic *montage* in order to demonstrate an idea.

This concept looks for new methods of expression, and new music presents them.

The form of the coming opera must differ so radically from existing forms that comparisons in the number of singers and the lack of elephants and elaborate costumes will not even come up. For this reason, the ideal locales would be smaller centers where the public has not yet learned to associate the idea of opera with the Metropolitan in New York, but where many music lovers are eager for a theater of music. Evidence of such eagerness may be found in the continued growth of the scattered and struggling summer theaters, no matter how primitive and amateurish many of these attempts still are.

Practical Suggestions

AN EXCEPTIONALLY systematic co-operation on the part of artistic and organizing forces is called for in the realization of such an ambition. One of the main difficulties lies in the problem of actually starting an enterprise of this kind. One cannot expect librettists and composers to sit down and produce what is needed if they do not know in advance whether, and if so how, their works are to be given. Scores and libretti are not written at random, but with an eye on the problems connected with the eventual performance. Yet it is difficult, on the other hand, to build up an organism involving a not inconsiderable financial investment before the material to be used is available.

However, organizational imagination in the United States should not find it impossible to start a project along these lines. The initial investment might not be too heavy. A traveling ensemble giving two or three performances in one town could surely subsist for eight or ten weeks on not more than three programs in a defined territory. If, as a beginning, several such groups were formed, each presenting different works, the repertories could be alternated between various parts of the country, thus furnishing the working plan for a year.

Of course, auditoriums seating two thousand to twelve thousand persons should be avoided, and it is possible that the smaller scale of operations involved in this plan would fail to interest the agencies which handle "big attractions"; but we must not forget that the basic idea is the creation of a new operatic style and not a plan to draw money out of people's pockets.

An opera and music school would be the logical central bureau of the movement, familiarizing all those concerned, from the outset, with the problems involved. One more reason why large stages are unsuitable for effective performances of new works is that these theaters are limited, in view of heavy overhead expenses, to the presentation of interpreters thoroughly trained in operatic tradition and thus needing a minimum of rehearsals.

New music cannot come into its own until composers have it in their power to educate young people in its spirit. If a school of the order under discussion were to operate for a sufficient length of time, its graduates could then branch out from the narrower field into larger institutions, orchestras, the radio, and so forth, and the perplexity which prevails in regard to new music would gradually be replaced by a more reasonable and a less shameful attitude.

We can assume that permanent establishment of the project would lead to widespread local organizations having similar aims, a highly desirable consummation and a sign that American soil is a fertile one for opera. The fertility would be indigenous, not foreign nor nourished by irrelevant influences. It is remarkable that Americans, extraordinarily antipathetic to the importation of articles or ideas which they consider unsuitable to their tastes, do not realize that the majority of their operatic ventures have been copied from European examples, and not even from the best of those. If a real American operatic "atmosphere" could be developed, it would, in turn, provide possibilities for large festivallike enterprises allied with the production of the new "grand" opera, which has lately come more and more into prominence, though still struggling against heavy odds.

When Salzburg ceased to be what it had been, people in different parts of the United States took up the question of reconstructing the same setting somewhere in America. The unique quality of the original Salzburg festival consisted of a combination of very special and partly imponderable elements found in exactly the right place at a propitious time. These components could not be reassembled elsewhere simply by engaging a good orchestra, a few prominent singers, and Toscanini to conduct the whole combination. Nor is it clear why a revival of the assembly should immediately have been attempted with glowing fervor. No matter how deserving the Salzburg festivals were, and regardless of their tangible use in an extramusical sense, it must be admitted that not one new concept was realized in them and that they were barren of a single new musical idea. For these reasons, Americans would do better to plan original and novel festivals of their own than to copy the Salzburg layout.

Perhaps some of my readers have misgivings about beginning the propagation of opera anew. In reality, the thought of starting again, from scratch, is less hazardous in opera than in any other form of art. For opera, being the youngest of all musical arts, is thereby far removed from any firmly established forms (if such there be), and, as we remember, owes its existence to completely artificial experiments. Therefore I fail to see why, on the basis of new experiments, opera should not enter upon another vigorous and vital epoch. Among all peoples, Americans should be the last to worry over tradition, since freedom from prejudice has always been one of their most esteemed and, we hope, imperishable virtues.

Public Subsidies or Private Sponsors?

WHENEVER operatic plans are discussed in the United States or in England, one is bound to hear the complaint that the public authorities do little, if anything, for music of any kind and for opera least of all. It is true that operatic activity in central Europe was based on subsidies granted by federal, state, or municipal governments (generally by the last-named); but we must not forget that the foundation for such support was laid in the days when the authorities represented imperial, royal, or other sovereign courts. In admitting that German opera houses had their "golden age" at the time of the Weimar Republic, we should remember that this hectic period was too short to furnish definite conclusions, based on its results, as to whether democratic administrations are, in the long run, the best sponsors of artistic ventures.

Economic crises of the last decades have prompted citizens in many countries to expect their governments to do everything for them. In fact, under the pressure of wartime and postwar calamities, governments have been forced to assume control of so much that formerly was left to private initiative that the average citizen is inclined to shrug his shoulders resignedly and say, "If the government is going to interfere with my movements right and left, it might as well take care of all the details." The danger here is that the state cannot give without taking. Consequently the man who expects too much from his government must be prepared for correspondingly large relinquishments. Doubtless this attitude has largely paved the way for the totalitarian states in Europe. One should be careful, too, in

surrendering cultural enterprises to government influence. In thinking of the backward and recalcitrant
stand of reigning classes in the face of spiritual processes, it is pleasant to imagine that the well-filled
coffers and the smoothly running machinery of a benevolent government ought to be available for the pro-
motion of culture. But such benevolence is never guaranteed for any specified length of time; and it will seldom, if ever, be possible to snatch back from the claws
of a malevolent regime the concessions that the public
had gladly granted to its sympathetic predecessor. Even
if we agree that it may be harder to win the support of
overcautious or unappreciative private individuals for
new ideas, we may still find it more expedient to depend on this than to rely on public officials.

American high schools, colleges, and universities
could perhaps be made the first fixed points around
which such an operatic organization as I have discussed
might revolve. In no fields are the admirable traits of
objectivity, modesty, ambition to learn, and desire for
new ideas so evident. These attributes constitute the
highest hope raised by the question of what we must
do. For the future of new music will depend entirely
on musical education.

New Educational Attempts and Their Danger

BY "MUSICAL education" I mean the teaching which
should be given to laymen. I have already mentioned
the necessity of special training for performers; what
the composer ought to learn can be gleaned from this
book. It is not my task to discuss here how instruction
of specialists should be organized in detail.

The musical teaching of laymen that I speak of be-

gins a little above the elementary grade. It is desirable
that people learn to read music, and it is not unreason-
able to ask that they should. By what method they
learn is of as little interest to musicians as the system
used in teaching penmanship would be to authors.
What we are emphatically interested in is what people
do with this primitive knowledge once they have acquired it, and especially how they can use it to reach a
living contact with the values inherent in new music.

Europeans have found that the music instruction
given to laymen in the latter part of the nineteenth
century did not lead to satisfactory results. The central
point in this pedagogy was the piano lesson, in which
children were drilled to learn a "piece" they could play
before assembled relatives on the occasion of grand-
mother's birthday. Generally the solo was a sentimental
or showy *morceau de salon* of a deteriorated Chopin-
Liszt type. Escaped from this refined torture, the pupils
found scarcely any other enjoyable use for their virtu-
osity than to try to play from memory the popular song
hits which had charmed them in beer gardens or vaude-
ville theaters. A reform was urgently needed, and much
has been done to place musical education on a better
basis.

The principal objective shared in all these manifold
attempts to improve educational conditions is to place
the musical activity of young people on a broader basis,
mostly with emphasis on directing their attention toward more adequate material. They should no longer
be forced to ape their elders with inadequate means,
but should occupy themselves with a type of material
which corresponds to their natural gifts and inclina-
tions and gives them a less stilted relationship to music.
Certainly the trend of these efforts is to be commended,

though they unfortunately have often led to a different kind of narrow-mindedness.

European reformers have frequently placed too great an emphasis on the element of amusement in learning, and so have missed the real aim of musical education, namely, the understanding and appreciation of music as a completely valid spiritual expression. Of course it is wrong to educate laymen as if they were destined to become professionals, and then to leave them suspended in a state of dissatisfied spiritual semicivilization, which is necessarily the only level they can reach. But, on the other hand, if education is whittled down to match the pupil's naturally limited ability, there exists the danger of opening up to him no more than a small sector of an unlimited territory. It is, to be sure, very nice for children to sing easy choruses, to blow on recorders, and to take part in school operettas; these simple performances will give them a pleasure they could not get out of piano exercises or the practice of pieces they dislike. Since, however, this gratifying activity and interest leaves precious little time in which to glance at the realm of music as a whole, the young people may be tempted in the end to see as music only what they can master with their slender efforts. And the obvious result is that their working acquaintance with "real" music is confined to the relatively easy instrumental pieces of the preclassical period and the type which is composed especially for them. Whatever lies between Bach and the present, is, for them, merely too hard to play. After the first World War, musical educationists in Germany built up a theory on this question of compulsion, declaring that the spirit of youth called for the use of either the old, concise, unemotional, and "unromantic" sort of music or for a new kind composed in the same "unromantic" vein. As a result, the *Spiel-musik* produced by Hindemith and a few others (mentioned in an earlier chapter) came to the fore.

I have no wish to repeat my criticism of the ideological background of the movement. Viewing education as an instrument for promoting better understanding, I can only say that in this way a dilettantism which had been regarded as an objectionable product of faulty nineteenth-century methods, and which one wanted to expel for good and all, came in again through the back door. The dilettante who has mastered a piano solo by Sinding well enough to jog around on it for the rest of his natural·life is actually an enemy of music, since he will judge the whole art from the shallow niche in which he is entrenched; but the trifler who sees only what interests him in the light of handicraft will not be much better. When the latter believes no music to be good unless it tramps imperturbably along in square meters, without emotion and within the narrow range of the recorder, his productive association with music will be no more worthy than that of our dabbler in Sinding.

In Praise of the True Amateur

IN FIGHTING the bad dilettante, and justly, we should not forget to praise the good one, for he carries the true message of a fully developed musical life. He is distinguished from the professional musician by a superiority to the imperfection of his performance. That is inevitable, as it is characteristic of him always to live a little beyond his artistic means and to be forever looking for something new, something outside the bounds of his capacities. Directly he starts to aim at perfection, to work out programs which he intends to "exhibit" in one way or another, he ceases to be a good amateur and is on the road to a miserable pseudoprofessionalism. Your bad dilettante loves his own ostentation, and is odious because he fails to notice, or will not admit, that there is no justification for it. As a lover of music in the full and literal sense of the word, the good amateur, on the other hand, woos the muse, grapples with her mysteries, and tries to grasp what is above his reach. His activity never becomes an end in itself, but serves always as an approach to a clearer understanding of the art and a more intimate relationship with it. When he struggles at home with his part in a difficult string quartet, he will not excuse his inability to master it with the complaint that it is "hardly music," but will be keen to hear a perfect performance of the work. And when he does, his past active occupation with the opus, even if insufficient, will help him to appraise its merit.

The aim of musical education, therefore, must be the cultivation of the good type of amateur. The bad type will then disappear automatically. We need intelligent, spiritually alert, and well-informed amateurs in the place of hybrid and vain virtuosi and dull craftsmen. In a word, we need the species of musical people I referred to in Chapter I. This means that musical education, seen in bold outlines, should treat *music as literature*. As a starting point, everyone should have as clear an idea of music, no matter how sketchy that idea may be, as he has of literature.

The man who does not suspect that Goethe lived some time after Shakespeare is indeed rare. Yet I have met plenty of men and women who have never heard, even at second hand, of the monumental Dutch music that accumulated during two centuries. In spite of the much-advertised esteem with which the public is supposed to regard music, musical history remains a special study for the initiated, and music itself is not sufficiently recognized as a spiritual expression on the same level as the plastic arts and literature.

The Importance of Playing the Piano

WE ARE introduced to literature and we learn to value it through *reading*. In music, reading is promoted or replaced by playing an instrument or by singing. When the trained musician sees any kind of music on the printed page, he can imagine how it will sound. But he finds the task easier when he can support his imagination with an audible performance. We cannot, nor should we, expect the reading of a score to be sufficient for the layman. But he should be so well coached in playing the piano that through it he can get some idea of how music of all kinds, including chamber works and the simpler orchestral and choral scores, will sound. To attain this end, piano teaching should be less concerned with dexterity of the fingers than with nimbleness of the eyes, intelligence, and mental agility. Sight reading and the playing of scores on the piano, scorned today in many conservatories as subsidiary subjects, should become centers of attention. Naturally, other instruments, too, ought to be studied, especially those which can be used in chamber music playing. But people who want to be musical—and why should there not be more of them than there are?—need to acquire this visual dexterity very early in their experience. Without the ability to read scores at the piano, the music lover will be denied access to the whole field of music, for only

through this means will its universal spiritual significance be opened to him.

The piano is the one easily available and sufficiently
flexible instrument through which the essence of music
in every form, from grand opera to the solo violin
sonata, can be potently distilled. A bassoon player may
be a valued member of many an ensemble, but his relation to music will be that of a specialist. It is the pianist
alone who can meet the art with the authority of a
sovereign.

It is vital that instructors never teach merely how to
play an instrument, whatever it may be, but always, and
above all, that they teach music. It is important to keep
the instrument in the place allotted to it by its name,
which the dictionary defines as "a tool; a utensil; an
implement," useful in the case of music for the representation of thought. As the thought is the focal point
of music, so should it be the focal point of musical education. All that interests the layman is what happens in
the composer's brain. Once he understands this, he is
certain to understand and love music. When everything
of an instrumental-technical nature is of secondary importance, even to the professional interpreter (since the
finest detail of technique is under the government of
the musical thought), the condition is so much the more
applicable to the amateur, who does not need to trouble
himself over mechanical perfection.

Above All: The Work

IN THE utopian state one would no longer meet dilet-
tantes who make music because they love to play the
violin, but amateurs who love music and perhaps play
the violin on that account. Music teaching would start

from the work of art and return to it, and pregnant
analysis of the opus would be the keynote of instruction.

I have explained in these pages that by "pregnant
analysis" I do not mean the customary methods of im-
parting "music appreciation." The matter is not one of
teaching the layman to learn a large number of rules
by rote, nor of his being able to determine whether
they have been correctly applied in the music he hears.
What he can and should be enabled to comprehend is
how the human spirit expresses itself through music,
and how musical thought is articulated and given form
and meaning.

If music were taught along these lines, one of the
most damaging abuses from which students now suffer,
namely, neglect of new music, would disappear. So long
as instruction is centered on the pupils' capacity to *perform,* new music will be proscribed. As I have shown in
a different connection, new music does not present any
peculiar difficulties once old works are comprehended.
Whoever understands what came from the mind of a
Bach or a Beethoven will not find that Berg and Bartók
harass him with unique propositions.

When this aim has been reached, musical education
will serve to bring contemporary man into a living and
significant relationship with the music of his time. Neglect of this vital task in musical teaching will result in
an increasing indifference toward music in general.
Such an indifference would prove less injurious to
music than to the entire structure of Western civilization, which cannot afford to renounce the art. In moods
of melancholy retrospection, the composer of today
often compares the status of his art to the restricted
place of literature in medieval times, when a few monks,

scattered among barbarians, were the lonely custodians of bookish culture. Like the monks, who knew that the nearest human beings capable of reading what they had written lived far away, so does the modern composer feel that he must travel many a weary mile to meet someone who understands what he has in his mind. Perhaps composers will be able to keep afloat on such an anonymous, subterranean stream for generations. But a civilization which is unconcerned over this state of things will have little cause to be satisfied with its picture as thrown on the screen of future history.

The Place of the Composer in Society

ONE can record with gratification the fact that circumstances in the United States are far more propitious than in Europe. Through the intervention of colleges, forming a link between the preparatory school and the university classes, a period of study has been ensured in which music is treated as a subject of general culture and yet with some degree of detail. In this way a good scaffolding is provided for the building of musical education. To be sure, that framework is not always supported by the right spirit. If it were, my American confreres would not continually complain that their position in the social body is unsatisfactory.

If I interpret these complaints correctly, they do not refer so pointedly to faulty performances or to financial returns, as to morale. American composers, who rightly bring forward the question of ethics, feel that they still are looked upon as more or less obscure purveyors of whatever new material a commercialized management needs whenever the old no longer suffices. The phenomenon is typical of a musical culture in its youth, and reminds us of what used to happen in Europe. The answer to the question of whether musical production in America has already become sufficiently influential to alter the existing state of affairs lies beyond the limits of my survey. But there can be no doubt that the composer's status in the imagination of society would change soon enough if new music were more strongly emphasized in musical education.

Again we must stress the point that if people would look at old music from the point of view of its creators, if they would learn to find in it the living realization of spiritual plans, they would immediately see the composer of our time in an illuminating light, and would perceive that he is modestly following his great predecessors in the path they opened up.

I have tried to show how matters stand here and now, and what problems are begotten by the position of present-day music. Doubtless these problems are very difficult, but that fact should stimulate us to tackle them. When an intrepid mountain climber was asked why he intended to attempt the ascent of Mount Everest, he replied, "Because it's there." The two greatest psychological dangers of our time are a frivolous optimism which rejects all problems, and a desperately smart nihilism which, *a priori,* regards their solution as impossible and much prefers to await the "inevitable" disaster. And in the latter case, the catastrophe is usually not long delayed.

Both these attitudes are unworthy of us. We are faced with a problem, and should proceed to its solution— *here and now.*

BOSTON, MASS., *October,* 1938.
ANN ARBOR, MICH., *June,* 1939.

APPENDIX

THE following list gives a selection of characteristic gramophone records recommended as illustrations of the respective passages of this book. Titles of additional records may be found in *The Gramophone Shop Encyclopedia of Recorded Music,* from which the American sales numbers of the listed records are quoted.

No records are listed here for the period from Bach to the end of the nineteenth century. Practically all important compositions of this epoch have been recorded. Moreover, the reader, who is probably more or less familiar with the standard works of the period, will not need special advice in this respect.

As to contemporary music, the selection of records given below mirrors clearly the strange situation of new music, discussed at great length in this book. It is most characteristic for this situation that we are not able to list a single record of one of Schoenberg's atonal compositions. And yet, deplorable as this may be, it is by no means so hopeless as it seems. By securing the services of artists devoted to new music and by using the method of subscription, a series of really "new" records, at least in the field of chamber music, could be brought out, without tremendous investment and most probably without financial risks. Can we hope for intelligent and benevolent co-operation on the part of the gramophone industry?

Preclassical Music (in approximately chronological order)

GREGORIAN CHANT (recorded by the Monks Choir of St. Pierre de Solesmes Abbey, 24 sides)	VM-87 (Alb.)
JOSQUIN DE PRÉS, Sacred Choruses	V-11677+

ORLANDO DI LASSO, Masses	V-80160
PALESTRINA, Masses	V-11680/1 +
	V-35941/4
GESUALDO, Madrigals	D-20162
MONTEVERDI, Madrigals	CM-218 (Alb.)
Fragments of operas	VM-496
	C-DB 500+
	V-21747

For more records of old music see *L'Anthologie Sonore*, a collection of records in six volumes, published under the direction of Dr. Curt Sachs.

Contemporary Music (in alphabetical order)

BARTÓK, String Quartet No. 1	VM-288 (Alb.)
String Quartet No. 2	VM-320 (Alb.)
Three Rondos on Folk Tunes (piano)	P-R 20434
BUSONI, Indianisches Tagebuch (piano)	C-69010
2 Sonatinas for Piano	FRM-23/4
DEBUSSY, Excerpts from "Pelléas et Mélisande" (opera)	VM-68 (Alb.)
La Mer (for orchestra)	VM-89 (Alb.)
HÁBA, Duo in the Sixth Tone System	C-DB 1307
HINDEMITH, String Quartet No. 3	V-15238/40
Symphony "Mathis der Maler"	T-E 1647/9
HONEGGER, Pacific 231 (for orchestra)	C-67998 D
Concertino (piano with orchestra)	V-8765
Excerpts from "Judith" (drama with music)	CM-X78
Le Roi David (oratorio)	D-25517/8
IVES, Orchestra Pieces	NMQR-1013
General Booth Goes to Heaven (song)	NMQR-1112
Six Songs	NMQR-1412
Sixty-seventh Psalm (a capella)	C-17139 D

MALIPIERO, Quartet	VM-397
MILHAUD, String Quartet No. 2	C-D 15183/6
L'Orestie d'Eschyle (orchestra and choir)	CM-X64
La Création du Monde (ballet)	CM-X18
3 Opéras Minutes (miniature operas)	CM-309
Scaramouche (duet for two pianos)	G-DB-5086
SATIE, Songs	C-9132 M
Parade (ballet)	BAM-16/7
SCHOENBERG, Gurre-Lieder (oratorio, composed as early as 1900!)	VM-127 (Alb.)
STRAWINSKY, Octet	C-68203/4 D
Ragtime (for chamber orchestra)	C-68300 D
L'Histoire du Soldat (theatrical music)	CM-184 (Alb.)
Les Noces (oratorio)	CM-204 (Alb.)
Le Sacre du Printemps (ballet)	CM-129 (Alb.)
Symphonie des Psaumes (oratorio)	CM-162 (Alb.)
Apollon Musagète (ballet)	D-25700/3
Jeu de Cartes (ballet)	T-SK 2460/2
WEBERN, String Trio	D-K 904
WEILL, Excerpts from "Die Dreigroschen-oper" (operetta)	U-AP 436/9

INDEX

Acoustics, 102, 201
Aeschylus, 89
Allgemeiner Deutscher Tonkuenstlerverein, 60
Amateur, 241, 287, 288, 290
America, 11, 64, 78, 80, 224, 263; Civil War in, 14; concerts in, 58; jazz music in, 257; music of, 79, 80, 293; opera in, 58, 276; radio in, 58, 59
Anthroposophy, ideas of, 164
Architecture, 90, 141, 175; European, 95; Arabic, 95, 96; Gothic, 76, 95
Articulation, 25, 138, 179, 227, 236, 241; free, 96, 97, 99, 101, 128, 169, 229
Aryan, 270
"Athematic" style, 78, 162, 163
Atonality, 71, 72, 80, 86, 108, 140, 152, 160, 164, 165, 167, 168, 191, 199, 200, 208, 216, 260; and jazz, 255, 257; and physics, 209, 211-13; and polytonality, 161, 162; and rhythm, 149; and twelve-tone technique, 175-77, 179, 183, 190; conservative trends in, 83, 84; definition of, 143, 144, 153; development of, 138, 139; early stage of, 157, 158; new forms in, 182; objections against, 142, 145, 146, 147, 166, 195; syntax of, 155, 156
Atonal music, 81, 82, 85, 86, 87, 141, 142, 149, 150, 151, 157, 159, 164, 165, 169, 170, 183, 188, 211

Attica, tragedies of, 90
Augmentation, 131
Austria, 80-82, 271; literature of, 83
Axioms, 203-07, 216

Bach, Johann Sebastian, 41, 73, 126, 127, 128, 129, 131, 188, 192, 211, 246, 247, 286, 291, 294; *Art of Fugue*, 127, 128; Cantatas, 92; *Well-tempered Clavichord*, 127
Balance, 83, 99, 100, 105, 127, 128, 152, 166, 167, 168, 169, 177, 178, 179, 255
Ballet, 62; Russian, 161
Bartók, Béla, 50, 78, 291
Basso continuo, 44
Bayreuth, 230; *Buehnenweihfestspiele* of, 56
Beethoven, Ludwig von, 27, 31, 33, 34, 42, 48, 49, 50, 83, 131, 132, 133, 134, 135, 136, 137, 165, 222, 225, 291; *Eroica*, 33; Fifth Symphony, 65; German dances, 134; last quartets, 34, 65, 133; Seventh Symphony, 226
Bel canto, 121, 220
Belgium, 58
Berg, Alban, 63, 157, 291; *Lulu*, 184; Violin Concerto, 184
Bergdorf-Goodman, 73
Berlin, 52, 272
Berlin, Irving, 64
Berlioz, Hector, 136
Binchois, Gilles, 117
Bizet, Georges: *Carmen*, 251